GREAT AMERICAN
VEGETARIAN

Also by Nava Atlas

Vegetariana

Vegetarian Celebrations

Vegetarian Soups for All Seasons

Vegetarian Express

Pasta East to West

The Vegetarian 5-Ingredient Gourmet

GREAT AMERICAN
VEGETARIAN

(A revised and updated edition of *American Harvest*)

Traditional and Regional Recipes
for the Enlightened Cook

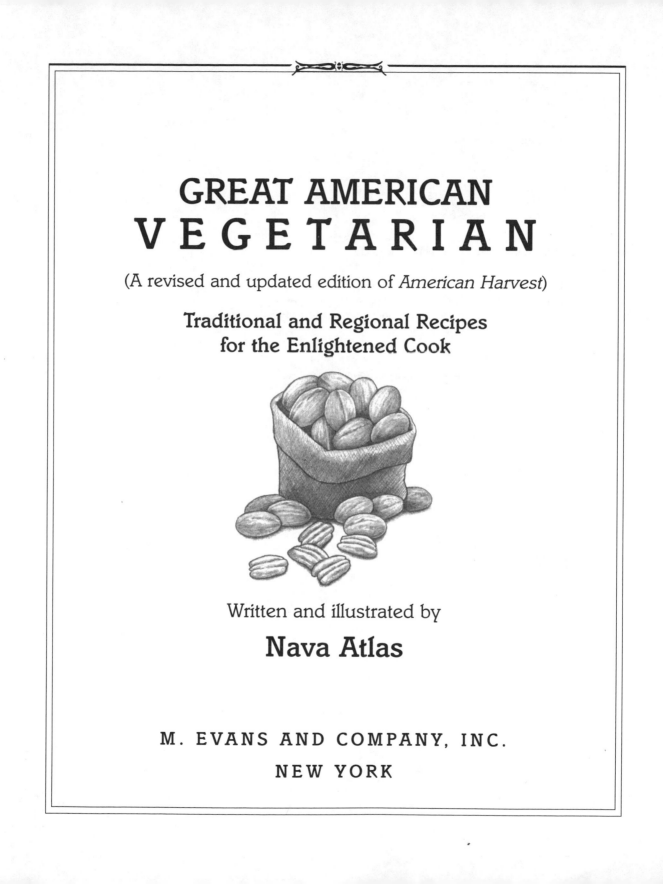

Written and illustrated by

Nava Atlas

M. EVANS AND COMPANY, INC.

NEW YORK

Great American Vegetarian
Traditional and Regional Recipes for the Enlightened Cook

Library of Congress Cataloging-in-Publication Data

Atlas, Nava.
    Great American vegetarian : traditional regional recipes for the
vegetarian enlightened cook / written and illustrated by Nava Atlas.
— 3rd ed.
      p.   cm.
    Rev. updated ed. of: American harvest. 1987
    Includes bibliographical references and index.

    1. Vegetarian cookery. 2. Cookery, American. I. Atlas, Nava.
American harvest. II. Title.
TX837.A845 1998
641.5'636—dc21   98-4717

10 9 8 7 6 5 4 3 2 1

For Chaim,
my partner in great adventures
along the highway of life

Creating this collection of lore and recipes handed down from the past and updated for the future has been a joy, since the information comes from diverse and fascinating sources. Many people contributed not only their knowledge, but also fond memories of the foods they grew up with, some of which have remained a part of their lives as an ongoing tradition.

Among the many people who offered information, I'd like to mention the following for contributing recipes, or for taking time from their busy schedules to talk to me about the foods of their region. Since it has been some years since I spoke to the following people for the first edition of this book, I'll mention their names only, since many have probably moved on from the places or positions at which they were at the time. Thanks to Suzanne Carney; the staff of the Coffee Pot Restaurant in New Orleans, the staff of Dip's Country Kitchen in Chapel Hill, Amina DaDa; Sharon Dowell; Barbara Freer, Alvaro Jurado, F. Leo Kendall, Barbara McPhail, Henry Nelson, Russ Parsons, and Anne Phillips. Special thanks go to Jane Lovato, who shared much about the foods of the Southwest.

No matter how many people one might talk to, it would be impossible to get a sense of the past without digging in to the books of those times. I'd like to acknowledge the New York Public Library, whose incredible collection of original old American cookbooks contributed much to this one. I'd also like to mention the following special libraries and institutions, whose collections and displays were not only highly informative but a pleasure to visit: The Atlanta Historical Society; Colonial Williamsburg (Virginia); the Historic New Orleans Collection, with special thanks to Jessica Travis; and the Walter C. Jackson Library of the University of North Carolina at Greensboro. Thanks also to Patrick Bunyan for his research contributions.

Finally, love and thanks to my husband, Chaim Tabak, for accompanying me on the original 6,500 miles of travels for this book (actually, he did most of the driving), and for his unwavering support throughout all the journeys since that time.

CONTENTS

FOREWORD TO THE NEW EDITION

When I first began researching *American Harvest* (the previous title of this book) in 1985, classic regional American cooking was *the* hot food trend. And though ethnic foods might be considered trendier today, the interest in American cookery has been sustained in a very satisfying way.

Familiar and exotic cuisines co-exist harmoniously everywhere that the food scene can be documented. In one magazine, an article on healthy all-American barbecues was juxtaposed with one on Asian noodles; in another, an article on lightened heartland cooking was side-by-side with an homage to Greek cuisine. Ethnic restaurants are proliferating, but regional American establishments continue to be just as popular as ever.

As a cook and a writer, I am enthused both about the wonderful ethnic cuisines that have become popular, as well as timeless all-American fare. This is a book that I've enjoyed using as much as I enjoyed writing it. To research it, my husband and I traveled 6,500 miles by car to talk to home cooks, short-order cooks, restaurant chefs, and to research at local historic sites (such as Colonial Williamsburg) and libraries. We especially fell in love with the Southwest and its spicy cuisine, but it was also fascinating to learn about the culinary traditions of New England, the South, New Orleans, and the Pennsylvania Dutch.

After ten years in print, it became apparent that the original edition needed a bit of fine tuning to bring it up to date. While much is timeless in the food world, some trends do change. For example, I wrote in the original text that fresh chiles are difficult to find outside the Southwest, which at the time was true enough. Other ingredients like cilantro and jícama were also rare finds. Happily, this is no longer the case; the heightened awareness of cuisines of all kinds has transformed supermarkets into virtual ethnic groceries.

I have added more than fifty new recipes to this new edition, including vegetarian versions of great classics that I was too timid to tinker with the first time around, including Jambalaya, Cincinnati Chili, Cajun Dirty Rice, and others. A sprinkling of soy-based meat analogs as well as soy alternatives to dairy are now represented here as well. More recipes for America's bounty of healthful crops are here, too, such as fresh greens, squashes, wild rice, berries, and more. You'll also find an expanded menu section, and finally, all the recipes, new and original alike, have been nutritionally analyzed.

This book has always held a fond place in my heart because it was so enjoyable to write and research. Doing this revised and updated edition has reaffirmed my appreciation of America's remarkable culinary heritage, and of the bountiful array of crops that makes every day an occasion for giving thanks.

INTRODUCTION

Oh! how my heart sighs for my own native land,
   Where potatoes, and squashes, and cucumbers grow;
Where cheer and good welcome are always at hand,
   And custards, and pumpkin pies smoke in a row;
Where pudding the visage of hunger serenes,
   And, what is far better, the pot of baked beans.

—*The New England Farmer,* 1829

Pick up any vegetarian cookbook and you'll likely find an enticing array of ethnic recipes. Italian, Chinese, and Indian are just a few of the cuisines whose influence has enlivened the vegetarian repertoire and made the meatless alternative more attractive to the general public than was the "soy beans and oats" school of the sixties. The appeal of ethnic foods has helped make us a nation of enlightened eaters, whether vegetarian or not. The emphasis on interesting combinations of fresh vegetables, exotic seasonings and delectable grain and legume dishes proved that a lighter diet is far from boring.

Just as all of these exotic new cuisines seemed to settle into a comfortable niche in this nation's eating habits, the early to mid-1980s saw a great resurgence of interest in regional and traditional American cookery. Seemingly overnight, a number of fascinating books and a proliferation of articles appeared on the subject, almost as a reminder to preserve and continue the tradition of down-home classics that developed, so to speak, in our own backyards. I enjoyed these writings—somehow, they made me feel warm and nostalgic, and evoked images of charming small towns and Thanksgiving at grandmother's. This was a strange effect to be worked on me, a child of immigrants, myself not even American born!

My interest led me to wonder whether a complete selection of American recipes, from soup to desserts, could be tailored to the healthful vegetarian kitchen. And of course, the answer is a resounding *yes*.

The criterion for choosing the recipes in this book was that they fit in with today's emphasis on healthy, lighter eating, with lots of fresh vegetables, fruits, grains, and legumes. Though these ingredients may not come immediately to mind when one thinks "American food," they once played a *major* role in the traditional diet. Prior to the turn of the twentieth century, meat was often just one component of a meal or a dish, rather than its focal point. It was this century's age of affluence that altered our national eating habits.

Wholesome recipes abound among the primary regional styles represented here, including those from New England, the South, the Pennsylvania Dutch, the Southwest, the Creole of New Orleans, and America's vast "heartland." Though the culinary approaches differ widely, there is a strong thread running through the recipes, represented by the use of fresh ingredients that are the basis of our native harvest.

This bountiful harvest includes beans and peas of every color; corn (used in a wide range of forms, from fresh kernels to snowy grits); an abundance of squashes, rice, sweet and white potatoes, an assortment of fruits that fill every manner of traditional dessert; and a cornucopia of vegetables for every season. From these ingredients come a profusion of dishes ranging from simple and earthy to exotic and elegant: Great whole-grain breads and muffins; warming soups, both plain and fancy; hearty grain and bean entrees; satisfying fruity desserts; and much more.

Now you can add to your repertoire of Italian pastas, Chinese stir-fries, and Indian curries an array of tempting homegrown classics such as Southwestern enchiladas, thick Creole soups, southern griddlecakes, and New England pies. And, as an added relish, you can sample the fascinating lore and literature that have accompanied the development of American cooking since its inception.

THE COLONIAL EDEN

The story of Colonial agriculture and cookery is familiar to those of us who were American schoolchildren. It begins with the well-known fact that the early European settlers, arriving in a vast, untamed land would have starved if not for the Native Americans' guidance. From them the colonists learned how to hunt the land, sky, and seas for game, fowl, and fish and to discover wild plants that yielded edible nuts, berries, and greens.

The greatest gift passed along to the settlers by the Native Americans was the ability to cultivate corn. No other single food item has had so great an impact on the development of American cookery. Corn quickly became a staple crop for the colonists, as it required little skill in cultivation. It grew well even in poor soil and produced a food that was as versatile as it was nutritious. As an added bonus, beans and squash could be grown among the corn rows, their vines and stalks intertwining. Corn, beans, and squash have long been known as "the three sisters" in many branches of Native American mythology; these life-sustaining crops are represented by three daughters of the Earth Mother who protect the harvest.

The early years of colonization were hardly paradise for the newcomers, fraught with the hardships of adjustment to a drastically different way of life. But, in time, the knowledge gleaned from the Native Americans, combined with the familiarity of the settlers with certain native crops that had been carried back to Europe by earlier travelers (these include several varieties of beans, sweet peppers, pumpkins and other squashes, and white and sweet potatoes) ensured that the new land would prove generous. Eventually the settlers added to these crops plants from seeds brought over from Europe, including several types of cabbage, lettuce, peas, and herbs.

By the early 1700s, two chroniclers of colonial Virginia set down descriptions of the agriculture of that area in exquisite detail, painting a picture of a veritable Eden of produce. In fact, William Byrd's *Natural History of Virginia* (1737) is subtitled, "or the Newly Discovered Eden." Byrd's report of what was being grown at the time makes today's supermarket offerings pale in comparison. Here is his description of what he refers to merely as "pot herbs," presumably a list of what was grown in some kitchen-gardens:

> *Turnips, carrots, beets, four species of cabbage, such as smooth savoy cabbage, curled red, curled green, as also beautiful cauliflower, chives, artichokes, radish, horseradish, many species of potatoes...parsnips...white and red garlic...smooth, curled and red lettuce, round and prickly spinach, two kinds of fennel...cultivated and wild rhubarb, sorrel, two kinds of cress, mustard, two species of parsley, very large and long asparagus of splendid flavor, white as well as red. There are many species of melons, Guinea, golden, orange, green, and several other sorts. There are three varieties of cucumbers, which are very sweet and good-tasting; four species of pumpkins...squashes are also very good, raw or cooked. All these are Indian vegetables or pot herbs; therefore [they are] not at all or imperfectly known. In addition, there are still many other garden stuffs, which would take too long to mention here.*

Byrd stresses the importance of corn as a staple crop for the multitudes:

> *This corn is very good in this land and is eaten by everyone, rich and poor. People consider it very healthful...Indeed most of the*

inhabitants plant almost nothing but corn for their household needs,
with which they are pleased and remain healthy besides. Their
intention in this is that it is much less trouble to plant and offers
more advantages than grain, since corn yields the planter in good
soil seven to eight hundredfold or still more.

Other grain crops mentioned are wheat, rye, barley, and oats, but none is emphasized or described as extensively as corn.

Robert Beverly's book on the same subject, *The History and Present State of Virginia* (1705), predates Byrd's by some years but offers an equally detailed description of the agricultural bounty of Virginia. The number of different types of fruit trees alone, with all their species and subspecies, is astonishing. He is able to identify, for example, twenty-five different types of pears! Like Byrd, Beverly tells of the importance of corn, relating it to the lives of Native Americans:

This Indian Corn was the Staff of Food, upon which the Indians did
ever depend; for when sickness, bad weather, war or any other ill
Accident kept them from Hunting, Fishing and Fowling; this, with the
Addition of some Peas, Beans and such other fruits of the Earth, as
were then in season, was the Families Dependence, and the Support
of their Women and Children.

Later in the same century, this surrounding of variety and abundance helped nurture the self-described Virginia "epicurean," Thomas Jefferson. Despite the fact that his career was devoted to law and politics, Jefferson's early ambition was to be a gentleman planter. His love of fine food seemed innate, and his creativity as a gardener is well documented in his *Garden Books* (1766-1824). In his gardens grew cucumbers, cabbage, spinach, sprouts, squashes, potatoes, artichokes, lettuce, cauliflower, eggplant, endive, onions, turnips, beets, and much more. Even ordinary vegetables were classified as to their exact variety: "Carrots from Pisa, Salmon radishes, Lattuga lettuce, Windsor beans, cluster peas..."

Jefferson also grew a wide variety of legumes, including the green peas that he so loved, as well as lentils, black-eyed peas, and several varieties of beans. His enthusiasm extended also to his lovely orchards, which bore a multitude of fruits and nuts. Jefferson's tables were set in such style and taste that it has been said that their quality, both in and out of the White House, has rarely been matched. His overseer, Bacon, commented that "He was never a great eater, but what he did eat he wanted to be very choice."

The first truly American cookbook to reflect the culinary diversity of its region was *The Virginia Housewife* by Mary Randolph, first published in 1824, which marked the end of the Jeffersonian era. Mrs. Randolph, a member of a prominent Virginia family, conveys a sense of the lavish diversity of local foods and a great sensitivity to the quality of ingredients. Although largely based on English cooking techniques, Mrs. Randolph's book includes a profusion of New World foods. Meat and fish abound in her pages, to be sure, but the sheer variety of fruits, vegetables, and grains used in her recipes dispels any notion of a universally lackluster early American table. Hearty breads, elegant desserts bursting with luscious berries and other fruits, pickles and relishes, and beautifully seasoned soups are other hallmarks of this landmark book on American cookery.

Mrs. Randolph's cookbook likely inspired some of the superb volumes that followed hers later in the nineteenth century, such as Eliza Leslie's *Directions for Cookery* and Maria Parloa's *Miss Parloa's Kitchen Companion* (1887). In poring over those as well as scores of other culinary volumes of that period, I discovered a fascinating world of sensible yet creative cooks who used our native harvest to its full advantage. Their words and ideas, forgotten for so long, have been rediscovered and proven timeless.

A VEGETARIAN'S-EYE VIEW OF AMERICAN REGIONAL CUISINES

In this collection, recipes from a wide range of sources are meshed together. What they have in common prevails, though, over their differences, since similar ingredients often wind their way from one cuisine to another. Of course, there are variations in seasoning from bland to fiery, preferences in cooking styles, and occasional ingredients that are unique to a particular region. No differences, though, subtle or obvious, will overshadow the freshness and basic unpretentiousness of the recipes as a whole. So, before all these recipes wind up under the umbrella of "American vegetarian," here is a brief description of the primary regional cuisines represented in this book, with a look at what each has to offer to the vegetarian palate.

NEW ENGLAND

Old New England—the phrase evokes images of small towns nestled among mountains, steepled white churches, and vibrantly colored autumn leaves. New England's food just as quickly brings to mind a set of firmly planted notions, such as the boiled dinner consisting of corned beef and root vegetables, codfish specialties, and seafood chowders. Getting beyond the obvious, though, this simple cuisine of Puritan roots has some worthy treasures to contribute to the vegetarian kitchen.

Colonial New England was not nearly as bountiful a land as the early Virginia described in previous pages. The reason is simple—the climate was harsher, and the soil was best suited to hardier crops. Further, fireplace cooking with "spider-legged" skillets and black iron pots, along with the Puritan penchant for simplicity, dictated that the most practical dishes were plain and long-cooking.

What I found most useful in the range of New England recipes was the number of ideas for preparing winter vegetables. The much-maligned parsnip is turned into an elegant and warming chowder. Similarly, such common vegetables as potatoes, cabbage, and beets are turned into comforting classics that take the doldrums out of cold-weather cooking.

Another nice contribution was a group of tasty, fortifying pancakes, sweetened with maple syrup, a New England perennial. The crowning touch of this region's staples are none other than its great American pies and fruit desserts. Brimming with apples, blueberries, cranberries, strawberries, pumpkin, squash, and bananas, these desserts make it possible to enjoy a sweet treat without feeling sinful!

THE PENNSYLVANIA DUTCH

The Pennsylvania Dutch are descendants of German immigrants who arrived in this country in the seventeenth century. Thus, the term Dutch is a misnomer, and actually a corruption of *Deutsch*, meaning "German." Their cookery developed as an adaptation of the German style applied to the agricultural and climatic conditions of the areas that they settled (mainly Pennsylvania, with pockets in Ohio, Indiana, and Iowa).

The Dutch were (and still are in large part) a self-sustaining farm people whose Amish and Mennonite branches are the best known. Their penchant for plain living and the isolation of farm life during long winters resulted in a style of cooking that is simple, filling, and nourishing.

It's a fascinating and underexplored cuisine, and the hardy crops basic to New England are equally prominent here. Scrapple and pepper pot might spring to mind immediately as characteristic Dutch dishes, but corn, potatoes, cabbage, apples, parsnips, and egg noodles form the basis of many hearty dishes that a vegetarian can enjoy. It's hard to go wrong with such classics as Corn Noodles, Dutch Succotash, Red Wine Cabbage, and Potato-Bread Stuffing, among others.

The true artistry of Dutch cooking, the ability to stretch home-grown food from season to season by drying, canning, and pickling (hence the famous relishes known as "the seven sweets and seven sours") is an art you might like to explore if Pennsylvania Dutch cookery captures your interest.

THE SOUTH

No other regional style can boast such a vast amount of specific ingredients as can Southern cookery. As described in the previous pages, colonial Virginia was a haven of produce, and this was true of many other parts of the South, with a climate so favorable to growing both wild and cultivated foods.

This variety of foods native to the Southern soil by way of the Native Americans was combined with the foods brought over as part of the slave trade from Africa (including okra, peanuts, and black-eyed peas). Prepare these foods in the earthy style of Southern African Americans or in the European manner of the wealthy planter families, and sometimes a little of both, and you have the basic components of southern cooking.

The repertoire of the South is very wide-ranging. The foods that are now the basis of "soul food" formed the core of the diet of African Americans from the days of slavery: greens, black-eyed peas, sweet potatoes, corn bread, grits, and various forms of salt meat. These foods and their preparation have survived to become an integral part of any "typical" Southern menu, crossing any boundary of class or race. Conversely, the penchant of the wealthier planters for "big eating," where quantity is almost as important as quality, is reflected in the menus of even the humblest of diners in the South today.

During my Southern travels, I noticed on any menu considered traditional, no matter how humble the establishment, a long list of daily vegetables, from which one could choose four or five at a set price. At one such place in South Carolina, the list read like this: lima beans, turnip greens with turnips, candied yams, pickled beets, cole slaw, crowder peas, hush puppies (fried cornmeal balls), and banana pudding. Other lists would include black-eyed peas, collard greens, string beans, corn, potato salad, cauliflower, and broccoli. Dessert standards were most always sweet potato pie and pecan pie. As vegetarians, we would have to avoid the beans (including string beans), peas, and greens because they are almost invariably "seasoned" with salt pork or bacon. This illustrates, however, the love of hearty food, and lots of it!

I've already mentioned quite a number of foods typical to Southern cooking and these played an important role in the recipes I chose for this collection. Many of my adaptations will lighten the dishes, keeping them low in fat and high in flavor. Of great interest to me were dishes made with sweet potatoes, a highly nutritious but underused crop, as well as those including the great variety of beans and peas that are a pillar of this region's cuisine.

Corn has played as crucial a role in Southern cooking as it has in most any other region's, producing many wonderful classics. Biscuits, corn breads and other hearty breads, griddlecakes, cole slaws, and fruity desserts were also among the generous bounty of great dishes from the South that fit in beautifully with this collection.

LOUISIANA: CREOLE AND CAJUN COUNTRY

William Makepeace Thackeray, the British author, found New Orleans to be "of all the cities in the world, where you can eat the most and suffer the least." New Orleans is the hub of Creole culture, and it is there that its distinctive cookery was born.

Creoles are the descendants of the Spanish and French settlers of Louisiana in its Colonial period. They're also the descendants of the West Indian or African blacks who settled the area or were taken as slaves. After centuries of the inter-mixing of these groups, it might suffice to say that a Creole is the descendant of a true native of Louisiana, no matter what color or extraction. This excludes the Cajuns, whose ancestors, the Acadians of Nova Scotia, settled and farmed Louisiana's lush Bayou country.

The Creole and Cajun cooking styles have much in common, with many over-lapping ingredients. Perhaps the essential difference might be summed up in say-ing that whereas the Creole aspires to elegance, Cajun cookery is its more rustic, earthy counterpart. It was much more difficult to extract from the latter typical dishes adaptable for vegetarians; almost always pungent and fiery, the Cajun repertoire makes constant use of the abundant sea life in the area. That, along with the use of peppery homemade sausage puts too distinct a stamp on Cajun dishes to have encouraged me to adapt but a few of them.

Creole cooking incorporates elements of French *haute cuisine*, the Spanish and African love of high seasoning, the West Indian way with exotic herbs, and the lavish supply of ingredients basic to the American South. Central to this style is the flair for seasoning, ranging from delicate to fiery, but always making a state-ment. The 1941 Works Progress Administration guide to Louisiana comments that "well-stocked as the larder may be, it is the seasoning that makes Creole food distinctive. Onions, garlic, bay leaf, celery, red, green, black and cayenne pepper, parsley, thyme, shallots, basil, cloves, nutmeg and allspice are used in different combinations."

New Orleans has long been known as an eater's city, but a vegetarian's paradise it's not. My husband and I loaded up on the fabulous breakfasts because we were rather limited for our other meals while in search of traditional fare—Creole restaurant cooking today is quite dominated by the abundant and diverse seafood of the area. Even the famous stuffed vegetables are usually filled with shrimp or crab.

Happily, but a bit too late in our visit, we discovered the I & I Creole Vegetarian Restaurant, then (in the mid-1980s) on Saint Peter Street, where we enjoyed owner Amina DaDa's interpretations of classics of the area and her stories of her efforts to introduce these adapted standards to a resistant public. More of her comments and recipe ideas are ahead.

Creole home cooking, much of it documented in charming turn-of-the century cookbooks, provided the basis for the recipes I've adapted. Great soups and vegetable dishes were high on my list of favorites, being perfect beneficiaries of the Creole genius for seasoning. Dishes incorporating another Louisiana staple, rice, were also welcome, especially when combined with beans, as in the famous Red Beans and Rice. Further, Creole is the only American cuisine that makes substantial use of eggplant, resulting in several nice recipes for it.

After a stroll in the French Quarter, there was no more pleasant way for my husband and myself to end the day than with a nice piece of aromatic Bread Pudding laced with a sauce of rum or whiskey. This seductive treat is included in the desserts chapter as a reminder of New Orleans' slightly decadent side.

THE SOUTHWEST

The Southwest, with its warm, languid days and cool desert nights, has produced a cuisine that is down-to-earth, yet at the same time, wonderfully exotic. Based on centuries-old food customs of the Pueblo Indians, it was influenced by the Spanish missionaries, who brought with them their preference for highly seasoned food. Combined with native ingredients and culinary influence from Mexico, the resulting cuisine is comprised of a rich, distinct range of recipes marked by simplicity and integrity. Of the beginnings of this regional style, Ana Bégué de Packman writes in *Early California Hospitality* (1938):

> **Far more fortunate were the colonists of New Spain than their**
> **English brothers who landed on the rocky shores of the New England**

coast. Here, on the western sun-kissed Pacific, the earth gave forth
bountifully of her green garlands of cress and pigweed, festooned
garlic heads, strings of red chile peppers, pearly corn, and pink beans.

"Tex-Mex," a popular term used to describe Southwestern food, is not one that I like to use; it's vague and often used as a catch-all. The debate is always a hot one, so to speak, over the differences between the cooking styles of Texas, New Mexico, Arizona, and California, as well as what developed north or south of the border. The recipes in this collection represent those that are common to the region in general, as well as those that have become popular in Southwestern-style restaurants everywhere.

The Southwest is an adventurous vegetarian's haven in a sea of coast-to-coast homogeneity. There's much to choose from, and many restaurants are lightening up the classics, such as preparing refried pinto beans without lard. These well-loved, ubiquitous *frijoles,* along with tortilla specialties such as *enchiladas* or *burritos* and rice, are often the basis of a hearty meal. Embellished with green chilies (lots of them!), tomatoes, onions, garlic, bell pepper, cheese, squashes, avocado, potatoes, and black beans, these form the basis for any number of exciting variations.

Tortilla specialties notwithstanding, the Southwest has also made quite a few lively contributions to this collection in the form of unusual egg dishes, well-seasoned soups, and robust salads, among others. If my preference for this region's cookery is evident, forgive me—it's irresistible, and once you've gotten hooked, you'll know what I mean.

NOTES ON INGREDIENTS

Here is a list of ingredients used commonly or occasionally in the recipes that warrant some discussion. Refer to this list for additional information that may come in handy.

FLOURS, MEALS, AND GRAINS

Buckwheat flour

This is used to make buckwheat cakes and has a very assertive flavor. Buy it in 1- or 2-pound bags at natural food stores.

Cornmeal

Although the commercial variety found in supermarkets is adequate, it has been bolted of its valuable germ and is not, to my mind, very flavorful. Try to find stone-ground or water-ground cornmeal at natural food stores. White or yellow cornmeal may be used interchangeably in the recipes.

Rice

I nearly always recommend brown rice, whose nutritious hull is intact, giving it a nutty flavor and preventing it from becoming starchy and sticky when cooking. Rice swells to about 3 times its original bulk when cooked. Quite often, the ratio of cooking water to rice is recommended at 2-to-1, but that never seems to do it for me; I prefer a 3-to-1 ratio. Bring the water to a simmer, then cover and simmer over low heat until the water has been absorbed, about 35 to 40 minutes.

Whole wheat flour and whole wheat pastry flour

Used in whole or part in bread and dessert recipes, respectively, buy these in bulk at natural food stores, or in 2- or 5-pound bags in supermarkets. I don't recommend using them interchangeably.

Unbleached white flour

This is used in part to lighten the texture of whole wheat or whole wheat pastry flour in breads and desserts and also as a thickener for sauces.

BEANS AND PEAS

An assortment of legumes are used in these recipes, including:
Black beans
Black-eyed peas
Chickpeas (garbanzos)
Cowpeas
Green peas
Navy or small white beans
Pinto beans
Red or kidney beans

Beans have finally seemed to shake their stigma as a fattening, poor man's food. A serving of beans or peas is very low in calories, and the fat content is almost nil! And few food groups are as versatile.

The cooking method I prefer is as follows: Sort and rinse the beans or peas and soak them overnight in plenty of water, or bring them to a simmer, then cover and let stand off the heat for an hour or so. When you're ready to cook them, drain and rinse them again and add water in at least one and one-half times their bulk. Cook over low heat, covered.

Pinto, red, and kidney beans require about 1½ to 2 hours. Black beans, navy beans, black-eyed peas, and cowpeas generally require 1 to 1½ hours. This will all vary according to how long you've soaked the beans, the temperature at which they are cooked, and even the altitude at which you live. I don't recommend cooking chickpeas from scratch. They take a long time to cook, and honestly, are not as tasty as their canned counterparts. Dried split peas are most often used in soups and don't require presoaking.

Test the beans occasionally toward the end of recommended cooking times; they should be soft and mealy when pressed between thumb and forefinger. You don't want them to be mushy, but neither should they be underdone—that makes them hard to digest.

Some other tips: Add salt only toward the end of the cooking (doing so sooner toughens the beans). Also, for more flavor and softer texture, add a small, halved onion and a tablespoon of canola oil to the water when you begin to cook the beans. Most beans generally yield from two and one-quarter to two and one-half times their original bulk when cooked, hence, 1 cup of dried beans will equal 2¼ to 2½ cups when cooked. Most beans freeze well, so cook extra, and save the flavorful cooking water to use as soup stock.

Canned beans

Many of the beans used in this book come in canned form. It makes sense to use canned beans when small amounts are needed, but not when a whole pound is called for, such as in Red Beans and Rice or Black Bean Soup. Choose a brand without additives. The only real drawback to canned beans is their high sodium content, so drain them well and rinse their salty brine.

Green peas, fresh

The season for fresh peas is late spring to early summer. Frozen green peas are a fine product, but it's fun to use fresh peas when they are in season, and to nibble on the raw peas while shelling them.

Lima beans

It's nearly impossible to find fresh lima beans, so the frozen variety (especially green baby lima beans) will do for most of the recipes here. They often come just underdone enough so that the further stewing and simmering required doesn't obliterate them. Dried white lima beans aren't called for in these recipes.

CORN AND CORN PRODUCTS

Fresh corn

Get into the habit of scraping corn kernels right off the cob instead of automatically using frozen corn. For most recipes, the corn is first cooked on the cob. While late summer is the season for fresh local corn, its season has been extended due to imported corn from Florida and elsewhere. This "seasonless" corn, in my experience, is surprisingly good and sweet. The sweet white corn of late summer is most delicious in recipes where corn is highlighted.

Frozen corn kernels

Frozen corn is certainly convenient, and for the most part is a good product, but I recommend using it only in dishes in which it isn't the main ingredient. Most corn recipes are just not worth making with anything but fresh, and I'll alert you as the occasions arise.

Grits (or hominy grits)

Quaker Oats grits and quick grits are the most readily available. Having eaten a lot of grits in the South, I find Quaker Oats' product to be fairly good. However, the stone-ground variety available from natural food stores is more flavorful.

Hominy, whole

Hominy results from soaking corn kernels until the hull comes off. This product, once exclusively in the domain of the Southwest, is now fairly easy to find in supermarkets. It comes in 1-pound cans and is shelved near other canned corn products.

Tortillas, corn or flour

Corn or flour tortillas are easy to find, usually in the dairy section in supermarkets or in the refrigerated section in natural foods stores. They are acceptable, though not as fresh and pliable as those you'd find in the Southwest.

MISCELLANEOUS INGREDIENTS

Bread crumbs

Rather than throwing out your slightly dried-out bread ends, put them to good use by making crumbs. Simply tear leftover bits of whole grain bread into small pieces and process them in a food processor until finely ground. For crunchier crumbs, first dry the bread out in the oven at a low temperature. I call for fresh bread crumbs in recipes for scalloped vegetables and in some desserts such as Apple Brown Betty (page 245).

Butter and margarine

I always agonize over the butter-versus-margarine issue due to the saturated fat and cholesterol content of the former and the trans-fatty acid problem of the latter. In this edition, I call for a choice of either whipped butter, since it is measure for measure less fatty and caloric than regular, or natural canola margarine. The latter is available in natural foods stores; it is at least free of all the additives contained in supermarket brands, is low in saturated fat, and is also more appropriate for dairy-free diets. I try to use either sparingly—just enough to impart buttery flavor where it is really warranted; whenever possible, I use canola oil or olive oil instead.

Cheeses

The recipes in this book call for either Cheddar or Monterey Jack cheese. When a small amount of cheese is needed, I'd rather use the whole-fat variety. On those rare occasions when cheese becomes a more prominent ingredient in a dish, I may opt for the reduced-fat kind. But reduced-fat cheeses just aren't as tasty, and for me, the non-fat stuff is unacceptable. If you use really fresh, well-flavored cheeses like sharp Cheddar, a little goes a long way. Soy-based cheeses are an option for those who are lactose intolerant or vegans; but they don't have as full a flavor, nor do they melt as well as do dairy cheeses.

Nuts

Most often used in these recipes (and in moderation) are pecans, with walnuts coming in second. Sunflower seeds are called for on occasion. If your kitchen is cool, store the nuts in tightly lidded jars at room temperature; otherwise store them in the refrigerator or freezer if they are not to be used up quickly.

Oils

How things change—I recommended safflower oil in the first edition of this book, as it was praised as the healthiest of oils at the time. Now the oil of choice is canola, and that's the one I call for most often. Olive oil never seems to go out of favor, and it works well in the Southwest's Spanish-influenced recipes. Extra virgin olive oil is most flavorful.

Vinegar

There are many varieties of vinegar available, but the one I prefer using for these home-grown recipes is apple cider vinegar. I've grown fond of its sweet-sour flavor and think it works nicely as an all-purpose vinegar.

SWEETENERS

Fructose

For anyone who wants to replace regular granulated white sugar for a sweetener that is a little gentler to the metabolism, I give fructose as an alternative ingredient. Available in natural foods stores, fructose is a concentrated sweetener made from fruit sugar. Use only about ½ the amount of fructose for a given amount of sugar.

Honey

Honey is used here on occasion when a distinctive sort of sweetness is needed in cooking or bread baking.

Light brown sugar

This common sweetener works well in the American-style treats in this book. However, for anyone who wishes to use a more natural sweetener, Sucanat (see below) is given as an alternative.

Maple syrup

Maple syrup is used here mainly as the sweetener for the griddlecakes in Chapter One. It's also compatible with sweet potato dishes, as in Baked Sweet Potatoes and Apples (page 191). Buy pure maple syrup that comes from New England or Canada. It's more expensive, but definitely worth it.

Molasses

The strong flavor of molasses can at first seem overpowering. If you can acquire a taste for it, so much the better, since it's the only common sweetener that has measurable nutritional value, being high in iron and other minerals. Organic unsulphured blackstrap molasses is a fine choice, as is Barbados molasses.

Sucanat®

The trade name for this product stands for *SUgar CAne NATural*, and as implied, it's made from natural evaporated cane juice. This tawny-hued sweetener has less sucrose, or simple sugar, content than granulated sugar. It is an especially good stand-in for brown sugar, but can also replace white sugar. It is used as a 1-to-1 replacement.

Chapter 1

BISCUITS, MUFFINS, AND GRIDDLECAKES

Who recalls when a girl could hardly wait till she got married so she could make some biscuits?

— Kin Hubbard
  Abe Martin on Things in General, 1925

This was a chapter I particularly enjoyed preparing, since like many people, I often slip into a serious "breakfast rut." Busy people frequently gulp down their morning coffee with a little something or other or skip breakfast altogether. In days past, breakfast was a substantial meal, meant as sustenance for a good day's work. Alice B. Toklas, in her cookbook, recalls that "the first food I remember from my childhood in San Francisco in the [eighteen] eighties is breakfast food..."

What a treat it is to wake up to hot whole-grain muffins or biscuits or a stack of pancakes. No doubt, a bit of planning is in order, since few people I know are going to get up early on a weekday morning before their long commute and whip up a batch of muffins! However, muffin batter and biscuit dough take little time to prepare and bake, so why not make some in the evening? It's a relaxing way to unwind, then you can refrigerate it, covered, until the morning. What a great way to start a day—with a fresh treat awaiting you in the kitchen.

Similarly, any griddlecake or pancake batter can be prepared the night before and cooked on the griddle in the morning. When was the last time you had golden brown homemade pancakes with maple syrup? If all else fails, though, there is always Sunday morning for a special and leisurely breakfast.

Muffins, biscuits, and griddlecakes all have European predecessors, but the American versions developed early and represented a distinct departure. They incorporated native grain products to great advantage, including cornmeal, hominy, rice, and buckwheat, as well as wheat flour when available. The earliest typically American griddlecake may have been made of cornmeal, milk, and eggs, first set down by Amelia Simmons in *American Cookery* (1796) as "Indian Slapjacks."

I don't want to leave the impression that the recipes in this chapter are only appropriate for breakfast. On the contrary, biscuits are a fixture of the traditional Southern meal, and muffins taste just as good at lunch. But for the most part, these treats are particularly suited to making our first meal of the day more enticing and less likely to fall by the wayside.

BUTTERMILK BISCUITS

Makes 12 to 15

Buttermilk biscuits are a Southern standard. However, there is no real standard recipe for them, as one cook's method can cause another to throw a fit. This recipe was handed down to a friend by her Aunt Burnace from Ellisville, Virginia. Burnace's use of oil rather than butter or shortening is a bit unorthodox, but it works very well.

1 cup whole wheat pastry flour
1 cup unbleached white flour
2 teaspoons baking powder
½ teaspoon baking soda
1 teaspoon salt
¾ cup buttermilk
¼ cup canola oil

Preheat the oven to 425 degrees.

In a mixing bowl, sift together the first 5 ingredients. Stir in the buttermilk and oil, a bit at a time, and work together to form a soft dough.

Turn the dough out onto a well-floured board. Knead for a minute or two, adding a small amount of flour if the dough is too sticky.

You can make the biscuits in one of two ways: Either roll the dough out to about a ½ inch thickness and cut it with a biscuit cutter 2 ½ inches in diameter; or just pinch the dough off in small bits, about 1½ inches in diameter, and pat into nice biscuit shapes. Place the biscuits on a lightly oiled baking sheet. Bake for 12 to 15 minutes, or until touched with golden brown on top. Transfer the biscuits to a rack or plate to cool.

Per Biscuit:
Calories: 100
Carbohydrates: 13 g

Total fat: 3 g
Cholesterol: 1 g

Protein: 2 g
Sodium: 166 mg

POTATO BISCUITS

Makes 1 dozen

Here are two biscuit recipes (the second one follows) that have a small quantity of mashed potato added to the dough. This excellent biscuit is from America's heartland. If you'd like to try a savory variation, add a teaspoon or so of mixed dried herbs to the dough.

1½ cups unbleached white flour
    or whole wheat pastry flour, or a
    combination
1½ teaspoons baking powder
½ teaspoon salt
3 tablespoons whipped butter or
    natural canola margarine
1 medium potato, cooked,
    peeled, and well mashed
    (about 1 cup)
½ cup low-fat milk or soymilk, or
    as needed

Preheat the oven to 400 degrees.

In a mixing bowl, combine the flour, baking powder, and salt. Work the butter in with the tines of a fork until the mixture resembles a coarse meal. Work in the mashed potato and enough milk to form a soft dough.

Turn the dough out onto a well-floured board. Knead for 2 to 3 minutes, adding a small amount of flour if the dough is too sticky. Divide the dough into 12 equal pieces and shape into balls.

Arrange the biscuits on a lightly oiled baking sheet and pat them down a bit to flatten. Bake for 20 minutes, or until the tops are golden and a toothpick inserted into the center of one tests clean. Transfer the biscuits to a rack or plate to cool.

Our living consisted almost invariably of coffee, and hot short cakes, called biscuits.

—John Palmer
Journal of Travels in the U.S., 1818

SWEET POTATO BISCUITS

Makes 1 dozen

I was pleased to have been able to enjoy these subtly sweet, traditional biscuits while visiting Virginia's Colonial Williamsburg.

1¾ cups unbleached white flour
    or whole wheat pastry flour,
    or a combination
½ cup unbleached white flour
2 teaspoons baking powder
½ teaspoon salt
3 tablespoons whipped butter or
    natural canola margarine
⅓ cup low-fat milk or soymilk
1 cup well-mashed sweet potato
3 tablespoons honey
¼ cup finely chopped walnuts or
    pecans, optional

Preheat the oven to 425 degrees.

In a mixing bowl, sift together the flours, baking powder, and salt. Work the butter in with the tines of a fork until the mixture has the texture of a coarse meal. Add the milk and sweet potato and work them in to form a soft dough.

Turn the dough out onto a well-floured board. Knead for 2 to 3 minutes, adding a small amount of flour if the dough is too sticky. Divide the dough into 12 equal pieces and shape into balls.

Arrange on a lightly oiled baking sheet and pat them down a bit to flatten. Bake for 15 minutes, or until a toothpick inserted into the center of one tests clean. Transfer the biscuits to a rack or plate to cool.

Calories: 127   Total fat: 3 g   Protein: 3 g
Carbohydrates: 23 g   Cholesterol: 6 g   Sodium: 94 mg

RICE MUFFINS

Makes 1 dozen

In South Carolina and Louisiana, the abundance of rice inspired cooks to use it as an ingredient in all kinds of baked goods. Here is an adaptation of Rice Muffins from an old Louisiana recipe. Serve these warm to accompany soup for lunch or supper or spread with preserves for breakfast.

1 cup whole wheat pastry flour

½ cup unbleached white flour

1½ teaspoons baking powder

1 teaspoon salt

2 eggs, well beaten

1 cup low-fat milk or soymilk

1 cup cold well-cooked brown rice

2 tablespoons melted whipped butter or natural canola margarine

Preheat the oven to 400 degrees.

In a mixing bowl, combine the flours, baking powder, and salt. In another bowl, combine the beaten eggs, milk, rice, and melted butter and stir together. Gradually add the wet ingredients to the dry and stir together vigorously until thoroughly blended.

Divide the batter evenly among 12 paper-lined muffin tins. Bake for 25 to 30 minutes, or until the muffins are lightly browned and a toothpick inserted into the center of one tests clean. When the muffins are cool enough to handle, transfer them to a plate or rack to cool.

Calories: 104	Total fat: 2 g	Protein: 4 g
Carbohydrates: 15 g	Cholesterol: 40 g	Sodium: 200 mg

The servant will bring you hot muffins and corn battercakes every 2 minutes.

—*Maryland Historical Magazine*, 1833

HOMINY MUFFINS

Makes 1 dozen

Adding cooked grits to muffins was a common baking trick in the nineteenth century, and not confined to Southern cookery. The grits give these muffins a nice moistness.

1½ cups water
¼ cup quick-cooking grits
1 tablespoon whipped butter or
    natural canola margarine
2 eggs, well beaten
1 cup low-fat milk or soymilk
1 tablespoon honey
1½ cups unbleached white flour
    or whole wheat
    pastry flour, or a combination
1¼ teaspoons baking powder
½ teaspoon salt

Preheat the oven to 350 degrees.

Bring the water to a simmer in a heavy saucepan. Sprinkle the grits in slowly, stirring constantly to avoid lumping. Cook over very low heat until done, about 3 to 4 minutes. Remove from the heat and stir in the butter to melt.

In a mixing bowl, combine the cooked grits with the beaten eggs, milk, and honey and stir together until well blended. Add the flour, baking powder, and salt and stir together until completely combined.

Divide the batter evenly among 12 paper-lined muffin tins. Bake for 25 minutes, or until the tops are golden and a toothpick inserted into the center of one tests clean. When the muffins are cool enough to handle, transfer them to a plate or rack to cool.

Calories: 102	Total fat: 2 g	Protein: 4 g
Carbohydrates: 17 g	Cholesterol: 38 g	Sodium: 111 mg

APPLE MUFFINS

Makes 1 dozen

Inspired by old recipes from both New England and America's heartland, these chewy muffins make a delightful change-of-pace treat for breakfast.

1 cup whole wheat pastry flour
¾ cup unbleached white flour
¼ cup wheat germ
2 teaspoons baking powder
½ teaspoon cinnamon
¼ teaspoon ground allspice or
   cloves
1 egg, well beaten
¼ cup packed light brown sugar
   or Sucanat
1 cup applesauce
¼ cup low-fat milk or soymilk
1 heaping cup peeled, finely
   diced apple
½ cup dark or golden raisins

Preheat the oven to 350 degrees.

Combine the first six ingredients in a large mixing bowl and stir together.

In another mixing bowl, combine the beaten egg with the sugar until it dissolves. Add the applesauce and milk and stir together until smooth. Gradually add the wet ingredients to the dry and stir together vigorously to form a smooth, stiff batter. Stir in the diced apple and raisins.

Divide the batter evenly among 12 paper-lined muffin tins. Bake for 25 to 30 minutes, or until the muffins are golden and a toothpick inserted into the center of one tests clean. When the muffins are cool enough to handle, transfer them to a plate to cool.

Calories: 130   Total fat: 0 g   Protein: 4 g
Carbohydrates: 26 g   Cholesterol: 18 g   Sodium: 13 mg

WILD BLUEBERRY-OATMEAL MUFFINS

Makes 1 dozen

Tiny wild blueberries from Maine make a brief appearance on produce stands in late June, but they're available year-round in the frozen food section of well-stocked supermarkets.

1¾ cups unbleached white flour or whole wheat pastry flour, or a combination

½ cup quick-cooking oats

1 teaspoon baking powder

1 teaspoon baking soda

1 egg, beaten

1 cup (8 ounces) vanilla or lemon low-fat yogurt

⅔ cup packed light brown sugar or Sucanat

¼ cup low-fat milk, or as needed

1 cup fresh or frozen wild blueberries

3 tablespoons finely chopped walnuts

Preheat the oven to 350 degrees.

Combine the flour or flours, oats, baking powder, and baking soda in a mixing bowl and stir together.

In another mixing bowl, combine the beaten egg, yogurt, brown sugar, and milk in another mixing bowl and stir together until well blended.

Make a well in the center of the flour mixture and pour in the wet mixture. Stir together vigorously until completely combined. The batter should be medium-thick. If it seems too stiff or dry, add a small amount of additional milk.

Divide the batter evenly among 12 paper-lined muffin tins. Bake for 20 to 25 minutes, or until the tops of the muffins are golden and a toothpick inserted into the center of one tests clean. When the muffins are cool enough to handle, transfer them to a plate or rack to cool.

| Calories: 143 | Total fat: 3 g | Protein: 5 g |
| Carbohydrates: 25 g | Cholesterol: 19 g | Sodium: 28 mg |

ORANGE-CRANBERRY MUFFINS

Makes 1 dozen

I don't know how the flavors of orange and cranberry became such a classic pairing, but somehow, they're a perfect team.

1 cup unbleached white flour
¾ cup whole wheat pastry flour
¼ cup wheat germ
2 teaspoons baking powder
½ teaspoon baking soda
½ teaspoon ground ginger
1 egg, beaten
⅓ cup light brown sugar or
    Sucanat
1 cup (8-ounce container) orange
    or lemon low-fat yogurt
½ cup fresh orange juice
½ teaspoon grated orange rind
1 cup chopped fresh or dried
    cranberries
3 tablespoons finely chopped
    walnuts, optional

Preheat the oven to 350 degrees.

Combine the first 6 ingredients in a mixing bowl and stir together. In another bowl, combine the remaining ingredients except the last two. Mix wet and dry ingredients and stir vigorously until well combined.

Stir the cranberries and optional walnuts into the batter. Divide the batter evenly among 12 paper-lined muffin tins. Bake for 20 to 25 minutes, or until the tops of the muffins are golden and a toothpick inserted into the center of one tests clean. When the muffins are cool enough to handle, transfer them to a plate or rack to cool.

Calories: 111   Total fat: 0 g   Protein: 4 g
Carbohydrates: 21 g   Cholesterol: 19 g   Sodium: 23 mg

BASIC BUTTERMILK PANCAKES

Makes 12 to 15

Pancakes have been an American tradition since early colonial times. The earliest of American cookbooks refer to them as "flapjacks," and over the years, dozens of varieties have developed. This basic recipe can be used as is or as a starting point for the recipes that follow.

1 cup whole wheat pastry flour
½ cup unbleached white flour
1 teaspoon baking powder
½ teaspoon baking soda
1 egg, beaten
2 cups buttermilk
Whipped butter or natural canola margarine
Maple syrup or all-fruit preserves

Combine the flours, baking powder, and soda in a mixing bowl. Make a well in the center and pour in the egg and the buttermilk. Stir vigorously with a whisk just until the batter is smooth. Don't overbeat.

Heat a nonstick griddle or a large, nonstick skillet that has been lightly coated with butter. Ladle on the batter in amounts enough to form thin cakes approximately 4 inches in diameter. Cook on both sides until golden brown. Serve hot with maple syrup or preserves.

Calories: 65	Total fat: 0 g	Protein: 3 g
Carbohydrates: 11 g	Cholesterol: 17 g	Sodium: 54 mg

Variation:

NEW ENGLAND CURRANT PANCAKES

Add ½ cup of lightly floured currants and ½ teaspoon of cinnamon to the basic buttermilk batter. Cook as directed above.

BANANA-PECAN PANCAKES

Makes 18 to 20

I first had these fabulous pancakes at the Coffee Pot restaurant in New Orleans, making for a memorable breakfast in their charming antiquated courtyard. I later discovered that they're fairly common not only in that area, but also in the Southwest.

1 recipe Basic Buttermilk
  Pancakes (page 39)
2 large bananas, thinly sliced
⅓ cup finely chopped pecans

½ teaspoon cinnamon
Whipped butter or natural canola margarine
Maple syrup or all-fruit preserves

Prepare the batter as directed for Basic Buttermilk Pancakes. Fold in the bananas, pecans, and cinnamon. Cook as directed in the recipe and serve hot with maple syrup or preserves.

Calories: 70	Total fat: 1 g	Protein: 3 g
Carbohydrates: 11 g	Cholesterol: 12 g	Sodium: 39 mg

MAINE RYE PANCAKES

Makes 12 to 15

This isn't a common recipe, but an interesting old one from New England. The combination of flours make for a filling and hearty breakfast.

¾ cup rye flour
½ cup whole wheat flour
¼ cup unbleached white flour
1 teaspoon baking powder
½ teaspoon baking soda
2 cups buttermilk
2 tablespoons molasses
Whipped butter or natural canola
    margarine
Maple syrup or all-fruit preserves

Combine the first 5 ingredients in a mixing bowl and stir together. Add the buttermilk and molasses and beat together until smoothly blended.

Heat a nonstick griddle or a large, nonstick skillet that has been lightly coated with butter. Ladle on the batter in amounts enough to form thin cakes approximately 4 inches in diameter. Cook on both sides until golden brown. Serve hot with maple syrup or preserves.

Calories: 70   Total fat: 0 g   Protein: 3 g
Carbohydrates: 14 g   Cholesterol: 1 g   Sodium: 53 mg

Women are going wild over the pancake hat.

—*Kansas City Times*,
September 1931

BUCKWHEAT CAKES

Makes 16 to 20 pancakes

An English traveler said in 1870, "It is hard for the American to rise from his winter breakfast without his buckwheat cakes." These pancakes are wholesome and filling and even look healthful. Since yeast is involved in the process, you must begin making them the night before.

1 cup low-fat milk or soymilk
1¼ cups lukewarm water
½ package active dry yeast
1½ cups buckwheat flour
½ cup whole wheat pastry flour
1 tablespoon molasses
½ teaspoon salt
½ teaspoon baking soda
Whipped butter or natural canola margarine
Maple syrup or all-fruit preserves

James Whistler, the noted American painter, was such a great fan of buckwheat cakes that he introduced them to London society. Perhaps it was his well-known mother, a fine cook, who introduced them to her son.

Scald the milk by bringing it to just below the boiling point. Combine it with the water in a mixing bowl and allow the mixture to cool to lukewarm. Sprinkle the yeast into the lukewarm mixture and let it stand for 10 minutes to dissolve.

Combine the buckwheat and whole wheat flours in another mixing bowl. Gradually add the wet mixture to the dry and stir vigorously until just well-combined. Cover and let the batter stand at room temperature overnight.

In the morning, whisk in the molasses, salt, and baking soda. Heat a nonstick griddle or a large, nonstick skillet that has been lightly coated with butter. Ladle on the batter in amounts enough to form thin cakes approximately 4 inches in diameter. Cook on both sides until golden brown. Serve hot with maple syrup or preserves.

Calories: 53   Total fat: 0 g   Protein: 2 g
Carbohydrates: 11 g   Cholesterol: 1 g   Sodium: 91 mg

LACE-EDGED CORNMEAL GRIDDLECAKES

Makes 12 to 15

Breakfast cakes made of cornmeal are traditional to old Southern home cooking. The contrasting flavor of crisp, cooked cornmeal and maple syrup or preserves is delightful. These are so named because when the griddle is really hot, bubbles burst on the edges of the cakes, thus forming a "lacy" effect.

1 cup boiling water

1 cup cornmeal

¼ cup unbleached white flour or whole wheat pastry flour

½ teaspoon salt

1 teaspoon baking powder

1 egg

1 cup low-fat milk or soymilk

Whipped butter or natural canola margarine

Maple syrup or all-fruit preserves

Pour the boiling water over the cornmeal in a heatproof bowl and let it stand for 10 minutes.

Combine the cornmeal with the flour, salt, baking powder, egg, and milk in a food processor. Process until completely smooth.

Heat just enough butter to coat the bottom of a nonstick griddle or a large, nonstick skillet. Ladle on enough batter to form thin, 3-inch cakes. Cook until golden brown and crisp on both sides. Serve hot with maple syrup or preserves.

Calories: 56   Total fat: 0 g   Protein: 2 g
Carbohydrates: 10 g   Cholesterol: 16 g   Sodium: 90 mg

RICE AND CORNMEAL GRIDDLECAKES

Makes 16 to 18

These wholesome griddlecakes, from a common old Southern recipe, make an uncommonly hearty and delicious breakfast.

½ cup cornmeal

½ cup whole wheat pastry flour or unbleached white flour

½ teaspoon baking soda

¼ teaspoon salt

1 cup well-cooked brown rice

2 eggs, well beaten

1 cup buttermilk

Whipped butter or natural canola margarine

Maple syrup or preserves

Combine the cornmeal, flour, soda, and salt in a mixing bowl. Stir in the rice, then add the eggs and buttermilk and stir vigorously until the mixture is well blended.

Heat a nonstick griddle or a large, nonstick skillet that has been lightly coated with butter. Ladle on the batter in amounts enough to form thin cakes 3 to 4 inches in diameter. Cook on both sides until golden brown. Serve hot with maple syrup or preserves.

Calories: 55	Total fat: 0 g	Protein: 2 g
Carbohydrates: 9 g	Cholesterol: 26 g	Sodium: 71 mg

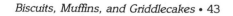

WILD BLUEBERRY GRIDDLECAKES

Makes 16 to 18 4-inch griddlecakes

Tiny wild blueberries are a delicious addition to griddlecakes. Buy them fresh during their fleeting season in mid- to late June, or look for them in the frozen food section of your supermarket all year around.

¾ cup cornmeal

¾ cup whole wheat pastry flour

½ cup unbleached white flour

1 teaspoon baking soda

2 cups buttermilk, or as needed

1 egg, beaten

2 tablespoons light brown sugar
   or Sucanat

1 cup wild blueberries

Whipped butter or natural canola
   margarine

Maple syrup

Combine the first 4 ingredients in a mixing bowl and stir together. Make a well in the center of the flours and pour in the buttermilk, beaten egg, and brown sugar. Stir together vigorously with a wooden spoon until the ingredients are just combined. Don't overbeat. Gently stir in the blueberries.

Heat a nonstick griddle or a large, nonstick skillet that has been lightly coated with butter. Ladle on the batter in amounts enough to form thin cakes approximately 4 inches in diameter. Cook on both sides until golden brown. Serve hot with maple syrup.

Calories: 77	Total fat: 0 g	Protein: 3 g
Carbohydrates: 14 g	Cholesterol: 14 g	Sodium: 68 mg

SQUASH OR PUMPKIN GRIDDLECAKES

Makes about 16 4-inch pancakes

Pumpkin or squash lend a cheery color and wonderful flavor to griddle cakes. Make these in the fall.

1 cup flour
1 tablespoon sugar
1 teaspoon baking powder
½ teaspoon cinnamon
Pinch of nutmeg
1 egg, beaten
¾ cup pureed cooked squash or
    pumpkin
1 cup low-fat milk or soymilk, or
    as needed
Whipped butter or natural canola
    margarine
Maple syrup

Combine the first 5 ingredients in a large mixing bowl. Combine the beaten egg with the pureed squash and milk in another mixing bowl and whisk together. Pour the wet mixture into the dry and stir together just until well blended.

Heat a nonstick griddle or a large nonstick skillet that has been lightly coated with butter. Ladle on the batter in amounts enough to form thin cakes approximately 4 inches in diameter. Cook on both sides until golden brown. Serve hot with maple syrup.

Calories: 43	Total fat: 0 g	Protein: 2 g
Carbohydrates: 8 g	Cholesterol: 14 g	Sodium: 13 mg

New Haven is celebrated for having given the name of "pumpkin heads" to all New Englanders. It originated from the "Blue Laws," which enjoined every male to have his hair cut round by a cap. When caps were not to be had, they substituted the hard shell of a pumpkin. Whatever religious virtue is supposed to be derived from the custom, I know not...

—The Rev. Samuel Peters
    General History of Connecticut, 1877

MR. MAYOR

Chapter 2
LOAF BREADS AND PAN BREADS

I was so exceedingly surprised at seeing on the table a great variety of beautiful-looking bread, made both from fine wheaten flour and Indian corn, that I exclaimed, "Bless me, we must be in Virginia!"

—George Featherstonhaugh
English traveler in the U.S., 1834

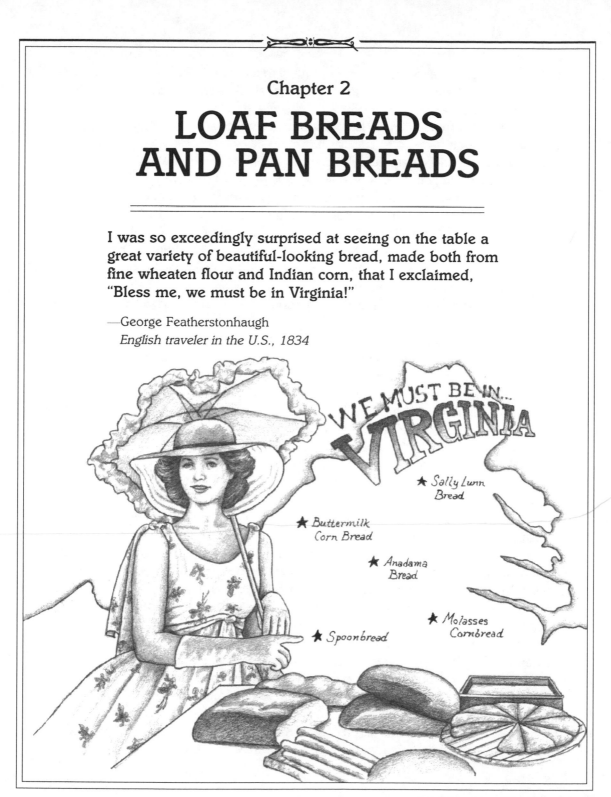

WE MUST BE IN... VIRGINIA

★ Sally Lunn Bread
★ Buttermilk Corn Bread
★ Anadama Bread
★ Molasses Cornbread
★ Spoonbread

The search for regional breads rewarded me with plenty of great basic ones as well as some with offbeat twists resulting in a uniquely American character. Southern breads containing rice or squash; Shaker breads with potatoes, herbs, and cheese; and a Southwestern corn bread filled with the ubiquitous hot chile are among the delightfully different.

Like so many other categories of American cooking, bread-making has its roots firmly planted in the Native American knowledge of corn that was passed along to the colonists. Thus, cornmeal was known well into the nineteenth century as "Indian meal." The preference for corn breads in early days was as much a matter of practicality as taste. Besides its being a hardier crop than wheat, it was better suited to grinding by the crude millstones used then. In addition, the yeasting process required for wheat breads was tedious, and homemade baking powders weren't always reliable. As time went on, wheat breads grew in popularity in the colonies but were still mixed with a portion of cornmeal, as in the case of Anadama Bread.

At Colonial Williamsburg, I had the opportunity to observe the old method of windmill-powered stone-grinding of corn. The rather coarse, uneven meal that results by this method is similar to the cornmeal produced before the 1850s. Maria Parloa writes longingly of the coarser meal in *Miss Parloa's Kitchen Companion* (1887), commenting that though it didn't keep as well due to its high moisture content, it had a sweet and delicious flavor. She lamented that as corn was made to dry more quickly at high temperatures and ground ever finer, "these changes in the meal have damaged it considerably and it is almost impossible to get the moist, sweet corn-bread of years gone by."

This might explain why the corn breads that came out best for me, with today's bland, commercially produced cornmeal, were those that contained plenty of "moisturizers" such as molasses, cheese, and lots of buttermilk.

Whole wheat flour in the nineteenth century was a bran-filled meal called Graham flour, named for the eccentric clergyman and health advocate, Sylvester Graham. But, as Karen Hess comments in her annotations to Mary Randolph's *Virginia Housewife* (1824), it's safe to venture that even the all-purpose flour of that era was not as finely bolted as it is today and must have contained a portion of the healthy germ and bran.

After learning to make the breads in this chapter, I was finally freed of the fear of making leavened breads. The extra time and effort was well rewarded by the sight of golden loaves bursting from their tins and the aroma of fresh bread in the house. For those of you who are too busy to make yeasted breads the old-fashioned way, or have no inclination to bread machines, there are several very satisfying and unusual quick breads to choose from here as well.

BUTTERMILK CORN BREAD

Makes 1 9-inch square loaf, about 12 servings

It's hard to think of a more classic American bread than corn bread. Almost all corn breads can be traced back to the Native Americans. As mentioned in the introduction to this chapter, cornmeal was called "Indian meal" well into the nineteenth century. Buttermilk corn bread is common to the South and New England.

1½ cups cornmeal

½ cup whole wheat pastry flour or
    unbleached white flour

1 teaspoon baking powder

1 teaspoon baking soda

1 teaspoon salt

2 eggs, well beaten

3 tablespoons light brown sugar
    or Sucanat

1¾ cups buttermilk

2 tablespoons melted whipped
    butter or natural canola
    margarine

The North thinks it knows how to make corn bread, but this is mere superstition.

—Mark Twain (1835–1910)

Preheat the oven to 425 degrees.

Combine the first 5 ingredients in a mixing bowl. In another bowl, beat the eggs together with the brown sugar, buttermilk, and melted butter. Pour the wet ingredients into the dry and stir vigorously until completely combined. Pour the mixture into a lightly oiled, shallow 9-by 9-inch aluminum pan.

Bake for 20 to 25 minutes, or until the edges turn golden and a knife inserted into the center tests clean. Allow the bread to cool in the pan just until warm, then cut into 12 squares to serve.

Per square:
Calories: 129   Total fat: 3 g   Protein: 4 g
Carbohydrates: 21 g   Cholesterol: 41 g   Sodium: 277 mg

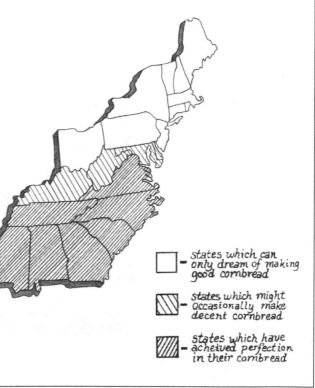

☐ - *states which can only dream of making good cornbread*

▨ - *states which might occasionally make decent cornbread*

▧ - *states which have acheived perfection in their cornbread*

MOLASSES CORN BREAD

Makes 1 9-inch square loaf, about 12 servings

Here's an Old South variety of corn bread. Combine it with a piece of sharp Cheddar cheese and some fresh fruit for a pleasant lunch.

1 cup cornmeal
½ cup whole wheat pastry flour
½ cup unbleached white flour
2 teaspoons baking powder
1 teaspoon salt
1 egg, well beaten
1 cup low-fat milk or soymilk
¼ cup molasses
2 tablespoons canola oil

Preheat the oven to 400 degrees.

Combine the first 5 ingredients in a mixing bowl. In another bowl, combine the beaten egg with the milk, molasses, and melted butter. Stir together until well mixed.

Add the wet ingredients to the dry and stir vigorously until completely combined. Pour the mixture into a lightly oiled, shallow 9- by 9-inch aluminum pan.

Bake for 20 to 25 minutes, or until a knife inserted into the center tests clean. Allow the bread to cool in the pan just until warm, then cut into 12 squares to serve.

Per square:
Calories: 133   Total fat: 4 g   Protein: 3 g
Carbohydrates: 23 g   Cholesterol: 19 g   Sodium: 204 mg

GREEN CHILE CORN BREAD

Makes 1 9-inch square loaf, about 12 servings

This is a Texan and Southwestern version of corn bread. It's a more contemporary recipe than the previous two, and still a very popular one. For real chile-heads, make this with the jalapeños to produce an incendiary bread. For those of you who are wary of breads that must be eaten with a fire extinguisher, do use milder chiles. Either way, this is a richly flavored treat.

1½ cups cornmeal

½ cup whole wheat pastry flour or
   unbleached white flour

1½ teaspoons baking soda

1 teaspoon baking powder

1 teaspoon salt

2 eggs, well beaten

1½ cups buttermilk

1 cup grated Cheddar cheese,
   reduced-fat if desired

1 to 2 jalapeño peppers, seeded
   and minced,
   or 1 4-ounce can chopped
   mild green chiles

½ cup cooked fresh corn kernels,
   optional

2 tablespoons melted whipped
   butter or natural canola
   margarine

Preheat the oven to 400 degrees.

Combine the first 5 ingredients in a mixing bowl and stir together. In another bowl, beat the eggs, then stir in the buttermilk. Add the wet mixture to the dry and stir together vigorously until well blended.

Stir in the grated cheese, jalapeños, and optional corn kernels. Pour the melted butter into a shallow, 9- by 9-inch baking pan and swirl it around to coat the bottom and sides. Pour the excess butter into the batter and stir it in.

Pour the batter into the pan. Bake for 20 to 25 minutes, or until the top is golden and a knife inserted into the center tests clean. Allow the bread to cool in the pan, then cut into 12 or more squares to serve.

Per square:
Calories: 162
Carbohydrates: 20 g

Total fat: 5 g
Cholesterol: 51 g

Protein: 7 g
Sodium: 387 mg

PINTO BEAN CORN BREAD

Makes 1 9-inch square loaf, about 12 servings

This hearty adaptation of a Native American recipe is good served with vegetable soups. Try it with Potato, Cheese, and Green Chile Soup (page 84).

1 cup cornmeal
½ cup whole wheat flour
½ cup unbleached white flour
1 teaspoon baking soda
1 teaspoon baking powder
½ teaspoon salt
1 egg, beaten
1 cup buttermilk
1 cup canned diced tomatoes, lightly drained
2 tablespoons canola oil
1 tablespoon light brown sugar or Sucanat
1 cup canned pinto beans, drained and rinsed
2 scallions, green parts only, thinly sliced

Preheat the oven to 400 degrees.

Combine the first 6 ingredients in a mixing bowl. In another bowl, combine the beaten egg with the buttermilk, tomatoes, oil, and brown sugar. Whisk together until well mixed.

Add the wet ingredients to the dry and stir vigorously until thoroughly combined. Stir in the beans and scallions. Pour the mixture into an oiled, shallow 9- by 9-inch aluminum pan.

Bake for 20 to 25 minutes, or until a knife inserted into the center tests clean. Allow the bread to cool in the pan just until warm, then cut into 12 squares to serve.

Per square:
Calories: 131
Carbohydrates: 22 g
Total fat: 2 g
Cholesterol: 1 g
Protein: 4 g
Sodium: 174 mg

If I asked a neighbor for some bread in an emergency, I should receive a pan of corn bread.

—Marjorie Kinnan Rawlings
Cross Creek, 1942

ANADAMA BREAD

Makes 2 loaves

One of the earliest of colonial American breads, Anadama Bread is still one of the finest. Its outstanding texture and flavor put it high on my list of favorites.

1 cup low-fat milk
1 cup boiling water
½ cup cornmeal
2 tablespoons whipped butter or natural canola margarine
1 teaspoon salt
¼ cup molasses
1 package active dry yeast
½ cup lukewarm water
3 cups whole wheat flour
1½ to 2 cups unbleached white flour

At dinner, the safest conversational opening is as follows: "Is that your bread, or mine?"

—Francis W. Crowninshield
Manners for the Metropolis, 1909

In a large heavy saucepan, scald the milk by heating it to just below the boiling point. Pour the boiling water into the saucepan. Sprinkle the cornmeal in slowly, stirring constantly to avoid lumping. Stir in the butter until it melts, then add the salt and molasses and mix well. Let the mixture cool to lukewarm.

Dissolve the yeast in the lukewarm water. Let it stand for 10 minutes, then stir gently. Pour it into the cornmeal mixture. Stir in the flours, a cup or so at a time, then turn the dough out onto a well-floured board. Knead for 8 to 10 minutes, or until the dough is smooth and elastic, adding a small amount of flour if the dough is too sticky.

Form the dough into a smooth round and set it in a floured bowl. Cover with a clean tea towel and let it rise in a warm place until doubled in bulk, about 1½ hours.

Punch the dough down, knead briefly, and divide into two parts. Shape into two loaves and place them in two oiled, 9- by 5- by 3-inch loaf pans. Let the dough rise again, covered and in a warm place, until doubled in bulk, about 1 hour.

Preheat the oven to 350 degrees. Bake the loaves for 45 to 50 minutes, or until the tops are golden brown and the bread sounds hollow when tapped. When the loaves are cool enough to handle, remove them from their pans and allow them to cool on a rack.

Per 3/4-inch slice:

Calories: 113	Total fat: 1 g	Protein: 3 g
Carbohydrates: 22 g	Cholesterol: 2 g	Sodium: 100 mg

SALLY LUNN BREAD

Makes 1 10-inch tube loaf or 2 small loaves

A bread with a strange name and a complicated history, this is another early colonial bread. The absence of any cornmeal might suggest that its use was more prevalent with the "upper crust," so to speak, since wheat flour was a more valuable commodity. The recipe is thought to have perhaps originated in England as a bun.

Sally Lunn recipes have been included in dozens of cookbooks from the early nineteenth to the mid-twentieth century, with all manner of additions and strange explanations for the name. This recipe is adapted from the one considered to be the classic, from Eliza Leslie's immensely popular nineteenth-century cookbook, Directions for Cookery. *She states simply that, "This cake is named after the inventress." This is a lovely and very light bread.*

1 cup low-fat milk or soymilk
¼ cup whipped butter or natural
   canola margarine
1 package active dry yeast
¼ cup lukewarm water
2 cups whole wheat flour
2 cups unbleached white flour
1 teaspoon salt
2 eggs, very well beaten

In a small saucepan, scald the milk by heating it to just below the boiling point. Stir in the butter to melt, then allow the milk to cool to lukewarm.

Dissolve the yeast in the lukewarm water and let it stand for 10 minutes, then stir gently. Pour it into the lukewarm milk mixture.

Combine the flours and salt in a mixing bowl. Make a well in the center and put in the well-beaten eggs followed by the wet mixture. Beat together vigorously with a wooden spoon until thoroughly blended. The dough should have the texture of a very heavy batter and will be sticky. Shape it into a fairly smooth round and place it in a very well-floured bowl. Cover with a clean tea towel and let it rise in a warm place until doubled in bulk, about 1½ hours.

With well-floured hands (the dough will still be sticky), punch the dough down. Turn it out, with the aid of a cake spatula, onto a well-floured board. Arrange the dough in an oiled, 10-inch tube pan or divide it in half and place it in two small oiled loaf pans. Let the dough rise again, covered and in a warm place, until doubled in bulk, about 1 hour.

Preheat the oven to 350 degrees. Bake the loaves for 45 to 50 minutes or until the tops are golden brown and the bread sounds hollow when tapped. When the loaves are cool enough to handle, remove them from their pans and allow them to cool on a rack.

Per 3/4-inch slice:
Calories: 158   Total fat: 4 g   Protein: 6 g
Carbohydrates: 25 g   Cholesterol: 38 g   Sodium: 173 mg

CAROLINA RICE AND WHEAT BREAD

Makes 2 loaves

Rice was a staple crop in South Carolina early in the state's history and, like the corn of other locales, worked its way into nearly every category of cooking and baking. Thus, the addition of rice or rice flour to breads is an early practice that originated in this region. This hearty bread is adapted from Sarah Rutledge's The Carolina Housewife *(1847), a book containing many recipes for breads combining rice with wheat. It's a delicious and healthful idea.*

½ cup raw brown rice

2 cups water

1 cup low-fat milk or soymilk

¼ cup whipped butter or natural
    canola margarine

2 tablespoons molasses or honey

1 package active dry yeast

¼ cup lukewarm water

3½ cups whole wheat flour

1½ cups unbleached white flour

1½ teaspoons salt

Cook the rice in the water until all the water is absorbed (this 4-to-1 ratio will cook the rice to a softer-than-usual texture), about 35 to 40 minutes.

Scald the milk by heating it to just under the boiling point. Remove from the heat and stir the butter in until it melts. Add the molasses and let the mixture stand until it is lukewarm.

Dissolve the yeast in the lukewarm water and let it stand for 10 minutes, then stir it gently. Add it to the lukewarm milk mixture and stir until well blended.

In a large mixing bowl, combine the flours and salt. Pour the milk mixture in, a little at a time, and stir it in until the flour is completely moistened. Add the cooked rice and work it in with your hands until the dough holds together.

Turn the dough out onto a well-floured board and knead for 10 to 12 minutes. This requires diligent working before it becomes elastic, due to the heaviness of the rice. Pat the dough into a smooth round and place it in a floured bowl. Cover with a clean tea towel and let the dough rise in a warm place until doubled in bulk, about 1½ hours.

Punch the dough down, divide it in half and shape into two loaves. Place them in two oiled, 9- by 5- by 3-inch loaf pans and allow them to rise again, covered and in a warm place, until doubled in bulk, about 1 to 1½ hours.

Preheat the oven to 350 degrees. Bake the loaves for 45 to 50 minutes, or until the tops are lightly browned and the bread sounds hollow when tapped. When the loaves are cool enough to handle, remove them from their pans and allow them to cool on a rack.

Per 3/4-inch slice:
Calories: 122
Carbohydrates: 22 g

Total fat: 2 g
Cholesterol: 4 g

Protein: 4 g
Sodium: 142 mg

PHILPY (Hot Rice Bread)

6 servings

This is an old South Carolinian recipe, the origin of whose odd name is obscure. The first recorded recipe may be that in The Carolina Housewife *(1847), attributed to Sarah Rutledge. It's great for breakfast with maple syrup.*

1 cup well-cooked brown rice
1 egg, well beaten
½ cup low-fat milk or soymilk
⅓ cup whole wheat pastry flour
  or unbleached white flour
½ teaspoon salt
½ teaspoon baking powder
2 tablespoons melted whipped
  butter or natural canola
  margarine
Maple syrup or all-fruit preserves

Q. My husband buys forty-five cents worth of mixed drinks every time I send him for a five-cent loaf of bread. How long will we keep our home?

A. It takes longer to drink up some homes than it does others. Try baking your own bread.

—Kin Hubbard
  Abe Martin's Almanack, 1911

Preheat the oven to 400 degrees.

Mash the rice as finely as possible with the tines of a fork. In a mixing bowl, combine the beaten egg with the milk, then stir in the mashed rice. Add the flour, salt, and baking powder and stir briskly until the mixture is smooth. Stir in the melted butter, then pour the mixture into a lightly oiled 9-inch pie pan.

Bake for 30 minutes, or until golden brown and set. Cut into 6 wedges and serve hot with maple syrup or preserves.

Calories: 109   Total fat: 3 g   Protein: 3 g
Carbohydrates: 14 g   Cholesterol: 44 g   Sodium: 200 mg

OLD-FASHIONED OAT BREAD

Makes 2 loaves

Breads containing rolled oats were once common in New England and in the Great Plains states such as Nebraska. The oats all but disappear during the baking process, but leave a subtly chewy texture to this hearty bread.

1½ cups rolled oats
3 tablespoons whipped butter or
    natural canola margarine
1 cup low-fat milk or soymilk
1 cup boiling water
1 package active dry yeast
¼ cup lukewarm water
⅓ cup molasses
3 cups whole wheat flour
1½ cups unbleached white flour
1½ teaspoons salt

Combine the oats with the butter in a large mixing bowl. In a small saucepan, scald the milk by bringing it to just below the boiling point. Pour both the scalded milk and the boiling water over the oats and stir to melt the butter. Let the mixture cool to lukewarm.

Combine the yeast with the lukewarm water in a small bowl and let stand for 10 minutes to dissolve. Add it along with the molasses to the oat mixture and stir together gently.

In another mixing bowl, combine the flours and salt. Stir the flour mixture into the oats mixture, a bit at a time, ending by using floured hands. When the dough holds together, turn it out onto a floured board and knead for about 7 minutes, adding a small amount of flour if the dough is too sticky. Pat into a smooth round and place the dough in a floured bowl. Cover with a clean tea towel and set in a warm place to rise until doubled in bulk, about 1½ hours.

Punch the dough down and knead on a floured board for 5 minutes, or until it is quite elastic. Divide the dough in half, shape into loaves, and place them in oiled, 9- by 5- by 3-inch loaf pans. Let the loaves rise again until doubled in bulk, covered and in a warm place, about 1 hour.

Preheat the oven to 350 degrees. Bake the loaves for 45 to 55 minutes, or until the tops are golden and the bread sounds hollow when tapped. When the loaves are cool enough to handle, remove them from their pans and allow them to cool on a rack.

Per 3/4-inch slice:
Calories: 126	Total fat: 2 g	Protein: 4 g
Carbohydrates: 23 g	Cholesterol: 3 g	Sodium: 146 mg

ZUNI QUICK BREAD

Makes 1 loaf

There are several types of Zuni Bread from different parts of the Southwest. What they have in common is that they're all hearty breads made with both wheat flour and cornmeal. I chose to adapt this quick version because I liked the idea of including sunflower seeds.

1¼ cups whole wheat pastry flour
½ cup unbleached white flour
⅓ cup cornmeal
2½ teaspoons baking powder
½ teaspoon baking soda
1 teaspoon salt
2 eggs, well beaten
1 cup buttermilk
3 tablespoons molasses
2 tablespoons canola oil
¼ cup toasted sunflower seeds

Preheat the oven to 350 degrees.

Combine the first 6 ingredients in a mixing bowl and stir together. In another bowl, combine the beaten eggs with the buttermilk, molasses, and oil and stir until well blended.

Add the wet ingredients to the dry and beat together vigorously to form a stiff batter. Stir in the sunflower seeds. Pour the mixture into an oiled, 9- by 5- by 3-inch loaf pan.

Bake for 45 to 50 minutes, or until the top is nicely browned and a knife inserted into the center tests clean. When the loaves are cool enough to handle, remove them from their pans and allow them to cool on a rack.

Per 3/4-inch slice:
Calories: 148
Carbohydrates: 20 g
Total fat: 5 g
Cholesterol: 36 g
Protein: 5 g
Sodium: 242 mg

[The Indians] make their Bread of the Indian corn, wild Oats, or the Sunflower.

—Robert Beverly
The History and Present State of Virginia, 1705

SHAKER HERB BREAD

Makes two loaves

Shaker cookery in America is perhaps best known for having been far ahead of its time in its creative use of culinary herbs. An old Shaker journal extols their merits by stating that "they stimulate appetite, they give character to food and add charm and variety to ordinary dishes." Herbs even found their way into the Shakers' marvelous breads. Presented here are two of the best-known examples.

1 cup low-fat milk or soymilk

3 tablespoons whipped butter or
   natural canola margarine

1 cup lukewarm water

3 tablespoons honey

1 package active dry yeast

4 cups whole wheat flour

1 cup unbleached white flour

2 teaspoons dried dill

½ teaspoon dried thyme

½ teaspoon dried marjoram

2 teaspoons caraway seeds

1½ teaspoons salt

Scald the milk by heating it to just below the boiling point. Stir the butter in until it melts, then combine the mixture in a large mixing bowl with the water and honey. Allow to cool to lukewarm, then sprinkle in the yeast. Let it stand for 10 minutes to dissolve, then stir gently.

In another bowl, combine the flours, herbs, and salt. Work this mixture into the wet mixture to form a soft dough. Turn the dough out onto a well-floured board and knead for about 8 minutes, adding a small amount of flour if the dough is too sticky. Pat into a smooth round and place in a floured bowl. Cover with a clean tea towel and set in a warm place to rise until doubled in bulk, about 1½ hours.

Punch the dough down, then turn out onto a floured board and knead for a minute or two. Divide the dough in half and shape into two loaves. Place them in oiled 9- by 5- by 3-inch aluminum loaf pans. Let them rise until doubled in bulk again, covered and in a warm place, about 1 hour.

Preheat the oven to 350 degrees. Bake the loaves for 45 to 50 minutes, or until the tops are golden and the bread sounds hollow when tapped. When the loaves are cool enough to handle, remove them from their pans and allow them to cool on a rack.

Per 3/4-inch slice:

Calories: 107	Total fat: 1 g	Protein: 3 g
Carbohydrates: 20 g	Cholesterol: 3 g	Sodium: 140 mg

POTATO-DILL BREAD

Makes 2 loaves

Another great Shaker bread utilizing their special touch with herbs, this is one of my favorites. It has a wonderful texture—very light and springy. Fresh dill is preferable, but you have the option of using dried dill if it's unavailable.

1 large potato, cooked, peeled, and well mashed (about 1½ cups)

1 cup warm water

1 package active dry yeast

¼ cup lukewarm water

¼ cup whipped butter or natural canola margarine

2 tablespoons light brown sugar or Sucanat

3 tablespoons minced fresh dill, or 1 tablespoon dried dill

3½ cups whole wheat flour

1 cup unbleached white flour

1½ teaspoons salt

Dill seed for topping, optional

Combine the mashed potato with the warm water in a bowl and stir until well blended. Dissolve the yeast in the water. Let it stand for 10 minutes, then stir gently.

In the meantime, cream the butter and sugar together in a large mixing bowl until light and fluffy. Slowly add the potato mixture, stirring vigorously to combine. Stir in the dissolved yeast and the dill.

In another bowl, combine the flours and salt, then stir the flour mixture, about a cup at a time, into the wet mixture. Once all the flour is in, work everything together with floured hands. Turn the mixture out onto a well-floured board. Knead for about 8 minutes, adding additional flour only as needed to form a light, elastic dough.

Pat the dough into a smooth round and place it in a floured bowl. Cover with a clean tea towel and let it rise in a warm place until doubled in bulk, about 1½ hours.

Punch the dough down, then divide it in half and shape into loaves. Place them in two oiled, 9- by 5- by 3-inch aluminum loaf pans. Let rise again until doubled in bulk, covered and in a warm place, about 1 hour. Sprinkle with the optional dill seed.

Preheat the oven to 350 degrees.

Bake the loaves for 45 to 50 minutes, or until the tops are golden and the bread sounds hollow when tapped. When the loaves are cool enough to handle, remove them from their pans and allow them to cool on a rack.

Per 3/4-inch slice:

Calories: 101	Total fat: 1 g	Protein: 3 g
Carbohydrates: 18 g	Cholesterol: 4 g	Sodium: 136 mg

SHAKER CHEDDAR BREAD

Makes 1 loaf

The favored cheese of New England is used to great advantage in this delicious quick bread from the archives of the Shakers of New Hampshire. Practically a cheese sandwich with the cheese built right in, this bread makes for a great brown-bag or picnic lunch with a salad and fresh fruit. It's also perfect teamed with hearty bean soups such as Black Bean Soup (page 72). This bread freezes beautifully, so you might like to double the recipe and make one loaf to have fresh and one to freeze for later use.

1½ cups whole wheat pastry flour

½ cup unbleached white flour

2 teaspoons baking powder

1 teaspoon salt

2 eggs, well beaten

⅓ cup applesauce

1 cup low-fat milk or soymilk

1½ cups firmly packed grated
   sharp Cheddar cheese

1 teaspoon dried dill, optional

Preheat the oven to 350 degrees.

Combine the flours, baking powder, and salt in a large mixing bowl.

In another bowl, combine the beaten eggs with the applesauce and milk. Whisk together until well blended. Add the wet mixture to the dry and stir vigorously until completely mixed. Stir in the cheese and optional dill.

Pour the mixture into an oiled, 9- by 5- by 3-inch aluminum loaf pan. Bake for about 50 minutes, or until the top is nicely browned and a knife inserted into the center tests clean. When the loaves are cool enough to handle, remove them from their pans and allow them to cool on a rack.

Per 3/4-inch slice:

Calories: 148	Total fat: 5 g	Protein: 8 g
Carbohydrates: 16 g	Cholesterol: 51 g	Sodium: 288 mg

QUICK BOSTON BROWN BREAD

Makes 1 loaf

The original recipe for this classic American bread calls for it to be steamed for several hours in a large tin can. Somehow I can't imagine today's cooks doing so. But the trio of whole grains in this bread is so appealing that I've devised a quicker route to an excellent result. This bread is so easy to make that it's the next best thing to using a bread machine. Make it while your favorite comforting soup is simmering on the stove.

¾ cup rye flour
¾ cup whole wheat flour
¾ cup cornmeal
1½ teaspoons baking soda
1 teaspoon salt
1½ cups buttermilk
½ cup maple syrup or molasses
2 tablespoons canola oil

Preheat the oven to 375 degrees.

Combine the first 5 ingredients in a large mixing bowl and stir together.

Make a well in the center of the dry ingredients and pour each of the wet ingredients into it. Stir vigorously until the wet and dry ingredients are completely combined.

Pour the batter into a lightly oiled, 9- by- 5- by 3-inch loaf pan. Bake for about 40 minutes, or until the top is golden brown and a knife inserted into the center of the loaf comes out clean. Cool on a rack briefly, then slice and serve while still warm.

Per 3/4-inch slice:
Calories: 147	Total fat: 2 g	Protein: 3 g
Carbohydrates: 27 g	Cholesterol: 1 g	Sodium: 298 mg

At family dinners, where the common household bread is used, it should never be cut less than an inch and a half thick. There is nothing more plebeian than *thin* bread at dinner.

—Charles Day
  Hints on Etiquette, 1843

It is not proper to shock your guests by serving them thin bread at dinner.

GOLDEN SQUASH OR PUMPKIN BREAD

Makes 1 loaf

The abundant squash crop of the Native Americans worked its way into every category of cookery, whether soups, desserts, or even breads. This moist and just slightly sweet quick bread is a contemporary interpretation of a traditional idea.

1¼ cups whole wheat pastry flour

½ cup unbleached white flour

2 teaspoons baking powder

½ teaspoon salt

1 teaspoon cinnamon

¼ teaspoon each: ground cloves
   and allspice or nutmeg

¼ cup wheat germ

2 eggs, well beaten

3 tablespoons canola oil

⅓ cup fresh orange juice

¼ cup packed light brown sugar
   or Sucanat

1 cup pureed cooked butternut
   squash or fresh pumpkin, or
   canned pumpkin

⅓ cup finely chopped pecans or
   walnuts

Preheat the oven to 350 degrees.

Combine the flours, baking powder, salt, and spices in a mixing bowl. Stir in the wheat germ. In another mixing bowl, combine the beaten eggs with the oil, orange juice, and sugar, stirring until the sugar dissolves. Add the pureed squash and stir until smooth. Gradually add the wet ingredients to the dry and stir vigorously until thoroughly blended. Stir in the nuts. Pour the mixture into an oiled, 9- by 5- by 3-inch aluminum loaf pan.

Bake for 45 to 50 minutes, or until the top is golden brown and a knife inserted into the center tests clean. When the loaves are cool enough to handle, remove them from their pans and allow them to cool on a rack.

Per 3/4-inch slice:

Calories: 152	Total fat: 7 g	Protein: 4 g
Carbohydrates: 19 g	Cholesterol: 36 g	Sodium: 103 mg

SOUTHERN SPOONBREAD

6 servings

Spoonbread is one of the most characteristic dishes of traditional Southern cooking. Really a cross between a pan bread and a soufflé, it is probably so named because you can scoop it out of its pan—or eat it—with a spoon. Here is the recipe at its most basic. Although it is delicious in this simple form, you might like to try adding bits of sautéed green or red bell pepper, onion, zucchini, or cooked corn kernels.

2 cups water

1 cup cornmeal

1 teaspoon salt

2 tablespoons whipped butter or natural canola margarine

1 cup low-fat milk or soymilk

3 eggs, separated, at room temperature

Preheat the oven to 375 degrees.

Bring the water to a very gentle simmer in a heavy saucepan or double boiler. Sprinkle the cornmeal in slowly, stirring constantly to avoid lumping. Add the salt and cook over very low heat, covered, for 20 minutes, stirring occasionally. Remove from the heat.

Stir the butter into the cooked cornmeal until it melts. Transfer the mixture into a mixing bowl. Stir in the milk, half at a time, followed by the egg yolks, stirring after each addition until well blended. If you choose to use any additional ingredients, such as the vegetables mentioned above, add them at this point.

Beat the egg whites until they form stiff peaks. Fold them gently into the batter, then pour the batter into an oiled, 1½-quart casserole or soufflé dish. Bake for 30 to 35 minutes, or until the top is golden and the spoonbread is set. Serve at once, scooping portions out with a large serving spoon. Any leftover spoonbread may be cut into squares once it is chilled and sautéed on all sides in a little butter until the outside is lightly browned and crisp.

Calories: 167	Total fat: 6 g	Protein: 7 g
Carbohydrates: 20 g	Cholesterol: 116 g	Sodium: 411 mg

Anybody that ever ate spoonbread, corn cakes or pones below Mason and Dixon's line knows that white corn is for folk and yellow for critters.

—*Christian Science Monitor, 1944*

Folks seem to love posing with white corn.

RICE AND CORNMEAL SPOONBREAD

6 servings

Rice and cornmeal, with their complementary mild flavors, were often combined in old South Carolina and Louisiana recipes such as this variation of the basic spoonbread. Consider the same vegetable variations I suggested for Southern Spoonbread on the previous page. Sautéed bell pepper is especially nice.

1½ cups water

½ cup cornmeal

1 teaspoon salt

2½ tablespoons whipped butter or natural canola margarine

1 cup low-fat milk or soymilk

2 eggs, separated, at room temperature

2 cups well-cooked brown rice

Preheat the oven to 375 degrees.

Bring the water to a very gentle simmer in a heavy saucepan or double boiler. Sprinkle the cornmeal in slowly, stirring constantly to avoid lumping. Add the salt and cook over very low heat for 20 minutes. Remove from the heat.

Stir the butter into the cooked cornmeal until it melts. Turn the mixture out into a mixing bowl. Add the milk, half at a time, followed by the egg yolks and cooked rice, stirring after each addition until well blended.

Beat the egg whites until they form stiff peaks. Fold them gently into the rice-and-cornmeal mixture. Pour the mixture into an oiled, 1½-quart casserole or soufflé dish. Bake for 30 to 35 minutes, or until the top is golden brown. Cut into squares to serve.

Calories: 195   Total fat: 6 g   Protein: 6 g
Carbohydrates: 28 g   Cholesterol: 83 g   Sodium: 399 mg

Critters find that yellow corn is perfect for tricks.

Chapter 3
SOUPS

It's the old pot that makes the good soup.
Les vieux pots font les bonnes soupes.

—Creole proverb

Making soup is, for me, a continual source of culinary wonder and delight. I wonder, at first, how a bunch of seemingly disparate elements will come together—and then I am delighted by how they ultimately become a harmonious blend of complementary flavors and textures.

Great soups have always been a mainstay of American cooking, from the chowders of early New England to the thick *potages* of New Orleans. The soups that follow represent a broad cross section of regional styles, their key ingredients reading like a list of our basic native harvest: Corn, beans, rice, squash, and white and sweet potatoes are among those staples that form the basis for many of these soups. Those everyday items are transformed to outstanding savor by the ingenuity of yesterday's cooks. This inventiveness also extends to the use of unexpected ingredients—have you ever had an eggplant soup, a peanut soup, an okra soup, or a soup laced with green chilies? These offbeat finds made for a very rewarding search for soul-satisfying soups for this chapter.

My single greatest source for outstanding soups was found in the old Creole home-cooking tradition of New Orleans. Culled primarily from late-nineteenth- and early-twentieth-century Creole cookbooks, I adapted some of these soups to the vegetarian kitchen by simply omitting a soup bone or chicken stock from the original recipe. Others are from that variety known as Lenten soups, which were completely meatless to begin with. In either case, the Creole genius for creative seasoning made the adaptation easy, since the soups are already packed with flavor.

Similarly, the other soups in this chapter were chosen for their ease of adaptation, where the removal of some scraps of meat or stock would not change their intrinsic character. You will find a good selection of hearty winter soups, whose ingredients are suited to the availability of such produce in the cold months, when warming soups are most wanted. Soups for every season will be found here, whether soothing or spicy, hot or chilled, and as diverse as the origins and influences that inspired their invention.

POTAGE MAIGRE D'HIVER
(Winter Fast-Day Soup)

8 or more servings

This recipe and the one following are old Creole Lenten soups, of which the 1901 edition of The Picayune's Creole Cookbook *says, "The Creoles excel in preparation of soups without meat, or fast-day soups, as they are called...which are in great vogue during the Lenten season." Here is a winter version of Potage Maigre, adapted from the aforementioned edition. What they both have in common is the use of green peas—dried for winter, fresh for summer.*

2 tablespoons canola oil

3 medium celery stalks, diced

1 large onion, chopped

2 cloves garlic, minced

7 cups water

2 vegetable bouillon cubes

2 cups dried split peas

2 bay leaves

2 medium carrots, sliced

2 medium turnips or 1 large
    parsnip, peeled and diced

½ teaspoon dried thyme

½ teaspoon dried mint

¼ cup chopped fresh parsley

2 cups chopped fresh spinach or
    dark green lettuce leaves

Salt and freshly ground black
    pepper

Heat the oil in a large soup pot. Add the celery, onion, and garlic and sauté over medium heat until the onion is golden. Add the water and bouillon cubes, split peas, and bay leaves. Bring to a simmer, then cover and simmer gently for 10 minutes.

Add the carrots, turnips, thyme, mint and parsley. Simmer for another 45 to 50 minutes, or until the peas are mushy and the vegetables tender. Add the spinach, and season to taste with salt and pepper. Simmer for another 15 minutes over very low heat.

If time allows, let the soup stand for an hour or so before serving, then heat through as needed. This soup thickens considerably as it stands. Add more water as needed and adjust the seasonings.

Calories: 176   Total fat: 3 g   Protein: 8 g
Carbohydrates: 27 g   Cholesterol: 0 g   Sodium: 122 mg

To have [peas] in perfection, they must be quite young, gathered early in the morning, kept in a cool place, and not shelled until they are ready to be dressed...

—Mary Randolph
  The Virginia Housewife, 1824

POTAGE MAIGRE D'ETE (Summer Fast-Day Soup)

6 to 8 servings

Another Creole Lenten soup, it's unclear whether this originated as a Creole soup or was adopted by the region, since I saw versions of it in widespread sources, from old Pennsylvania Dutch cookbooks to the charming nineteenth-century Whistler's Mother's Cookbook (she called it "Soup Maigre").

2 tablespoons canola oil

2 large onions, quartered and thinly sliced

1 large celery stalk, finely diced

A handful of celery leaves

1 large head romaine lettuce, or 2 small heads Boston or Bibb lettuce, thinly shredded

5 cups water

1 vegetable bouillon cube

1 cup fresh green peas, steamed

1 cup peeled, seeded, and grated cucumber

¼ cup chopped fresh parsley

Salt and freshly ground black pepper

Potato Dumplings (page 91), optional

Reduced-fat sour cream or plain low-fat yogurt for topping, optional

Heat the oil in a large soup pot. Add the onions and sauté over medium heat until translucent. Add the diced celery and continue to sauté until the onion is golden. Add the celery leaves, lettuce, water, and bouillon cube. Bring to a simmer, then simmer gently, covered, for 10 to 15 minutes, or until the lettuce is wilted but still has a bit of crunch.

Add the peas and grated cucumber. Adjust the consistency with a bit more water or stock if the soup seems crowded.

Season to taste with salt and pepper. Simmer over very low heat for another 10 minutes. Serve hot with Potato Dumplings, if you'd like, or cold with a scoop of sour cream or yogurt.

Calories: 81   Total fat: 3 g   Protein: 2 g
Carbohydrates: 9 g   Cholesterol: 0 g   Sodium: 52 mg

RED BEAN SOUP

6 to 8 servings.

This thick, filling soup is an old Creole standard. It's a perfect choice for a soup-and-salad supper, teamed with a good bread and a light dessert.

1 pound dry red or kidney beans
1 medium onion, finely chopped
1 clove garlic, crushed or minced
2 bay leaves
2 large celery stalks, diced
A handful of celery leaves, chopped
1 cup chopped ripe tomatoes (substitute drained canned tomatoes if necessary)
½ teaspoon dried thyme
A few grains cayenne pepper, or to taste
1 tablespoon canola oil
1 large onion, quartered and thinly sliced
3 tablespoons dry red wine or sherry, optional
Salt and freshly ground black pepper
Thinly sliced lemon for garnish

Rinse and sort the beans and soak them overnight in plenty of water in a large soup pot. Or, for the quick-soak method, bring the beans and water to cover to a boil in a large soup pot, then cover and let stand off the heat for an hour or so. In either case, drain and rinse the beans and return them to the soup pot. Cover the beans with water in about double their volume. Add the onion, garlic, and bay leaves. Bring to a simmer, then cover and simmer gently over low heat for 1½ hours.

Stir in the celery and its leaves, tomatoes, thyme, and cayenne pepper. Simmer for another hour or more, or until the beans are quite tender. Remove from the heat and discard the bay leaves.

With a slotted spoon, transfer half of the solid ingredients to a food processor and process (in batches if necessary) to a coarse puree. Stir the puree back into the soup pot.

Heat the oil in a small skillet. Add the onion and sauté until it is golden brown. Stir the onion into the soup along with the optional wine and season to taste with salt and pepper. Return to very low heat for 10 to 15 minutes. Garnish each serving with 2 thin lemon slices.

Calories: 134	Total fat: 2 g	Protein: 6 g
Carbohydrates: 21 g	Cholesterol: 0 g	Sodium: 16 mg

Sometimes you sow red beans, and white beans grow.

—Creole Proverb akin to "the best laid plans..."

BLACK BEAN SOUP

6 to 8 servings.

I'm quite fond of black beans, so I was pleased to add this classic Southern soup (with distinctive Creole overtones) to my repertoire. Original recipes most often included some meat, such as ham, but with the robust flavor of the bean and the assertive seasonings, it will not be missed.

1 pound dried black beans
1 cup chopped onion
2 large carrots, chopped
2 large celery stalks, diced
2 or 3 cloves garlic, crushed or
   minced
3 tablespoons fresh parsley
   leaves
2 bay leaves
1 teaspoon dried basil
½ teaspoon dried thyme
¼ teaspoon each: ground cloves
   and allspice
¼ cup dry sherry
Salt and freshly ground black
   pepper
1 tablespoon canola oil
1 large onion, quartered and
   sliced
Thinly sliced lemons for garnish
Finely chopped fresh parsley for
   garnish

Rinse and sort the beans and soak them overnight in plenty of water in a large soup pot. Or, for the quick-soak method, bring the beans and water to cover to a boil in a large soup pot, then cover and let stand off the heat for an hour or so. In either case, drain and rinse the beans and return them to the soup pot. Cover the beans with water in about double their volume. Add the chopped onion, carrots, celery, garlic, and seasonings. Simmer for another 1 to 1½ hours, or until the beans are quite soft.

With a slotted spoon, scoop out 1½ cups of black beans, avoiding scooping out the other vegetables as best as you can. Set aside.

Discard the bay leaves. With a slotted spoon, transfer the solid ingredients to a food processor (in batches if necessary). Use about 1/4 cup of the cooking liquid per batch. Process until smoothly pureed, then return the puree to the soup pot along with the reserved beans. Add the sherry and season to taste with salt and pepper. Return to low heat.

Heat the oil in a small skillet. Add the sliced onion and sauté over low heat until golden brown. Stir the sautéed onion into the soup. Simmer for 5 minutes more.

Garnish each serving with two lemon slices and a bit of chopped parsley. This soup keeps very well for several days, and the flavor improves as it stands.

Calories: 143	Total fat: 2 g	Protein: 6 g
Carbohydrates: 22 g	Cholesterol: 0 g	Sodium: 20 mg

CREOLE EGGPLANT SOUP

6 servings

From an old Creole recipe, this unusual soup was a favorite discovery on my cross-country travels. This recipe is courtesy of the famous Commander's Palace restaurant in New Orleans, which still serves it occasionally. It's believed that the soup originated locally due to the abundance of the eggplant crop in the region.

1½ tablespoons canola oil

1 large onion, chopped

3 medium celery stalks, diced

1 clove garlic, minced

1½ tablespoons unbleached white flour

2 large potatoes, peeled and finely diced

1 large eggplant (about 1½ pounds), peeled and finely diced

1 tablespoon finely chopped fresh basil, or 1 teaspoon dried basil

1 teaspoon curry powder

¼ teaspoon dried thyme

1 cup low-fat milk or soymilk

Salt and freshly ground black pepper

2 to 3 tablespoons chopped fresh parsley

Heat the oil in a large soup pot. Add the onion, celery, and garlic and sauté over medium-low heat, stirring frequently, for 10 minutes. Add a small amount of water if the mixture begins to seem dry. Sprinkle in the flour and cook, stirring, for another minute or so.

Add the potatoes and eggplant to the soup pot along with enough water to cover all but about an inch of the vegetables, leaving them above the water line. Bring to a simmer, stir well, then cover and simmer gently until the potatoes are just tender, about 15 minutes.

Add the basil, curry powder, and thyme and simmer another 25 minutes. Stir in the milk, more or less as needed to achieve a nice consistency, and season to taste with salt and pepper. Simmer for another 5 to 10 minutes over very low heat. Stir in the parsley and serve.

Calories: 154	Total fat: 4 g	Protein: 3 g
Carbohydrates: 27 g	Cholesterol: 2 g	Sodium: 47 mg

POTAGE CRECY (Carrot Soup)

6 to 8 servings

This clove-scented Creole soup has a cheerful orange color, and if good, fresh carrots are used, a subtly sweet flavor. It's a real spirit-lifter in the winter, awakening and nourishing the dulled senses. Serve with fresh warm bread or top with crisp croutons.

2½ tablespoons canola oil, divided

2 large onions, chopped

2 cloves garlic, minced

2 medium turnips or parsnips, peeled and diced

2 medium celery stalks, diced

1 14- to 16-ounce can diced tomatoes

1½ pounds carrots, peeled and chopped

2½ cups water

1 teaspoon dried basil

¼ teaspoon dried thyme

3 or 4 whole cloves or ¼ teaspoon ground cloves

1½ to 2 cups low-fat milk or soymilk

Salt and freshly ground black pepper

3 tablespoons finely chopped fresh parsley

Juice of ½ lemon

Heat 1½ tablespoons of the oil in a large soup pot. Add the onions and sauté over low heat until they begin to turn golden. Add the garlic, turnips, celery, tomatoes and liquid, and about two thirds of the carrots. Set aside the remaining carrots.

Stir in the water and seasonings and bring to a simmer. Cover and simmer gently until the vegetables are tender but not mushy, about 25 to 30 minutes. Remove from the heat.

With a slotted spoon, transfer the cooked vegetables, along with a little of the cooking liquid, to a food processor. Process (in batches if necessary) to a smooth puree and return to the soup pot. Stir in enough milk to achieve a medium-thick consistency. Return to low heat.

Heat the remaining oil in a small skillet. Sauté the reserved carrots over medium heat until they are golden and nearly tender. Stir them into the soup, then season to taste with salt and pepper. Stir in the parsley and lemon juice and serve once the soup is well heated through.

Calories: 146	Total fat: 6 g	Protein: 4 g
Carbohydrates: 20 g	Cholesterol: 3 g	Sodium: 103 mg

POTAGE CRESSONIER
(Potato and Watercress Soup)

6 servings

This simple but elegant Creole soup is a good one to make a day ahead, since its flavor develops quite nicely. Serve it hot or cold.

2 tablespoons canola oil
1 large onion, chopped
2 cloves garlic, minced
6 cups peeled, diced potatoes
2 cups vegetable stock, or water
    with 1 vegetable bouillon cube
2 large bunches of watercress
    (about 4 to 5 packed cups)
2 cups low-fat milk or soymilk
Salt and freshly ground black
    pepper

Heat the oil in a large soup pot. Add the onion and garlic and sauté over medium heat until the onion is translucent. Add the potatoes and stock. Bring to a simmer, then simmer gently, covered, until the potatoes are just tender, about 15 minutes. Add the watercress and simmer for another 10 minutes. Remove from the heat.

Transfer approximately two thirds of the solid mixture to a food processor with a little of the liquid. Process (in batches if necessary) until smoothly pureed and stir the mixture back into the soup pot. Add the milk and season to taste with salt and pepper. Return to medium-low heat and simmer just until thoroughly heated through. Adjust the consistency with more milk if necessary. Let the soup stand off the heat for an hour or so, then heat through before serving, or cool and refrigerate, then serve chilled.

Calories: 205
Carbohydrates: 33 g
Total fat: 5 g
Cholesterol: 3 g
Protein: 5 g
Sodium: 108 mg

Many cooks do not appear to be alive to the fact that the less pretentious they make a soup the more certain it is to give satisfaction, and of all cooking, nothing is easier to do well and nothing more difficult to do badly, than soup-making—too much pains being productive of the same results as too many cooks.

—Godey's Lady's Book, 1870

SWEET POTATO SOUP

6 servings

A warming soup with an appealing golden color, this was likely developed to take advantage of the bumper crop of sweet potatoes so common to the South. Their natural sweetness gives this soup a surprising flavor twist.

2 tablespoons canola oil

2 large onions, chopped

2 medium carrots, diced

1 large celery stalk, diced

A handful of celery leaves

5 heaping cups peeled, diced
   sweet potato

2 bay leaves

¼ teaspoon dried thyme

¼ teaspoon ground nutmeg

1 cup low-fat milk or soymilk,
   or as needed

Salt and freshly ground black
   pepper

Heat the oil in a large soup pot. Add the onions, carrots, and celery and sauté over low heat until the onions begin to turn golden. Add the celery leaves, sweet potato dice, and enough water to barely cover the vegetables. Bring to a simmer, then add the bay leaves, thyme, and nutmeg. Cover and simmer gently for about 15 to 20 minutes, or until the sweet potatoes and vegetables are tender.

With a slotted spoon, transfer about half of the solid ingredients to a food processor or blender along with a little of the liquid. Process (in batches if necessary) until smoothly pureed, then stir back into the soup pot. Add the milk, more or less as needed to achieve a medium-thick consistency.

Season to taste with salt and pepper. Simmer over very low heat for another 10 minutes. Serve at once, or let stand for an hour or so off the heat, then heat through before serving.

Calories: 218

Total fat: 5 g

Protein: 3 g

Carbohydrates: 40 g

Cholesterol: 2 g

Sodium: 46 mg

PARSNIP CHOWDER

6 servings

*Although the word "chowder" origi-
nates from the French chaudière,
meaning "kettle," chowders have
come to represent a variety of all-
American soups. Most chowders are
associated with New England, as is
this recipe, and are usually characterized by a milk base with the addition
of potatoes and other vegetables or
seafood. Parsnips are hardy winter
roots whose mild flavor is perfect for
this soothing cold-weather soup.*

1½ tablespoons canola oil
1 cup chopped onion
4 medium potatoes, peeled and
  finely diced
1 pound parsnips, peeled and
  diced
3 cups vegetable stock, or water
  with 1 vegetable bouillon cube
2 cups low-fat milk or soymilk
3 tablespoons finely chopped
  fresh parsley
1 to 2 tablespoons finely chopped
  fresh dill, to taste
Salt and freshly ground black
  pepper

Heat the oil in a large soup pot. Add the onion
and sauté over medium heat until golden.
Add the potatoes, parsnips, and stock. Bring
to a simmer, then cover and simmer gently
until the potatoes and parsnips are tender,
about 20 minutes.

With a slotted spoon, transfer two cupfuls
of the potatoes and parsnips to a shallow
bowl. Mash well and stir them back into the
soup. Add the milk, parsley, and dill. Season
to taste with salt and pepper. Simmer over
very low heat for 10 minutes, or until heated
through.

Serve at once, or let the soup stand off the
heat for an hour or so, then heat through
before serving.

Calories: 214	Total fat: 4 g	Protein: 5 g
Carbohydrates: 38 g	Cholesterol: 3 g	Sodium: 103 mg

**Seasonings for soups may be varied to
suit tastes. The simplest many have
only pepper and salt, while the richest
may have a little of every savor, so
delicately blended that no one is
conspicuous. The best seasoning is
that which is made up of the smallest
quantity from each of many spices. No
measure can be given, because the
good soup-maker must be a skillful
taster.**

—*The Buckeye Cookbook,* 1883

CREAM OF ASPARAGUS SOUP

6 servings

Asparagus has been a much-loved kitchen-garden vegetable since colonial times. Asparagus soups appeared regularly in early cookbooks, often rubbed through a sieve to produce a puree.

2 pounds asparagus
1½ tablespoons canola oil
1 large onion, chopped
1 clove garlic, minced
1 large potato, finely diced
2½ cups vegetable stock, or water with 1 vegetable bouillon cube
1 teaspoon dried dill
½ teaspoon dried basil
Pinch of nutmeg
½ to 1 cup low-fat milk or soymilk
Salt and freshly ground black pepper

Cut about an inch off the bottoms of the asparagus stalks and discard. Scrape off any tough skin with a vegetable peeler. Cut the stalks into approximately 1-inch pieces. Set aside the tips for later use.

Heat the oil in a large soup pot. Add the onion and garlic and sauté until the onion is golden. Add the asparagus pieces, potato, stock, dill, basil, and nutmeg. Bring to a simmer, then cover and simmer gently until the asparagus and potatoes are tender, about 15 minutes. Remove from the heat.

With a slotted spoon, transfer the solid ingredients to a food processor. Process (in batches if necessary) until smoothly pureed, then stir back into the soup pot. Return to low heat. Add enough milk to achieve a medium-thick consistency, then season to taste with salt and pepper.

Steam the reserved asparagus tips until they are tender-crisp. Stir them into the soup and simmer over very low heat for another 5 minutes. Serve at once, or let the soup stand off the heat for an hour or so to develop flavor, then heat through before serving.

Calories: 120	Total fat: 4 g	Protein: 4 g
Carbohydrates: 16 g	Cholesterol: 1 g	Sodium: 73 mg

Pray, how does your asparagus perform?

—John Adams (1735-1826), in a letter to his wife, Abigail

OKRA-RICE SOUP

6 to 8 servings

A true Southern classic, this soup was as commonplace in the nineteenth century as it is unusual today. Despite the "throw-everything-into-the-pot" simplicity of the recipe, the result is a wonderfully complex blend of flavors and textures—thanks mainly to the unique character of okra. This thick soup is closely related to a Creole gumbo, and tastes great served with hot Buttermilk Biscuits (page 31).

1½ tablespoons canola oil
2 medium onions, chopped
2 medium celery stalks, finely
    diced
5 cups water
6 medium ripe juicy tomatoes,
    chopped
4 cups fresh small okra, stemmed
    and sliced ½ inch thick
1 medium green bell pepper,
    chopped
⅔ cup raw brown rice
3 tablespoons chopped fresh
    parsley
2 bay leaves
1 teaspoon dried thyme
¼ teaspoon dried red pepper
    flakes,
or ⅛ teaspoon cayenne pepper,
    or to taste
Salt and freshly ground black
    pepper

Heat the oil in a large soup pot. Add the onions and celery and sauté over low heat until the onions are golden. Add the water, followed by all the remaining ingredients(even the small amount of red pepper or cayenne given here will produce a distinct spiciness, so use your discretion!).

Bring to a simmer, then cover and simmer gently for about an hour, stirring occasionally, until the rice is cooked and the vegetables are tender. Serve at once, or let the soup stand for an hour or so, then heat through as needed. This soup will thicken considerably as it stands. Adjust the consistency if necessary with a bit more water and correct the seasonings, but let it remain very thick.

Calories: 142	Total fat: 3 g	Protein: 3 g
Carbohydrates: 24 g	Cholesterol: 0 g	Sodium. 28 mg

Hot soup at table is very vulgar; it either leads to an unseemly mode of taking it, or keeps people waiting too long whilst it cools. Soup should be brought to table only moderately warm.

—Charles Day
   Hints on Etiquette, 1843

TOMATO-BARLEY SOUP

8 servings

Barley soups seem to have been quite common in the nineteenth century. I noticed them on a number of old restaurant menus as well as cookbooks of that period, though there didn't seem to be any standard recipe. This hearty, full-flavored soup was inspired by a recipe from The Virginia Housewife *(1824) by Mary Randolph.*

2 tablespoons canola oil
2 large onions, quartered and
    thinly sliced
¾ cup pearl barley, rinsed
2 medium carrots, peeled and
    sliced
2 medium turnips or 1 medium-
    large potato, peeled and diced
2 large celery stalks, diced
1 28-ounce can diced tomatoes
2 bay leaves
5 cups water
3 tablespoons chopped fresh dill
Salt and freshly ground black
    pepper

Never allow butter, soup or other food to remain in your whiskers. Use the napkin frequently.

—Hill's Manual of Social and Business Forms, 1879

Heat the oil in a large soup pot. Add the onions and sauté over low heat until they are golden. Add the barley, carrots, turnips, celery, tomatoes and their liquid, bay leaves, and water. Bring to a simmer, then cover and simmer gently for 1¼ hours, stirring every 20 minutes or so. The barley and vegetables should be done, or nearly so.

Add the dill, and season to taste with salt and pepper. Simmer, covered, for another 10 to 15 minutes, or until the barley is puffy and the vegetables are tender but not mushy. Adjust the consistency with more water if necessary. The soup will thicken as it stands. Adjust the liquid and seasonings as needed, but let the soup stay nice and thick.

Calories: 104	Total fat: 3 g	Protein: 2 g
Carbohydrates: 16 g	Cholesterol: 0 g	Sodium: 35 mg

SPLIT PEA SOUP WITH BARLEY AND VEGETABLES

8 servings

Split pea soup, an American classic, is high on my list of great comfort foods.

1½ tablespoons canola oil

1 medium onion, finely chopped

2 to 3 cloves garlic, minced

2 medium celery stalks, diced

1 large or 2 medium carrots, diced

10 cups water, divided

1 pound green split peas, rinsed and sorted

½ cup pearl barley

2 bay leaves

2 teaspoons Mrs. Dash or other salt-free herb-and-spice seasoning mix

½ teaspoon ground cumin

Salt and freshly ground pepper to taste

Heat the oil in a large soup pot. Add the onion, garlic, celery, and carrots. Sauté over medium heat for 8 to 10 minutes, or until the onions are soft and golden.

Add 8 cups of the water and all the remaining ingredients except salt and pepper. Bring to a simmer, then simmer gently, covered, for 30 minutes. Stir and add the remaining 2 cups of water. Simmer for another 40 to 45 minutes, or until the barley is tender and the peas are mushy. Serve at once, or let the soup stand for an hour or two, then heat through before serving.

Note: The soup thickens considerably as it stands. Add more water as needed, then taste to correct the seasonings.

Calories: 130   Total fat: 3 g   Protein: 5 g
Carbohydrates: 21 g   Cholesterol: 0 g   Sodium: 16 mg

TORTILLA SOUP

6 servings

There are many variations on this Southwestern classic, the common denominator being that the soup is ladled over strips of crisp corn tortilla. It's a light and pleasant way to begin a meal with a Southwestern theme.

1 tablespoon olive oil
1 large onion, chopped
2 to 3 cloves garlic, minced
½ medium green bell pepper, finely diced
½ cup white rice
6 cups water
1 vegetable bouillon cube
6 corn tortillas
1 medium zucchini or yellow squash, diced
1 14- to 16-ounce can diced tomatoes
1 4-ounce can chopped mild green chiles
½ teaspoon each: ground cumin and dried oregano
Salt and freshly ground pepper to taste

Heat the oil in a large soup pot. Add the onion and garlic and sauté over medium heat until they are golden. Add the bell pepper, rice, water and bouillon cube. Bring to a simmer, then simmer gently, covered, for 15 minutes.

In the meantime, preheat the oven to 400 degrees. Cut the tortillas into strips about ½ inch wide by 1½ inches long. Arrange on a baking sheet and bake for about 15 minutes, or until they are crisp and dry. Remove from the oven and set aside until needed.

Add the squash, tomatoes, chiles, cumin, and oregano to the soup pot and stir. Continue to simmer for another 10 to 15 minutes, or until the rice and squash are tender. Season to taste with salt and pepper. If you wish, let the soup stand for an hour or two before serving, then heat through when needed.

When ready to serve, divide the tortilla strips among 6 serving bowls and ladle some soup into each. Serve at once.

Calories: 154   Total fat: 3 g   Protein: 4 g
Carbohydrates: 27 g   Cholesterol: 0 g   Sodium: 11 mg

ZUCCHINI CHOWDER

6 servings

The recipe for this excellent Southwestern soup comes from by a friend who grew up in San Antonio, Texas. He remembers having had it while growing up, and added that it was quite typical in the area. Serve it with Zuni Quick Bread (page 58) or Buttermilk Corn Bread (page 49).

1 tablespoon canola oil

1 heaping cup chopped onion

2 cloves garlic, minced

1 large green bell pepper, diced

1 cup chopped ripe tomato

7 to 8 cups diced zucchini

½ teaspoon each: dried oregano, ground cumin, chili powder

1½ cups low-fat milk or soymilk, or as needed

½ cup grated Monterey Jack cheese

2 tablespoons minced fresh cilantro or parsley

Salt and freshly ground black pepper

Heat the oil in a medium skillet. Add the onion and garlic and sauté over medium heat until the onion is translucent. Add the bell pepper and continue to sauté until it is tender-crisp. Add the tomato and sauté for another 2 minutes or so, just until it has softened somewhat.

Place the zucchini dice in a large soup pot or Dutch oven with about an inch of water. Cover and steam over moderately low heat until the zucchini is just tender, lifting the lid frequently to stir so that it cooks evenly. Remove 1½ cups of the zucchini and set aside.

Transfer the skillet mixture and the remaining zucchini to a food processor and process (in batches if necessary), until smoothly pureed. Return the puree to the pot along with the reserved zucchini, seasonings, and enough milk to achieve a medium-thick consistency.

Bring to a gentle simmer, then sprinkle in the grated cheese and the cilantro or parsley. Season to taste with salt and pepper. Simmer over very low heat for 10 minutes more, then serve.

Calories: 134	Total fat: 5 g	Protein: 6 g
Carbohydrates: 15 g	Cholesterol: 11 g	Sodium: 91 mg

Many people make a disgusting noise with their lips, by inhaling their breath strongly whilst taking soup— a habit which should be carefully avoided.

—Charles Day
Hints on Etiquette, 1843

POTATO, CHEESE, AND GREEN CHILE SOUP

6 servings

I discovered this robust soup in a number of Southwestern cafés and was glad to learn that it's a regional standard.

1½ tablespoons olive oil
1 large onion, chopped
2 to 3 cloves garlic, crushed or minced
4 large potatoes, peeled and diced
1 large green bell pepper, finely chopped
1 heaping cup finely chopped ripe tomatoes
5 cups vegetable stock or water
1 cup cooked fresh or thawed frozen corn kernels
1 small hot fresh chile, seeded and minced, or 1 4-ounce can chopped mild green chiles
½ teaspoon each: ground cumin and dried oregano
1½ cups grated Monterey Jack cheese
Salt and freshly ground black pepper

Heat the oil in a large soup pot. Add the onion and garlic and sauté over medium heat until the onion is golden. Add the remaining ingredients, except the cheese and salt and pepper. Bring to a simmer, then cover and simmer gently until the potatoes are tender, about 20 minutes.

Mash enough of the potatoes against the side of the pot with the back of a wooden spoon to thicken the base. Simmer over very low heat for another 10 to 15 minutes.

Slowly sprinkle in the grated cheese, stirring until it blends in. Season to taste with salt and pepper and simmer over low heat, stirring frequently, for another 5 minutes. Serve at once or let the soup stand off the heat for an hour or so, then heat through before serving.

Calories: 264   Total fat: 11 g   Protein: 10 g
Carbohydrates: 29 g   Cholesterol: 25 g   Sodium: 166 mg

Wrong way to finish soup: Slurping from tipped bowl is unseemly & noisy.

COLD AVOCADO SOUP

4 to 6 servings

This quick and easy Southwestern soup is refreshing on a hot summer day. Serve with Taco Salad (page 107) for a light, cool summer meal.

2 large ripe avocados
1½ cups low-fat milk
1 cup buttermilk
1 small green bell pepper, finely chopped
2 scallions, minced
2 to 3 tablespoons minced fresh cilantro
Juice of ½ lemon
½ teaspoon ground cumin
Salt and freshly ground black pepper

It is usual to commence with soup...when all are seated, send a plate of soup to everyone. Do not ask if they will be helped, as everyone takes it, of course.

—An American Lady
True Politeness, 1853

Peel the avocados. Mash one of them well and finely dice the other one. Place the mashed avocado in a serving bowl and add ½ cup of the milk. Stir together until smooth, then add the diced avocado and all the remaining ingredients, and stir again until well blended. Cover and refrigerate the soup for an hour or so, or until needed, then serve chilled.

Calories: 192	Total fat: 11 g	Protein: 6 g
Carbohydrates: 17 g	Cholesterol: 5 g	Sodium: 68 mg

Correct way to finish soup: Licking the bowl is both quiet & dignified.

PUREE OF CHICKPEA SOUP

6 servings

This flavorful traditional soup of the Southwest can be made with very little effort.

1 tablespoon olive oil
1 heaping cup chopped onion
2 to 3 cloves garlic
5 cups well-cooked chickpeas
    (about 1¾ cups raw), or 2
    20-ounce cans, drained and
    rinsed
1 14- to 16-ounce can diced
    tomatoes
2 cups vegetable stock or water
1 teaspoon each: dried oregano
    and ground cumin
½ teaspoon ground coriander
Salt and freshly ground black
    pepper
1 cup grated cheddar cheese,
    reduced-fat if desired, optional
Chopped fresh cilantro or parsley
    for garnish

Heat the oil in a large soup pot. Add the onion and garlic and sauté over medium heat until the onion is golden. Remove from the heat.

Set aside 1½ cups of the chickpeas. Place the rest in a food processor along with the onion mixture, the tomatoes, and ½ cup of the stock. Process until smoothly pureed. Stir the puree back into the soup pot along with the reserved chickpeas, the remaining stock, and the seasonings. Slowly bring to a simmer, then simmer, covered, very gently for 15 minutes.

If using the cheese, sprinkle it in, a little at a time, stirring each time until it melts. Garnish each serving with some chopped cilantro or parsley.

Calories: 264   Total fat: 5 g   Protein: 11 g
Carbohydrates: 42 g   Cholesterol: 0 g   Sodium: 17 mg

It is not correct to allow guests to wear fancy hats while eating soup.

SQUASH AND CORN CHOWDER

6 to 8 servings

This recipe is an adaptation of a Native American classic. The perfect time to make it is in the late summer and early autumn, when the first of the squash harvest dovetails with the last of the local sweet corn crop.

1 medium butternut squash
   (about 1½ pounds)
1 tablespoon olive oil
1 cup chopped onion
2 medium potatoes, scrubbed
   and diced
2 bay leaves
½ teaspoon dried thyme
½ teaspoon dried summer savory
Vegetable stock or water
2½ to 3 cups cooked fresh corn
   kernels (from 3 medium ears)
1 cup low-fat milk or soymilk
Salt and freshly ground black
   pepper

With a sharp knife, cut the squash across the center of the rounded part. Remove the seeds and stringy fibers. Slice the squash into ½-inch rings, then pare each ring and chop into small dice.

Heat the oil in a large soup pot. Add the onion and sauté over medium heat until golden. Add the squash, potatoes, all the seasonings, and enough stock or water to cover all but about an inch of the vegetables. Bring to a simmer, then cover and simmer gently until the squash and potatoes are tender, about 20 to 25 minutes.

With a slotted spoon, transfer 2 heaping cups of the solid ingredients to a shallow bowl, mash them well, and stir them back into the soup. Add the corn kernels and enough milk to achieve a medium-thick consistency. Season to taste with salt and pepper and simmer over very low heat for another 10 to 15 minutes.

Serve at once, or if time allows, let the soup stand off the heat for an hour or so, then heat through before serving. This may also be made a day ahead, since it flavors nicely overnight.

Calories: 164	Total fat: 2 g	Protein: 4 g
Carbohydrates: 32 g	Cholesterol: 1 g	Sodium: 27 mg

We dined on Indian corn and Squash soop, and boiled bread.

—John Bartram
Observations in his Travels, 1751

BUTTERNUT SQUASH AND APPLE SOUP

6 servings

Everything about this soup says "fall harvest"—from its warm golden color to its slightly sweet, fresh flavor. Once you've got the squash baked, it's a soup that cooks fairly quickly.

1 large butternut squash
2 tablespoons canola oil
1 large red onion, chopped
4 cups peeled, diced Macintosh
   apple
4 cups water
1 vegetable bouillon cube
½ teaspoon ground ginger
¼ teaspoon ground nutmeg
2 cups low-fat milk or soymilk,
   or as needed
Salt and white pepper to taste

Preheat the oven to 400 degrees.

Halve the squash lengthwise with a sharp knife and scoop out the seeds and fibers. Place cut side up in a shallow baking dish and cover tightly with foil. Bake for 45 to 50 minutes, or until tender. Set aside until cool enough to handle.

Heat the oil in a soup pot. Add the onion and sauté over medium-low heat until golden, about 8 to 10 minutes.

Add the apple, water, bouillon cube, and spices. Bring to a simmer, then simmer gently, covered, until the apples are soft, about 10 minutes.

In a food processor, puree the squash with ½ cup of the milk until completely smooth. Transfer to a bowl.

Transfer the apple-onion mixture to the food processor and puree until completely smooth. Transfer both this and the squash puree back into the soup pot and stir together. Add the remaining milk, using a bit more if the puree is too thick.

Bring the soup to a simmer once again, then cook over low heat for another 5 to 10 minutes, or until heated through. Season to taste with salt and white pepper. Serve at once, or let the soup stand off the heat for an hour or two, then heat through before serving.

Calories: 206	Total fat: 6 g	Protein: 4 g
Carbohydrates: 34 g	Cholesterol: 3 g	Sodium: 97 mg

CAJUN CORN SOUP

6 servings

This beautiful, creamy soup is perfect for taking advantage of summer's bumper crop of sweet corn. Serve it either hot or cold.

6 medium ears uncooked fresh
   corn
2 tablespoons canola oil, divided
1½ cups chopped onions
3 cloves garlic, minced
3 cups water
¼ teaspoon dried red pepper
   flakes, or to taste
¼ teaspoon dried thyme
1 tablespoon whipped butter or
   natural canola margarine
1 large green or red bell pepper,
   finely diced
1 cup low-fat milk or soymilk
Salt to taste

Before starting the soup, scrape the corn kernels off the cob with a sharp knife. Set aside.

Heat 1½ tablespoons of the oil in a large soup pot. Add the onions and garlic and sauté over low heat until the onions are lightly golden. Add the corn kernels, water, red pepper flakes (this amount will produce a nippy spiciness, so adjust to your taste) and thyme. Bring to a simmer, then cover and simmer gently until the corn kernels are tender but not overdone (the time this takes will vary depending on the variety and freshness of corn used, so check frequently). Remove from the heat.

With a slotted spoon, transfer half of the solid ingredients to a food processor along with a small amount of the liquid. Process (in batches if necessary) until smoothly pureed and stir back into the soup pot.

Heat the remaining oil in a small skillet. Add the green or red pepper and sauté until it is touched with brown. Stir it into the soup, followed by enough milk to achieve a medium-thick consistency. Season to taste with salt. Return to low heat for 5 minutes. Serve at once or allow to cool and refrigerate, then serve chilled.

Calories: 146   Total fat: 7 g   Protein: 3 g
Carbohydrates: 18 g   Cholesterol: 6 g   Sodium: 25 mg

PENNSYLVANIA DUTCH CORN AND CABBAGE SOUP

6 or more servings

Several standard Pennsylvania Dutch ingredients are combined in a pleasant soup. Serve it with Potato Dumplings (recipe follows) to make it heartier.

1 tablespoon canola oil
1 large onion, chopped
2 tablespoons unbleached
   white flour
4 cups finely shredded cabbage
1 large potato, finely diced
3 cups fresh uncooked corn
   kernels (from 3 to 4 ears)
1 heaping cup chopped ripe
   tomatoes, or the equivalent of
   canned diced tomatoes,
   drained
4½ cups vegetable stock, or 4½
   cups water with 2 vegetable
   bouillon cubes
1½ teaspoons mixed dried herbs
   of your choice
½ cup low-fat milk or soymilk,
   or as needed
Salt and freshly ground black
   pepper
Potato Dumplings (recipe
   follows), optional
Minced fresh parsley for garnish

Heat the oil in a large soup pot. Add the onion and sauté over medium heat until golden. Sprinkle in the flour and stir it in until blended. Add the cabbage, potato, corn kernels, tomatoes, and stock. Bring to a simmer, sprinkle in the herbs, then cover and simmer gently until all the vegetables are tender, about 30 minutes.

Stir in the milk more or less as needed to achieve the desired consistency. Season to taste with salt and pepper and simmer for another 10 minutes over very low heat. Allow the soup to stand off the heat for an hour or so before serving to develop flavor, then heat through before serving. Place 2 or 3 dumplings in each bowl if desired, ladle the soup over them, and garnish with a sprinkling of parsley.

Calories: 154   Total fat: 2 g   Protein: 4 g
Carbohydrates: 28 g   Cholesterol: 1 g   Sodium: 124 mg

It is best to plant corn once the Baltimore orioles appear.

—American folk-belief

POTATO DUMPLINGS

Makes about 18 dumplings

These dumplings are easy to make and give soups an extra measure of the filling goodness that Pennsylvania Dutch cooking is known for. It's a good way to use up leftover mashed potato.

1 cup well-mashed potato
1 egg, beaten
½ cup whole wheat flour
½ cup unbleached white flour
½ teaspoon salt
½ teaspoon baking powder
Pinch of nutmeg

Combine the mashed potato with the beaten egg in a mixing bowl. In another bowl, stir the flours together with the salt, baking powder, and nutmeg. Work this mixture into the mashed potato mixture, a little at a time, to form a soft dough. If time allows, chill the dough, which will make it easier to work with.

With floured hands (the dough will be slightly sticky), shape the dough into 1-inch balls. Bring water to a boil in a large, deep saucepan. Drop the dumplings gently into the water, one by one. Cook only half at a time if necessary so that they are not on top of one another. They will drop to the bottom at first; after a minute or so, gently nudge them with a wooden spoon so that they don't stick. Simmer steadily for 10 minutes, then remove each dumpling with a slotted spoon.

Per dumpling:

Calories: 40	Total fat: 0 g	Protein: 1 g
Carbohydrates: 8 g	Cholesterol: 12 g	Sodium: 64 mg

VIRGINIA PEANUT SOUP

6 servings

Peanuts were originally cultivated by ancient South Americans, very possibly of Brazil, and enjoyed a remarkably long trip to many parts of the world before returning to our colonial shores. Not until George Washington Carver promoted it in the latter part of the nineteenth century, however, did it become an important crop. Some attribute this famous Southern soup to him. Admittedly rich, this soup has an intense and unusual flavor and is good either hot or cold. Here's my interpretation.

1 tablespoon canola oil
1 cup chopped onion
2 large celery stalks, finely diced
3 medium carrots, thinly sliced
3 tablespoons dry white wine
2½ tablespoons unbleached
     white flour
4 cups water or vegetable stock
A few grains of cayenne pepper
⅔ cup reduced-fat or natural-style
     peanut butter
1½ cups low-fat milk or soymilk
Salt and freshly ground black
     pepper
Chopped roasted peanuts for
     garnish, optional
Minced fresh parsley for garnish

Heat the oil in a large soup pot. Add the onion, celery, carrots, and wine. Cook over low heat, stirring frequently, until the onion is golden. Sprinkle in the flour and continue to cook, stirring constantly, until the entire mixture begins to turn a light golden brown.

Add the water and bring to a simmer. Cover and simmer gently over low heat until the vegetables are tender, about 10 to 15 minutes. Spoon the peanut butter into the pot and whisk it in briskly until blended with the liquid. Stir in the milk or soymilk and season to taste with salt and pepper. Simmer very gently for another 10 minutes or so, stirring occasionally.

If time allows, let the soup stand off the heat for an hour or so to allow the flavors to blend, then heat through before serving. Garnish each serving with some chopped peanuts, if desired, and parsley.

Calories: 170	Total fat: 7 g	Protein: 9 g
Carbohydrates: 15 g	Cholesterol: 3 g	Sodium: 65 mg

At the turn of the century, the word peanut was used to describe petty or mean-spirited politics. The *New York Evening Post* put it this way in a 1909 edition: "They used to talk about 'peanut politics' at Albany, but a peanut is too large and respectable an object to yield comparison for yesterday's action of the Senate."

Chapter 4
SALADS AND RELISHES

If a gentleman with whom you are acquainted has dressed a salad, and offers the plate to you, take what you want, and immediately return to him the remainder; and do not pass it on to persons in your vicinity. It is *his* privilege and not *yours* to offer it to others, as he has had the trouble of dressing it.

—Eliza Leslie
The Behavior Book, 1853

Finding interesting regional salads to include in this chapter was not as simple as I had imagined. In old cookbooks, the salad chapter often seemed to be there because it was obligatory. And in my travels, I was often disappointed not to find a single salad with regional interest on any given menu. I don't believe, though, that this is because yesterday's cooks were unimaginative salad makers. To the contrary, I'm inclined to think that since salads can be so improvisational, relying on what's fresh or available, salad recipes just weren't as standardized as, say, a recipe for corn muffins. Thus, there was little need for setting them down in writing.

Several of the nineteenth-century cookbooks I explored devoted more space to giving advice on dressing, rather than making, a salad. If you think about it, this is perfectly reasonable. After all, if you had just returned from your kitchen garden with fresh chervil, watercress, savoy cabbage, or any of the other well-loved greens of those days, would you need obsessive instructions on what or how much to use? No, you'd likely want to wash, dress, and season your greens, then eat them at once!

Old cookbooks were full of stern or frivolous advice, too. Maria Parloa, in her *Kitchen Companion* (1887), warns, "A vegetable salad may be a thing of beauty or an indistinct mixture and uninviting dish." A depression-era cookbook from Wichita urges us to arrange a salad "daintily."

A fairly arduous search resulted in this selection of pleasing salads. Many use vegetables usually reserved for cooking, as well as beans and grains in colorful, well-seasoned ways. The list of ingredients reads like a "who's who" (or should I say "what's what") of American staples: Cabbage, potatoes, corn, peas, pinto beans, rice, avocados, and even Jerusalem artichokes and tortillas. You'll find regional variations of what must be the number-one great American salad—coleslaw—as well as more exotic selections from most every locale around the country.

CABBAGE AND PEPPER SLAW

4 to 6 servings

Cole slaw (from the Dutch, "kool," cabbage, "sla," salad) is, to my mind, the quintessential all-American salad, with regional variations all over the country. One that I especially enjoy is this recipe, one of several Southern varieties, in which the slaw is dressed in oil and vinegar. As it stands, it almost becomes a pickled cabbage relish.

5 cups firmly packed coarsely shredded cabbage
1 large green or red bell pepper, cut into thin julienne strips
1 large celery stalk, finely chopped
1 small onion, minced
2 tablespoons capers, optional

Dressing:
1 tablespoon canola oil
⅓ cup apple cider vinegar
½ teaspoon salt
1 teaspoon granulated sugar
½ teaspoon celery seed or dill seed
Freshly ground black pepper

Combine the cabbage with the next 4 ingredients in a serving bowl. Combine the dressing ingredients in a small bowl and let stand until the salt and sugar dissolve. Mix well and toss together with the cabbage mixture. Refrigerate for at least two hours before serving, stirring occasionally to distribute the dressing.

Calories: 60
Carbohydrates: 8 g
Total fat: 3 g
Cholesterol: 0 g
Protein: 1 g
Sodium: 233 mg

They prefer cabbages to roses.

—George W. Curtis
The Potiphar Papers, 1853

NORTH CAROLINA RELISH SLAW

4 to 6 servings

A friend who grew up in the western part of North Carolina contributed this lively cole slaw recipe.

2½ cups packed finely shredded white cabbage
2½ cups packed finely shredded red cabbage
1 large carrot, grated
⅓ cup sweet pickle relish
2 scallions, minced
½ cup Tofu Mayonnaise (below), or commercially prepared tofu mayonnaise
2 teaspoons prepared mustard
1 to 2 tablespoons lemon juice
Salt and freshly ground black pepper

Combine all the ingredients in a serving bowl. Season to taste with the lemon juice, salt, and pepper. Toss until thoroughly mixed. Serve at once or refrigerate for an hour or two before serving to allow the flavors to blend more thoroughly.

Calories: 62
Carbohydrates: 11 g
Total fat: 1 g
Cholesterol: 0 g
Protein: 2 g
Sodium: 300 mg

The tables was soon spread and garnished, from pepper-castor to cold-slaw.

—*Knickerbocker Magazine, 1842*

TOFU MAYONNAISE

Makes about 1 cup

This quick and easy dressing is a more healthful stand-in for oil-and-egg-based mayonnaise.

1 cup coarsely mashed soft or silken tofu
Juice of ½ lemon
1 teaspoon prepared mustard
½ teaspoon salt

Combine all the ingredients in a food processor. Process until completely smooth and creamy. Transfer to a lidded container and refrigerate any unused portion.

Per 2 tablespoons:
Calories: 17
Carbohydrates: 1 g
Total fat: 1 g
Cholesterol: 0 g
Protein: 1 g
Sodium: 152 mg

CREAMY COLE SLAW

4 to 6 servings

This mild and pleasant slaw is based on the New England variety. It's a good complement to the flavor of sweet-and-sour dishes such as Baked Barbecue Beans (page 132).

4 cups firmly packed finely shredded cabbage
1 medium carrot, finely grated
¼ cup chopped fresh herbs of your choice

Dressing:
⅓ cup reduced-fat sour cream
½ cup plain low-fat yogurt
1 tablespoon apple cider vinegar
½ teaspoon salt
½ teaspoon dry mustard
Freshly ground black pepper to taste

Combine the cabbage, carrot, and herbs in a serving bowl. In a small mixing bowl, combine all the dressing ingredients and stir together until completely blended. Pour over the cabbage mixture and toss together until thoroughly mixed. Serve at once or cover and refrigerate an hour or so until needed.

Calories: 57   Total fat: 2 g   Protein: 2 g
Carbohydrates: 7 g   Cholesterol: 3 g   Sodium: 252 mg

Throughout the nineteenth and early twentieth centuries, cabbage enjoyed a colorful life as an expression of slang. For example, it was used as a word to describe money or bank notes. As a verb, "to cabbage" meant to obtain dishonestly. In the 1940s, cabbage was a word for a young girl; Billy Rose wrote in a 1947 newspaper column, "The little cabbage spoke up for her generation."

PICNIC POTATO SALAD

Serves 6 to 8

Next to cole slaw, I can't think of a salad more all-American than potato salad. And I can't imagine a picnic that would be complete without it.

6 large red-skinned potatoes, scrubbed

1 6-ounce jar artichoke hearts, with liquid

1 red bell pepper, cut into short strips

1 cup frozen green peas, thawed

1 small zucchini, thinly sliced

2 tablespoons each: minced fresh parsley and fresh dill

2 scallions, thinly sliced

¾ cup plain low-fat yogurt

¼ cup Tofu Mayonnaise (page 96), or commercially prepared tofu mayonnaise

2 teaspoons Dijon-style mustard

1 tablespoon white wine vinegar

Salt and freshly ground black pepper

Cook or microwave the potatoes in their skins until tender but still firm. When cool enough to handle, dice them, but don't peel them. Transfer to a large mixing bowl and let cool to room temperature.

Pour the liquid from the artichoke hearts over the potatoes. Chop the artichokes and add them to the potatoes along with the red pepper, peas, zucchini, herbs, and scallions. Stir together gently.

In a small bowl, combine the yogurt, mayonnaise, mustard, and vinegar. Stir together and pour over the potato mixture. Toss gently until thoroughly mixed. Season to taste with salt and pepper. Serve at once or cover and refrigerate until needed.

Calories: 173	Total fat: 2 g	Protein: 4 g
Carbohydrates: 32 g	Cholesterol: 2 g	Sodium: 135 mg

PENNSYLVANIA DUTCH CORN RELISH

6 to 8 servings

This recipe is closely related to one of the famous "seven sweets and seven sours," as Pennsylvania Dutch relishes are known. I've also seen this referred to as "Amish Corn Salad." Simple to make, it's as colorful as it is tasty.

4 cups cooked fresh corn kernels
   (from 5 medium ears)
1 medium green bell pepper, cut
   into narrow, 1-inch strips
1 medium red bell pepper, cut
   into narrow, 1-inch strips
1 cup finely shredded cabbage
1 small onion, halved and thinly
   sliced

Dressing:
1 tablespoon canola or olive oil
¼ cup apple cider vinegar
1 tablespoon honey
½ teaspoon dry mustard
½ teaspoon celery seed or dill
   seed
Salt and freshly ground black
   pepper

Combine the first 5 ingredients in a serving bowl. Combine the dressing ingredients in a small bowl and stir until well blended. Pour the dressing over the corn mixture and toss well. Cover and allow to marinate, refrigerated, for several hours. Stir occasionally to distribute the dressing.

Calories: 117   Total fat: 2 g   Protein: 2 g
Carbohydrates: 22 g   Cholesterol: 0 g   Sodium: 7 mg

And out in Iowa, where the black loam is twenty feet deep, the corn grows so high they have to climb ladders to get down the ears.

—Max Adeler (1847-1915)
  Ten Tall Tales

CORN AND TOMATO SALAD

6 servings

A pleasant combination of two of summer's premier bumper crops.

4 cups cooked fresh corn kernels
  (from 5 medium ears)
3 medium firm ripe tomatoes,
  diced
1 large carrot, peeled and diced
1 large celery stalk, diced
1 small red bell pepper, diced
¼ cup chopped fresh parsley
1 scallion, minced

Dressing:
Juice of ½ lemon
2 to 3 tablespoons apple cider
  vinegar, to taste
1½ tablespoons canola or olive oil
1 tablespoon honey
¼ teaspoon dried dill
Pinch of dried thyme
Salt and freshly ground pepper

Combine the salad ingredients in a serving bowl. Combine all the dressing ingredients in a small bowl and stir together until well blended. Pour over the salad and toss well. Season to taste with salt and pepper. Serve at once, or cover and refrigerate for an hour or two before serving. Stir occasionally to distribute the dressing.

Calories: 155   Total fat: 3 g   Protein: 3 g
Carbohydrates: 28 g   Cholesterol: 0 g   Sodium: 22 mg

**One for the cutworm
One for the crow
One for the blackbird
And three to grow**

—American corn-planting rhyme

GREEN PEA AND CHEDDAR CHEESE SALAD

4 to 6 servings

Here is a salad that pleases both the eye and the palate. I enjoyed it several times while traveling through some of the heartland states—namely Kansas, Oklahoma, and Iowa. Not having seen any recipes for it in any old Midwestern cookbooks, I concluded that it must be a relatively recent invention. Its constant ingredients seem to be the peas, cheese, and celery, with additional, varying ingredients. This is my version, a composite of those that I sampled.

2 cups fresh shelled green peas, steamed (or substitute thawed frozen petit peas)
1 cup mushrooms, sliced and steamed
1 cup firmly packed grated cheddar cheese, reduced-fat if desired
1 large celery stalk, finely diced
1 small red bell pepper, finely diced
5 or 6 radishes, halved and sliced
1 to 2 tablespoons minced fresh dill, or 1 teaspoon dried
1 tablespoon olive oil
3 tablespoons white wine vinegar
Salt and freshly ground black pepper

Combine all the ingredients except the salt and pepper in a serving bowl and toss well. Season lightly with salt and pepper and toss again. Serve at once.

Calories: 222   Total fat: 7 g   Protein: 12 g
Carbohydrates: 26 g   Cholesterol: 16 g   Sodium: 241 mg

You are welcome, dear, welcome as green peas in June, or radishes in March.

—Ann S. Stephens
  Fashion and Famine, 1854

"TEXAS CAVIAR"
(Marinated Black-Eyed Pea Salad)

6 servings

Black-eyed peas have been an important staple of Southern cookery since they came to Southern shores as part of the slave trade from Africa. This appetizing salad hails from traditional Texas home cooking, its name reflecting the high esteem bestowed on black-eyed peas.

4 cups cooked black-eyed peas (about 1⅓ cups raw), or 2 1-pound cans, drained and rinsed
1 large green bell pepper, cut into narrow, 1-inch strips
2 to 3 scallions, chopped
⅓ cup chopped fresh parsley
2 tablespoons olive oil
¼ cup apple cider vinegar
½ teaspoon dried oregano
½ teaspoon dried basil
Salt and freshly ground black pepper
Dark green lettuce leaves

Combine all the ingredients, except the lettuce leaves, in a serving bowl and toss well. Cover and allow the salad to marinate, refrigerated, for several hours. Stir occasionally.

When ready to serve, arrange each serving on a bed of 2 or 3 lettuce leaves.

Calories: 179	Total fat: 5 g	Protein: 8 g
Carbohydrates: 26 g	Cholesterol: 0 g	Sodium: 6 mg

Her menu, in which corn-bread, dried fruit and black-eyed pease...figured as the principle dishes.

—T.N. Page
Red Rock, 1898

MENU
Corn-bread;
Dried fruit, all sorts;
Black-eyed pease,
in great abundance.

CORN AND FIELD PEA CHOW-CHOW

Serves 6

A chow-chow can be loosely defined as a relish of mixed ingredients with a piquant and/or pickled flavor.

2 cups cooked field peas (about ¾ cup raw), or substitute 1 1-pound can black-eyed peas, drained and rinsed
2 cups cooked fresh or frozen corn kernels
½ medium green bell pepper, finely diced
½ red bell pepper, finely diced
1 fresh small hot chile, seeded and minced, optional
1 small onion, minced, or 2 scallions, thinly sliced
2 to 3 tablespoons minced fresh cilantro or parsley
¼ cup chopped green olives

Dressing:
1 tablespoon olive oil
Juice of 1 lime
1 teaspoon prepared mustard
2 tablespoons undiluted apple juice concentrate
Salt and freshly ground black pepper

Combine all the ingredients for the salad in a serving bowl and stir together.

Combine the ingredients for the dressing in a small bowl and stir together. Pour over the salad and stir well. Season to taste with salt and pepper.

Cover and refrigerate for an hour or so before serving. Stir occasionally to distribute the dressing.

Calories: 158   Total fat: 2 g   Protein: 5 g
Carbohydrates: 27 g   Cholesterol: 0 g   Sodium: 137 mg

SUMMER SQUASH, GREEN BEAN, AND CHICKPEA SALAD

6 servings

This appealing mix of steamed vegetables and chickpeas is adapted from Early California Hospitality *(1938), a collection of Mission recipes of the Southwest.*

2 small yellow summer squashes
2 cups green beans, trimmed and
   cut into 1-inch pieces
1 1-pound can chickpeas,
   drained and rinsed
2 scallions, finely chopped
2 to 3 tablespoons chopped fresh
   parsley or cilantro
2 tablespoons olive oil
Juice of ½ lemon
2 to 3 tablespoons white wine
   vinegar, to taste
Salt and freshly ground black
   pepper
½ teaspoon dried oregano
Dark green lettuce leaves

Scrub the squashes, cut them in half lengthwise, and slice them 1/4 inch thick. Steam them until they are tender-crisp. At the same time, steam the green beans separately until tender-crisp. Once done, rinse the vegetables immediately under cold water and allow to drain for a few minutes in a colander.

Combine the squash and string beans in a large serving bowl along with all the remaining ingredients except the lettuce. Toss well, cover, and refrigerate for several hours. Stir occasionally to distribute the marinade. Arrange each serving on 2 or 3 lettuce leaves.

Calories: 188   Total fat: 6 g   Protein: 7 g
Carbohydrates: 26 g   Cholesterol: 0 g   Sodium: 8 mg

PINTO OR KIDNEY BEAN SALAD

4 to 6 servings

Teamed with warm flour tortillas or corn bread, this makes a great lunch or picnic dish.

4 cups cooked pinto or kidney beans

2 large celery stalks, finely diced

1 small green or red bell pepper, finely diced

2 scallions, minced

3 tablespoons chopped fresh cilantro or parsley

¼ cup reduced-fat sour cream or plain low-fat yogurt

2 teaspoons prepared mustard

1 tablespoon olive oil

2 tablespoons apple cider vinegar

½ teaspoon each: dried oregano and ground cumin

Salt and freshly ground black pepper

Tomato wedges

Combine the first 5 ingredients in a serving bowl. In a small bowl, combine the sour cream, mustard, oil, vinegar, oregano, and cumin. Stir together until well blended, then add to the bean mixture and toss well. Add salt and pepper to taste and toss again. Garnish with the tomatoes.

Calories: 183   Total fat: 3 g   Protein: 8 g
Carbohydrates: 29 g   Cholesterol: 1 g   Sodium: 81 mg

As much alike as if they'd been kidney beans, shelled out of the same pod.

—Ann S. Stephens
High Life in New York, 1844

CONTEMPORARY THREE-BEAN SALAD

8 servings

Classic three-bean salad gets a contemporary twist with balsamic vinegar, cilantro, and sunflower seeds.

2 cups green beans, trimmed and cut into 1-inch pieces
1 1-pound can chickpeas, drained and rinsed
1 1-pound can kidney beans, drained and rinsed
1 to 2 scallions, thinly sliced
¼ cup chopped fresh cilantro

Dressing:
Juice of ½ lemon or lime
3 tablespoons white or dark balsamic vinegar
1½ tablespoons honey
2 tablespoons olive oil
½ teaspoon dried oregano
½ teaspoon dried basil
Freshly ground pepper to taste
2 medium firm, ripe tomatoes, diced, optional
2 to 3 tablespoons roasted sunflower seeds for topping

Steam the green beans until tender-crisp. Drain and rinse them until cool. Combine them with the next 4 ingredients in a serving bowl and stir together.

Combine the ingredients for the dressing in a small bowl and mix together until well blended. Pour over the bean mixture and toss well. Cover and allow to marinate, refrigerated, for several hours before serving, stirring occasionally.

Just before serving, stir in the optional diced tomatoes. Or simply sprinkle the sunflower seeds over the top and serve.

Calories: 234   Total fat: 6 g   Protein: 10 g
Carbohydrates: 35 g   Cholesterol: 0 g   Sodium: 7 mg

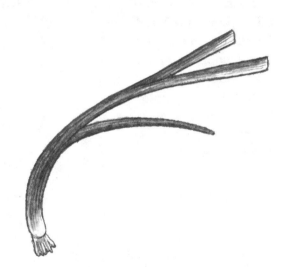

TACO SALAD

4 to 6 servings

I first had this salad at a friend's home in Washington, D.C., then later discovered it in Southwestern restaurants. Now it's popular everywhere. Incorporating all the lively flavors of tacos, this tasty salad is quick and easy to prepare, and is a perfect choice when you'd like a hearty main-dish salad.

4 corn tortillas
2 medium firm ripe tomatoes, chopped
1 large green bell pepper, chopped
¼ cup black olives, chopped
2 scallions, thinly sliced
1 cup grated cheddar or Monterey Jack cheese
1 cup cooked pinto or kidney beans
Dark green lettuce, torn, as needed

Dressing:
⅓ cup thick tomato juice
1 tablespoons olive oil
2 tablespoons red wine vinegar
½ teaspoon each: chili powder and dried oregano
¼ teaspoon salt
Freshly ground black pepper

Cut the tortillas into strips about ½ by 2 inches long. Heat a large skillet and toast the tortilla strips over medium heat, stirring frequently, until they are dry and crisp.

Combine the remaining salad ingredients in a serving bowl. Use lettuce as needed, according to the number of servings needed.

Combine the dressing ingredients in a small bowl and stir together until well blended. Pour over the salad, toss well, and serve at once.

Calories: 239   Total fat: 11 g   Protein: 11 g
Carbohydrates: 23 g   Cholesterol: 20 g   Sodium: 228 mg

If possible, when combining vegetables, have those which are of a delicate flavor form the body of a salad, using only a small proportion of those with strong flavor.

—Maria Parloa
Miss Parloa's Kitchen Companion, 1887

WALDORF SALAD

4 servings

A famous American salad, this crunchy mixture of apples, walnuts, and celery supposedly originated— and took its name from—the Waldorf Astoria hotel in New York City.

2 medium Granny Smith apples, cored and diced (don't peel)
Juice of ½ lemon
2 large celery stalks, diced
½ cup dark raisins
¼ cup chopped walnuts
½ cup thinly sliced red onion, optional
⅓ cup Tofu Mayonnaise (page 96), or commercially prepared soy mayonnaise
Pinch of nutmeg
Dark green lettuce leaves or mesclun (mixed baby lettuces), as desired

Combine the apples and lemon juice in a mixing bowl and toss together. Add the remaining ingredients, except the lettuces, and toss well.

Line four salad plates or shallow salad bowls with a few lettuce leaves and divide the salad over them. Serve at once.

Calories: 200　　Total fat: 8 g　　Protein: 2 g
Carbohydrates: 20 g　　Cholesterol: 0 g　　Sodium: 151 mg

COBB SALAD

6 servings

Another old restaurant-inspired salad, this one is said to have had its origins at the Brown Derby restaurant in Los Angeles. The original recipe calls for diced chicken or turkey, several slices of crisp-cooked bacon, and a few chopped hard-cooked eggs. Sometimes, some crumbled bleu cheese is added—now that's what I would call "the cholesterol special"! Avocado is also a characteristic ingredient, and that has been retained, though I've eliminated the eggs and replaced the meats with soy-based analogs.

6 slices soy bacon substitute (see note)

4 to 6 ounces baked marinated tofu or soy "turkey" or "chicken"-style deli slices, diced (see note)

1 medium firm, ripe avocado, pitted and diced

Juice of ½ lemon

2 medium firm, ripe tomatoes, diced

6 cups torn dark green lettuce leaves

Low-fat dressing of your choice (French or Catalina are good with this)

Crisp-cook the "bacon" according to package directions. Remove to a plate. When cool enough to handle, cut into small sections, about ½ inch in length.

Combine the "bacon" with the tofu in a serving bowl. In another small bowl, toss the avocado dice with the lemon juice, then add them to the serving bowl, along with the tomatoes and lettuce. Toss well with the dressing of your choice, then serve at once.

Note: Bacon substitute (such as Lightlife Fakin' Bacon), baked marinated tofu, and soy deli slices are available in well-stocked supermarkets or natural foods stores.

Per serving, not including dressing:

Calories: 109	Total fat: 7 g	Protein: 4 g
Carbohydrates: 8 g	Cholesterol: 0 g	Sodium: 267 mg

As a Back Bay friend was saying, "You just don't find service like this anymore," one of the servitors clearing off an adjoining table let an almost complete avocado salad slip off a plate and onto the floor where it lay totally bewildered for a good ten minutes.

"There's a salad on the floor," I said to our waiter at length, which precipitated a hubbub as the herbaceous material was removed.

—Richard Bissell
How Many Miles to Galena? 1968

GUACAMOLE

Makes about 2 cups; serves 8 or more as an appetizer

This recipe was contributed by a friend who grew up in San Antonio. He gives standard guacamole a special touch with the addition of roasted tomatoes and bell peppers, which imparts a subtly smoked taste. Serve alongside or as part of Southwestern tortilla dishes, or as an appetizer with crisp tortilla chips.

1 medium firm ripe tomato

1 small green bell pepper

2 large very ripe avocados

Juice of ½ lemon

1 clove garlic, crushed, optional

2 tablespoons finely minced
    fresh cilantro

½ teaspoon ground cumin

Salt and freshly ground black
    pepper, to taste

1 tomatillo, finely chopped, or 1
    small hot green chile, seeded
    and minced, optional

Roast the tomato and green pepper under a broiler. Turn on all sides until the skins are quite blistered. Let them cool in a paper bag.

In the meantime, peel and mash the avocados in a mixing bowl. Stir the lemon juice in immediately. Add the remaining ingredients.

Slip the skins off the cooled tomato and green pepper and chop them finely. Add them to the avocado mixture, avoiding adding too much of the tomato's liquid. Mix well and serve.

Calories: 133   Total fat: 9 g   Protein: 2 g
Carbohydrates: 10 g   Cholesterol: 0 g   Sodium: 7 mg

WILD RICE CONFETTI SALAD

Serves 4 to 6

Wild rice makes an earthy, nutty back-drop for a salad. I love taking wild rice salads on picnics and hikes.

¾ cups wild rice, rinsed
2¼ cups water or vegetable stock
1 green bell pepper, finely diced
1 cup cooked fresh or thawed
　frozen corn kernels
1 large carrot, finely diced
1 10- to 12-ounce jar roasted red
　peppers, liquid reserved
2 scallions, minced
2 to 3 tablespoons chopped fresh
　parsley or cilantro

Dressing:
Reserved liquid from red peppers
Juice of ½ lemon or lime, or more
　to taste
1 tablespoon undiluted orange
　juice concentrate
1 tablespoon olive oil
Salt and freshly ground black
　pepper
Dark green lettuce leaves

Combine the wild rice with the water in a small saucepan and bring to a simmer. Simmer gently, covered, until the water is absorbed, about 35 minutes. Transfer the wild rice to a serving container and let it cool.

Combine the wild rice with the vegetables and parsley. Combine the reserved liquid from the roasted peppers with the remaining dressing ingredients in a small bowl and stir together. Pour over the wild rice mixture and toss well.

Season to taste with salt and pepper and serve each portion over a lettuce leaf or two.

Calories: 124	Total fat: 3 g	Protein: 3 g
Carbohydrates: 24 g	Cholesterol: 0 g	Sodium: 97 mg

Wild rice is actually the seed of a tall aquatic grass that is unrelated to rice, nor is it a grain at all. Indigenous to parts of North America, most of our crop is harvested by Native Americans in and around Minnesota and other Great Lakes States. Wild rice thrives in fresh-water lakes or rivers.

JERUSALEM ARTICHOKE SALAD

4 to 6 servings

Jerusalem artichokes are bumpy tubers that are neither related to the common artichoke, nor have anything to do with Jerusalem. They're the root of a sunflower, first noted in 1605 as a garden crop of the Native Americans of Cape Cod. A unique, nutritious vegetable, they may be used raw or cooked. In flavor and texture, they are reminiscent of a cross between potatoes, turnips, and water chestnuts. Jerusalem artichokes are occasionally marketed under the name "sunchokes" and are abundant in early fall.

1 pound Jerusalem artichokes
2 scallions, finely chopped
2 tablespoons fresh mint leaves, minced, or 2 teaspoons dried
2 to 3 tablespoons minced fresh dill
1½ tablespoons olive oil
3 to 4 tablespoons red wine vinegar, to taste
1 tablespoon honey
3 tablespoons toasted sunflower seeds
2 cups chopped dark green lettuce leaves

Scrub the Jerusalem artichokes well. Trim off any excessively dark or knobby spots, but you don't have to peel them. Cut them into thin, bite-sized pieces and place them in a serving bowl along with the scallions, mint, and dill.

In a small bowl, combine the oil, vinegar, and honey and stir together until well blended. Pour this over the artichoke mixture and toss well. Serve at once, or cover and refrigerate for an hour or so. Give the mixture one good stir during this time, then again just before serving.

Calories: 158
Carbohydrates: 20 g
Total fat: 6 g
Cholesterol: 0 g
Protein: 3 g
Sodium: 6 mg

JÍCAMA SALAD WITH ORANGES, CILANTRO, AND PUMPKIN SEEDS

4 to 6 servings

A perfect way to dress up a hearty Southwestern meal. Jícama (pronounced HIC-uh-ma), once confined to the Southwest, has recently become far easier to find in produce sections everywhere.

1 medium jícama, peeled and cut into narrow 1½-inch-long strips
3 to 4 clementines or other small seedless oranges, sectioned
4 ounces mesclun greens
¼ cup chopped fresh cilantro

Dressing:
Juice of ½ lime
1 tablespoon olive oil
2 tablespoons undiluted apple juice concentrate
3 tablespoons toasted pumpkin seeds

Combine the jícama, orange sections, greens, and cilantro in a serving bowl and stir together. Combine the dressing ingredients in a small bowl and stir together. Pour the dressing over the salad and toss together. Scatter the pumpkin seeds over the top and serve at once.

Calories: 124
Carbohydrates: 21 g
Total fat: 3 g
Cholesterol: 0 g
Protein: 2 g
Sodium: 16 mg

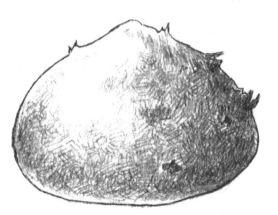

CRANBERRY-APPLE RELISH

8 or more servings

This relish adds vivid color to fall harvest meals, and is a nice change of pace from jellied cranberry sauces for holiday meals.

1 12-ounce bag fresh cranberries
4 sweet cooking apples (such as Cortland), peeled and diced
½ cup light brown sugar or Sucanat
¼ cup apple juice
½ teaspoon cinnamon
¼ teaspoon ground ginger
Pinch of allspice or nutmeg
¼ cup golden raisins

Combine all the ingredients except the raisins in a large saucepan. Stir together; bring to a simmer, then simmer gently, covered until the cranberries have burst and the apples are tender, about 20 to 25 minutes.

Stir in the raisins and allow to cool, uncovered. Transfer to a serving container and serve at room temperature.

Calories: 112   Total fat: 0 g   Protein: 0 g
Carbohydrates: 26 g   Cholesterol: 0 g   Sodium: 5 mg

Chapter 5
EGGS

It takes longer to hard-boil a man or a woman than an egg.

—F.L. Allen
Only Yesterday, 1931

Eggs, the folkloric symbols of new life and one of nature's most perfect foods, have for some time been a subject of controversy. Many of us are modifying our intake of eggs until it is clearer just how dietary cholesterol affects us. Some studies have suggested that saturated fat is a greater culprit in raising serum cholesterol than is dietary cholesterol—i.e., foods like eggs. But until all the evidence is in, moderation is always a good approach.

I enjoy eggs, but prefer to be cautious—I prepare them as a main dish only very occasionally. The recipes here are devised so that each serving contains at most one or one and a half eggs. I've chosen a small but select group of recipes that are unique and exciting.

Dominating this brief (but hopefully pithy) chapter are classic egg recipes from the Southwest, most of which I sampled while traveling there. The presentation of eggs in that beautiful region is quite invigorating and creatively embellished with the characteristic ingredients of the region—notably the "Spanish" seasonings of tomatoes, chiles, and garlic. Quite often, eggs are served in one way or another within, on top of, or surrounding tortillas.

Second in line with interesting egg recipes are those from the Creole tradition of New Orleans, whose gift for seasoning makes any recipe really special. In most other places, though, I found that, as an old American saying goes, "eggs is eggs," although all across the South and through Texas, a morning meal of scrambled egg with grits was something I looked forward to with great relish.

HUEVOS RANCHEROS (Ranch-Style Eggs)

4 servings

Huevos Rancheros is perhaps the most widely traveled of Southwestern egg dishes, having settled into breakfast menus in restaurants (Southwestern-style or otherwise) from coast to coast. There are several ways of preparing it, subject to regional variation. In New Mexico, the eggs are smothered with pure, incendiary green or red chiles; while the spiced tomato-based sauce used in the following recipe is a California-style variation. Great for brunch or even as a light supper, this basic recipe for four can be easily doubled to serve eight.

Sauce:

1 tablespoon olive oil
1 medium onion, chopped
1 clove garlic, minced
1 small green or red bell pepper, diced
1 heaping cup diced ripe tomatoes, or 1 cup canned diced tomatoes, drained
1 cup thick tomato sauce
1 small fresh hot chile, or 1 4-ounce can chopped mild green chiles
1 tablespoon minced cilantro, optional
½ teaspoon dried oregano
¼ teaspoon ground cumin
Salt, to taste

Whipped butter or natural canola margarine
4 eggs
4 corn tortillas
1 cup grated cheddar or Monterey Jack cheese, optional
1 medium firm ripe avocado, sliced, for garnish, optional

Heat the oil in a medium-sized saucepan. Add the onion and garlic and sauté over medium-low heat until the onion is translucent. Add the bell pepper and continue to sauté until the onion is golden. Add the remaining sauce ingredients and simmer over low heat, covered, for 15 minutes.

Using just enough butter to cover the bottom of a small skillet, fry each egg individually to everyone's liking.

To assemble, pass each tortilla briefly through the sauce to soften (tongs are good for this), then place each on an individual plate. Top each tortilla with a fried egg, followed by some sauce and, if desired, a sprinkling of grated cheese. Garnish with avocado slices if desired. Serve at once.

Calories: 231   Total fat: 11 g   Protein: 10 g
Carbohydrates: 24 g   Cholesterol: 213 g   Sodium: 447 mg

MEXICAN OMELET

4 servings

I would rather that this were more correctly named "New Mexican Omelet," as this recipe comes from the Apple Tree Restaurant in Taos. Their cook explained that it's simply a generic name for this local omelet featuring specific ingredients in varying presentations.

Filling:

1 tablespoon olive oil
2 cups chopped ripe tomatoes
3 to 4 scallions, thinly sliced
2 tablespoons minced fresh
    cilantro
½ teaspoon dried oregano
Salt and freshly ground black
    pepper

6 large eggs, beaten
2 tablespoons low-fat milk
2 tablespoons whipped butter or
    natural canola margarine
1 cup grated Monterey Jack
    cheese
1 recipe Green Chile Sauce
    (page 227)
Reduced-fat sour cream for
    topping, optional
Extra sliced scallions for garnish

Heat the oil in a small skillet. Add all the filling ingredients and sauté over medium-low heat for 2 minutes or so, just until the tomato is somewhat softened. Cover and set aside.

Beat 3 of the eggs well with 1 tablespoon of the milk. Heat half of the butter in a 10-inch, nonstick skillet. When the skillet is hot enough to make a drop of water sizzle, pour in the eggs. As the eggs begin to set, lift the sides with a spatula and tip the skillet to allow the uncooked eggs to run underneath. When the top is fairly set, arrange half of the filling on one side of the omelet, sprinkle half the cheese over it, and fold the other side over. Slide the omelet out onto a plate and cover with a matching plate to keep warm. Repeat with the remaining eggs, milk, margarine, filling, and cheese.

Cut each omelet in half and arrange the portions on 4 serving plates. Spoon some chile sauce over them, followed by a small dollop of sour cream, if desired. Garnish each omelet with a little of the scallion. Serve at once.

Calories: 391	Total fat: 27	Protein: 20 g
Carbohydrates: 14 g	Cholesterol: 357 g	Sodium: 541 mg

EGGS WITH AVOCADO SAUCE

4 to 6 servings

In several New Mexican restaurants, I sampled egg dishes enlivened with avocado pieces, either inside or atop the eggs. The combination is decidedly rich, but the blend of flavors is seductive. This is my interpretation, a composite of those that I tried, presented as a flat omelet.

2 tablespoons whipped butter or natural canola margarine, divided

½ medium red bell pepper, finely chopped

2 to 3 scallions, minced

1 to 2 teaspoons minced fresh hot green chile, optional

1 large firm, ripe avocado, finely diced

Juice of ½ lemon

1 tablespoon finely chopped cilantro or fresh parsley

½ cup reduced-fat sour cream

½ teaspoon ground cumin

6 large eggs, beaten

2 tablespoons low-fat milk

Salt and freshly ground black pepper

Heat ½ tablespoon of the butter in a medium skillet. Add the bell pepper, scallions, and optional green chile. Sauté over low heat until they have softened a bit.

Toss the avocado with the lemon juice and add to the skillet mixture along with the cilantro, sour cream, and cumin. Cook, stirring, just until the mixture is heated through. Remove from the heat and cover.

Beat the eggs well with the milk and add a little salt and pepper. Heat the remaining butter in a nonstick skillet. When hot enough to make a drop of water sizzle, pour in the eggs. As the eggs begin to set, lift the sides with a spatula and tip the skillet to allow the uncooked eggs to run underneath. Do this until the eggs are set on top. Slide the eggs out onto a serving plate. Spread the avocado mixture over the eggs, then cut into 4 or 6 wedges to serve.

Calories: 236　　Total fat: 18 g　　Protein: 10 g
Carbohydrates: 8 g　Cholesterol: 267 g　Sodium: 98 mg

You can't unscramble scrambled eggs.

—American proverb

MIGAS (Scrambled Eggs with Tortillas)

4 to 6 servings

Migas *literally means "crumbs" in Spanish. This quick, tasty Southwestern standard was developed as a way to use bits of stale leftover tortillas.*

6 corn tortillas, cut into 1-inch
   squares
1 tablespoon canola or olive oil
1 small onion, minced
1 clove garlic, minced
1 small green bell pepper, diced
2 medium ripe tomatoes, diced
1 teaspoon ground cumin
Salt and freshly ground black pepper
6 large eggs, well beaten
2 tablespoons low-fat milk

Heat a large skillet. Toast the tortilla pieces over medium-high heat, stirring often, until they are dry and crisp. Transfer them to a plate.

Heat the oil in the same skillet. Add the onion and garlic and sauté over medium-low heat until the onion is translucent. Add the bell pepper and continue to sauté until the onion is golden. Add the tomatoes and sauté just until they have softened a bit. Stir in the tortilla pieces, add the cumin and some salt and pepper to taste. Turn the heat up so that the skillet becomes very hot. Beat the eggs with the milk and pour into the skillet. Scramble until the eggs are set. Serve at once.

Calories: 223
Carbohydrates: 20 g
Total fat: 11 g
Cholesterol: 256 g
Protein: 11 g
Sodium: 92 mg

There is a best way of doing everything, even if it be to boil an egg.

—Ralph Waldo Emerson (1803-1882)

BREAKFAST BURRITOS

4 servings

I enjoyed Breakfast Burritos, which are basically scrambled eggs wrapped in soft flour tortillas, in several locales across the Southwest. I'd like to rename them "Brunch Burritos," since I'm not quite ready for green chiles until 11:00 a.m.!

6 large eggs, beaten
2 tablespoons low-fat milk
Salt and freshly ground black
　　pepper
1½ tablespoons whipped butter or
　　natural canola margarine

8 burrito-size (10-inch) flour
　　tortillas, warmed
1 recipe Green Chile Sauce
　　(page 227)
1 cup grated cheddar cheese,
　　reduced-fat if desired

Preheat the oven to 350 degrees.

Beat the eggs well with the milk. Season with a bit of salt and pepper. Heat the butter in a large skillet. Pour in the eggs and scramble them until they are done. Distribute the eggs among the tortillas, arranging them in the center of each. Fold the tortillas as instructed in the illustration for folding burritos on page 214.

Spread a small amount of the sauce over the bottom of a lightly oiled large shallow baking dish. Arrange the burritos, seam side down, in the baking dish and distribute the remaining sauce evenly over them. Sprinkle with the grated cheese and bake for 15 to 20 minutes, or until the cheese is bubbly.

Calories: 576	Total fat: 28	Protein: 28 g
Carbohydrates: 51 g	Cholesterol: 349 g	Sodium: 990 mg

POTATO OMELET

4 servings

Here's another great Southwestern egg specialty in the form of a flat omelet, known as a torta. This omelet of potatoes and green chiles is a common one, and is as simple as it is satisfying.

1½ tablespoons canola or light olive oil

1 medium onion, finely chopped

1 large potato, cooked or microwaved, then peeled and finely diced

1 small fresh hot chile, seeded and minced, or 1 4-ounce can chopped mild green chiles

Salt and freshly ground black pepper

6 eggs, beaten

2 tablespoons low-fat milk

½ cup grated Monterey Jack cheese

Salsa Ranchera (page 225) or store-bought salsa

Heat the oil in a 10-inch nonstick skillet. Add the onion and sauté over medium-low heat until golden. Add the potato and continue to sauté for about 2 minutes. Stir in the chile and add a little salt and pepper. Sauté until everything is heated through. Distribute the mixture evenly over the bottom of the skillet and turn the heat up to medium-high.

Beat the eggs well with the milk. When the skillet is hot, pour the eggs in. As the eggs begin to set, lift the sides with a spatula and tip the skillet to allow the uncooked eggs to run underneath.

When the eggs are set on top, sprinkle on the cheese and cover. Cook until the cheese is bubbly. Slide the omelet out onto a serving plate. Cut into 4 wedges to serve. Pass around salsa for topping.

Calories: 285	Total fat: 17 g	Protein: 15 g
Carbohydrates: 16 g	Cholesterol: 332 g	Sodium: 190 mg

Eggs is like autos—th' minute we pay less than th' top price we git int' cheap construction.

—Kin Hubbard
Abe Martin on Things in General, 1925

CALIFORNIA OMELET

4 servings

This is another simple flat omelet or torta, nicely flavored with the standard Spanish seasonings.

2 teaspoons olive oil
1 medium onion, chopped
2 cloves garlic, minced
1 small green or red bell pepper, diced
1 cup chopped ripe tomatoes
1 small fresh hot chile, seeded and minced, or 1 4-ounce can chopped mild green chiles
½ teaspoon dried oregano
Salt and freshly ground black pepper
5 eggs, beaten
2 tablespoons low-fat milk
1 tablespoon whipped butter or natural canola margarine

Heat the oil in a small skillet. Add the onion and garlic and sauté until the onion is translucent. Add the bell pepper and sauté until it is tender-crisp and the onion is golden. Add the tomatoes, chile, oregano, and salt and pepper to taste. Sauté until the tomatoes are soft and their liquid is reduced, about 8 minutes. Remove from the heat.

Beat the eggs well with the milk in a medium-sized mixing bowl. Stir the skillet mixture into them.

Heat the butter in a 10-inch nonstick skillet. When the skillet is hot enough to make a drop of water sizzle, pour in the egg mixture. When the eggs begin to set, lift the edges with a spatula and tip the skillet to allow the uncooked eggs to run underneath. When the omelet is firm, cover and cook until the top is completely set. Slide the omelet out onto a serving plate and cut into wedges to serve.

Calories: 180   Total fat: 12 g   Protein: 10 g
Carbohydrates: 9 g   Cholesterol: 273 g   Sodium: 97 mg

EGGS CREOLE

4 servings

In old Creole cookbooks this preparation is likely to be called Spanish Eggs. It's a bit different from, but certainly related to, the Spanish-influenced omelets of the Southwest, such as previous two. I encountered this as "Eggs Creole" at the Coffee Pot Restaurant in New Orleans, so that will be its name here, too.

1½ tablespoons canola oil
1 small red bell pepper, finely
   chopped
2 cups coarsely chopped
   mushrooms
2 to 3 scallions, finely chopped
1 large firm ripe tomato,
   chopped
¼ cup chopped fresh parsley
1 teaspoon paprika
Dash of dried thyme
Salt and freshly ground black
   pepper
6 eggs, well beaten

Heat the oil in a 10-inch nonstick skillet. Add the bell pepper, mushrooms, and scallions and sauté over medium heat, stirring occasionally, until they soften, about 6 to 8 minutes. Add the remaining ingredients except the eggs and cook until the tomatoes are soft.

Turn the heat up to medium-high. When the skillet is hot enough to make a drop of the egg sizzle, pour the eggs in. Let them set a bit, then scramble gently until they are done. Serve at once.

Calories: 184	Total fat: 13 g	Protein: 11 g
Carbohydrates: 5 g	Cholesterol: 320 g	Sodium: 108 mg

Think of our little egg-shell of a canoe, tossing across that great lake.

—Henry David Thoreau
The Maine Woods, 1862

EGGS NEW ORLEANS

6 servings

Here's another nice Creole egg dish common to old New Orleans cookbooks. What makes it unique is that the eggs are broken whole over the sauce and baked.

1½ tablespoons canola oil
1 small onion, finely chopped
1 large celery stalk, finely diced
1 small green bell pepper, finely chopped
2 cups chopped ripe tomatoes, or 1 14- to 16-ounce can diced tomatoes, lightly drained
1 teaspoon paprika
¾ cup soft whole-grain bread crumbs
Salt and freshly ground black pepper
6 eggs
¾ cup grated mild white cheese of your choice
1½ tablespoons minced fresh parsley

Preheat the oven to 325 degrees.

Heat the oil in a medium-sized skillet. Add the onion and celery and sauté over low heat until the onion is translucent. Add the bell pepper and sauté until the onion is golden. Add the tomatoes and paprika and cook until the tomatoes soften a little. Stir in the bread crumbs and season to taste with salt and pepper.

Transfer the mixture to a lightly oiled 9- by 13-inch baking pan and spread evenly. Carefully break each egg at even intervals over the sauce. Sprinkle with the grated cheese and then with the parsley. Bake for 20 minutes, or until the eggs are set. Cut into squares to serve, making sure that everyone gets just one yolk.

Calories: 209
Carbohydrates: 9 g
Total fat: 13 g
Cholesterol: 226 g
Protein: 12 g
Sodium: 218 mg

Tew make a hen lay 2 eggs a day, reazon with her; if that dont dew, threaten to chastize her if she dont.

—Josh Billings
Josh Billings Farmers' Alminax, 1870

Chapter 6
BEANS AND RICE

Boston runs to brains as well as to beans and brown bread.

—William Cooper Brann (1855-1898)

Most of the varieties of beans used today can be traced back to ancient South American civilizations, whose knowledge traveled early to their North American counterparts. Robert Beverly said of the Native Americans in *The History and Present State of Virginia* (1705), "They eat all sorts of Pease, Beans, and other Pulse, both parched and boiled."

Rice came to our shores later, introduced to the young colony of South Carolina as a gift of seed from Madagascar. It soon became their major crop and staple food. By the early 1700s, rice had made its way to Louisiana, whose marshy lands were perfect for its cultivation. Louisiana eventually overtook South Carolina as a rice-growing state and to this day rice is a must on any true Creole table.

What is fascinating about these staple crops is the regularity with which they've worked their way into nearly every regional cuisine (although potatoes become more widely used than rice as one goes further north, especially in the Pennsylvania Dutch and New England repertoires). Even more interesting is how the regional styles vary these basics, producing a seemingly endless variety of delicious dishes. I think, for example, of a typical meal I would sit down to in New Mexico—a plate of enchiladas accompanied by pinto beans and *arroz* (Mexican rice).

Then there are those wonderful Southern dishes that combine beans or peas with rice, such as Hoppin' John (black-eyed peas and rice), Cuban-influenced Black Beans and Rice, and the New Orleans classic Red Beans and Rice. These were easy to adapt—the original recipes may have contained a small bit of meat which was simply omitted, leaving a dish still packed with flavor and high in protein.

Beans and rice must have played at least as great a role in the diet of earlier Americans as they do in today's vegetarian diet. As plant-based proteins, they are part of the foundation of a healthful repertoire, just as they must have been in the earlier American diet, which did not become so meat-centered until the twentieth century.

FRIJOLES REFRITOS (Refried Pinto Beans)

6 to 8 servings

Few dishes are more basic to Southwestern cuisine than the beloved Frijoles. A good helping of them is a standard sight at lunch, dinner, and sometimes even breakfast. Here's a simple vegetarian preparation (though they're no longer prepared with lard as often as they once were, still, do ask if you have them in a restaurant). Serve these alongside the Southwestern egg dishes in Chapter 5, or any of the tortilla specialties in chapter 9 that don't themselves contain beans.

1⅔ cup raw pinto beans
1 large onion, chopped
1½ tablespoons olive oil, divided
1 teaspoon salt
½ cup grated Monterey Jack
    cheese

Soak the beans overnight. Drain and rinse them and place them in a large soup pot or Dutch oven with plenty of fresh water. Add the onion and ½ tablespoon of the oil, bring to a boil, then cover and simmer over very low heat until the beans are quite tender, about 1½ to 2 hours. A good test of the desired texture is to press a bean between the thumb and forefinger; if it feels soft and mealy, it is done. Drain and store the beans until they're needed.

When you are ready to "refry" the beans, heat the remaining oil in a large nonstick skillet. Add the cooked pinto beans and fry over medium heat, stirring frequently, for 10 minutes. Mash the beans coarsely with a mashing implement. Add the salt and cook, covered, adding small amounts of water until the beans have the consistency of a very thick sauce about 10 minutes. Sprinkle in the cheese and cook until it is completely melted, then serve.

| Calories: 190 | Total fat: 5 g | Protein: 9 g |
| Carbohydrates: 25 g | Cholesterol: 7 g | Sodium: 350 mg |

That's the bean called pink, called *frijole*, called the Mexican strawberry.

—*This Week Magazine*, March 1949

pink   frijole   Mexican Strawberry

FRIJOLES BORRACHOS
(Beer-Stewed Pinto Beans)

6 or more servings

The word borracho *was a nineteenth-century north-of-the-border term for a drunkard, and so the name of this recipe literally means "drunken pinto beans." Simmering the pintos in beer and fresh cilantro gives them a unique flavor. Use a jalapeño if you'd like some heat to this dish. Using milder chiles allows the flavor of the cilantro to be more pronounced. This is an exceptional accompaniment to* Huevos Rancheros *(page 117).*

1 tablespoon olive oil
1 cup chopped ripe tomatoes or
    diced canned tomatoes, lightly
    drained
2 large scallions, chopped
4 cups cooked pinto beans
    (about 1⅔ cups raw), or 2
    1-pound cans, drained and
    rinsed
½ cup beer
⅓ cup chopped fresh cilantro
1 jalapeño pepper, seeded and
    minced, or 1 4-ounce can mild
    green chiles
Salt, to taste

Heat the oil in a large skillet. Add the tomatoes and scallions and sauté over moderately low heat for 2 minutes. Add the remaining ingredients and stir together, then simmer, covered, over low heat for 30 minutes. If there is too much liquid in the skillet at this time, cook, uncovered, until it thickens up.

Note: You may use the directions for cooking the pinto beans given in the previous recipe. Cook them until they are tender, but still hold their shape. Do all the steps up to the refrying.

Calories: 199   Total fat: 2 g   Protein: 9 g
Carbohydrates: 33 g   Cholesterol: 0 g   Sodium: 6 mg

Next to rhy bread, beans hav been called by the poets and philosophers the cumfort, and staff ov life. The bean iz all food, thare is no more waste in them, than thare iz in a pint ov cold water, when a man is auphull dry. Beans are all colors, and most shapes, flat, round, oblong, square and 3 cornered, and a quart ov them put in a pot, and biled 2 hours, will meazzure a gallon, and a haff, when they cum out. This makes them a better dividend paying seed than enny thing we kno ov.

—Josh Billings
   Old Probability, Perhaps Rain, Perhaps Not, 1879

SPANISH-STYLE GARBANZOS

6 servings

Garbanzos, better known as chick-peas, were one of the foods brought by the early Spanish settlers to the Southwest. This is a standard preparation—simple, but very aromatic and satisfying.

2 tablespoons olive oil

2 medium onions, chopped

3 cloves garlic, minced

4 cups well-cooked chickpeas
   (about 1⅔ cups raw),or 2
   1-pound cans, drained and
   rinsed

2 cups chopped ripe tomatoes
   with ¼ cup water, or 1 14- to
   16-ounce can diced tomatoes

½ teaspoon each: dried oregano,
   dried basil, and ground cumin

¼ cup minced fresh cilantro or
   parsley

Salt and freshly ground black
   pepper

Hot cooked rice

Heat the oil in a large skillet. Add the onions and sauté over medium heat until translucent. Add the garlic and continue to sauté until the onions begin to turn golden. Add the chickpeas, tomatoes, oregano, basil, and cumin. Bring to a simmer, then cover and simmer gently for 20 minutes, stirring once or twice.

Stir in the cilantro, then season to taste with salt (taste first; you may not need any) and lots of pepper. Serve over hot cooked rice in bowls.

Calories: 248   Total fat: 7 g   Protein: 9 g
Carbohydrates: 37 g   Cholesterol: 0 g   Sodium: 15 mg

They will meazzure a gallon and a haff when they come out.

Put a quart ov beans in a pot and bile 2 hours.

BAKED BARBECUE BEANS

6 servings

A friend from Iowa recommended this recipe, noting that the contrast of the subtly sweet and tart flavors makes it a popular side dish at cookouts in that region.

1 tablespoon canola oil
1 medium onion, chopped
2 cloves garlic, minced
1 cup thick tomato sauce
1/4 cup molasses, light brown
    sugar, or Sucanat
2 tablespoons apple cider
    vinegar
1 1/2 teaspoons dry mustard
1 teaspoon paprika
1/4 teaspoon ground ginger
A few grains of cayenne pepper
Salt to taste
4 cups cooked navy beans
    (about 1 2/3 cups raw), or 2
    1-pound cans, drained and
    rinsed

Preheat the oven to 325 degrees.

Heat the oil in a deep, heavy saucepan. Add the onion and sauté over low heat until translucent. Add the garlic and continue to sauté until the onion is lightly browned. Add the remaining ingredients except the beans and simmer for 10 minutes.

Combine the sauce with the beans in a 1½-quart baking casserole and mix well. Bake, covered, for 45 minutes, then for an additional 15 minutes, uncovered.

Calories: 261	Total fat: 2 g	Protein: 10 g
Carbohydrates: 49 g	Cholesterol: 0 g	Sodium: 267 mg

HEARTY RED BEAN CHILI

6 servings

Perhaps the most exalted of all north- and south-of-the-border inventions is the dish that's known far and wide simply as "Chili." Originally, Chile con Carne was a very simple stew of meat with green chiles. Later, it evolved to include beans, spices, and sometimes vegetables. As chili cook-offs gained popularity, there seemed to be no end to the variations one could play on the theme.

1 tablespoon olive oil
2 medium onions, chopped
2 cloves garlic, minced
1 large green bell pepper, finely
    chopped
4 cups cooked kidney or red
    beans (about 1 2/3 cups raw),
    or 2 1-pound cans, drained
    and rinsed
1 28-ounce can diced tomatoes
1 to 2 jalapeño peppers, seeded
    and minced, or 1 4-ounce can
    mild chopped green chiles
1 teaspoon each: chili powder,
    dried oregano, and ground
    cumin
Salt, to taste
Hot cooked rice, optional
Grated sharp cheddar cheese for
    topping, reduced-fat if desired,
    optional

Heat the oil in a large soup pot. Add the onion and garlic and sauté over medium heat until the onion is golden. Add the remaining ingredients except the salt and optional ingredients. Simmer gently, covered, for 30 minutes, stirring occasionally.

Add salt to taste and adjust the other seasonings. Serve on its own or over rice in bowls, garnished with the optional cheddar cheese.

Calories: 220   Total fat: 2 g   Protein: 11 g
Carbohydrates: 38 g   Cholesterol: 0 g   Sodium: 17 mg

BLACK BEAN CHILI

6 servings

Here's a delectable version of chili using black beans. Serve with Green Chile Cornbread (page 51) and a tossed salad.

1½ tablespoons olive oil
1 cup chopped onion
2 to 3 cloves garlic, minced
1 medium red bell pepper, diced
1 medium yellow summer
    squash, diced
4 cups cooked black beans
    (about 1⅔ cups raw), or 2
    1-pound cans, drained and
    rinsed
1 28-ounce can diced tomatoes
1 or 2 small fresh hot chiles,
    minced, or 1 4-ounce can
    chopped mild green chiles
1 teaspoon ground cumin
½ teaspoon dried oregano
¼ cup chopped fresh cilantro
Salt, to taste

Heat the oil in a large soup pot. Add the onion and garlic and sauté over medium heat until the onion is golden. Add the remaining ingredients except the cilantro and salt. Bring to a simmer, then cover and simmer gently for 20 to 25 minutes, or until the vegetables are tender.

Stir in the cilantro and season to taste with salt. Serve at once or let stand off the heat for an hour or two, then heat through before serving.

Calories: 228	Total fat: 4 g	Protein: 11 g
Carbohydrates: 37 g	Cholesterol: 0 g	Sodium: 15 mg

Wish I'd had time for one more bowl of chili.

—Kit Carson's alleged last words

CINCINNATI "CHILI MAC"

6 servings

Cincinnati chili can be made with varying ingredients and seasonings, but it's always served with spaghetti. Often, a touch of sweet spices such as cinnamon or allspice are added. The result: a hybrid recipe that's uniquely American.

1 tablespoon olive oil

1 cup chopped onion

1 medium green bell pepper, diced

1 medium red bell pepper, diced

1 small fresh hot chile, seeded and minced, optional

1 14- to 16-ounce can diced tomatoes

1 14- to 16-ounce can crushed tomatoes

4 cups cooked red or pink beans (about 1 2/3 cups raw), or 2 1-pound cans, drained and rinsed

1 to 2 teaspoons chili powder, to taste

1 teaspoon each: ground cumin and dried oregano

1/2 teaspoon ground cinnamon

1/4 teaspoon ground allspice, optional

8 to 10 ounces spaghetti

Garnishes (all optional):

Diced ripe tomatoes

Chopped onion or scallions

Grated cheddar cheese, reduced-fat if desired, or cheddar-style soy cheese

Heat the oil in a large saucepan or stir-fry pan. Add the onion and sauté over medium heat until translucent, then add the bell peppers and continue to sauté until the onion is golden.

Stir in the remaining ingredients except the spaghetti and garnishes and bring to a simmer. Simmer gently, covered, for 20 minutes.

In the meantime, bring water to a boil in a large pot. Cook the spaghetti until al dente, then drain.

For each serving, place a small amount of spaghetti in a wide, shallow serving bowl and top with some of the chili. If desired, top with any or all of the suggested garnishes.

Calories: 318	Total fat: 3 g	Protein: 12 g
Carbohydrates: 59 g	Cholesterol: 0 g	Sodium: 64 mg

RED BEANS AND RICE

8 servings

If one had to choose a single truly characteristic dish of New Orleans, it would be hard to come up with one more renowned than Red Beans and Rice. A dish that has been around long enough to have become established in local folklore, it is also one that even today graces many New Orleans restaurant menus. Vegetarians visiting New Orleans should be aware that "red and white," as it has come to be known, is often made with spicy smoked sausage.

2 cups (1 pound) raw red or
    kidney beans
1 tablespoon canola oil
2 large onions, chopped
1 medium green bell pepper,
    finely diced
2 large celery stalks, diced
2 cloves garlic, minced
1 cup canned diced tomatoes
2 small bay leaves
1 heaping tablespoon peanut
    butter
3 tablespoons chopped fresh
    parsley
2 tablespoons chopped fresh
    basil leaves, or 1½ teaspoons
    dried
½ teaspoon dried thyme
Salt and freshly ground black
    pepper
Cayenne pepper to taste
Hot cooked rice

Sort and rinse the beans, then soak the beans overnight in plenty of water to cover. Before cooking them, drain the beans, then place them in a soup pot with water in about 1½ times their volume. Bring to a simmer and add the oil, onions, bell pepper, celery, garlic, tomatoes, and bay leaves. Cover and simmer over low heat for 1 hour.

At this point the water level should be just below the beans and vegetables. Add a bit more water if necessary to bring it to that level. Add the peanut butter and seasonings and simmer for another 1½ hours, stirring occasionally. At this point there should be a thick, sauce-like consistency to the liquid. Mash a small amount of beans against the side of the pot with a wooden spoon. Cover and cook until most of the beans have burst and are very soft. The resulting consistency should be thick and saucy. Remove the bay leaves and serve over hot cooked rice.

With 1/2 cup rice per serving:

Calories: 297	Total fat: 3 g	Protein: 11 g
Carbohydrates: 54 g	Cholesterol: 0 g	Sodium: 16 mg

Local lore on Red Beans and Rice tells us that to eat this dish on Monday was supposed to bring good luck. Conversely, the expression, "I am on the red and white" meant that one was broke.

JAMBALAYA

6 to 8 servings

Spicy bits of soy "sausage" lend an authentic flair to this simple vegetarian take on a Creole-Cajun classic. Many supermarkets now carry this versatile product, either in the produce section near the tofu products, or in the frozen foods section. Serve with coleslaw and fresh corn bread for a hearty, satisfying supper.

3 cups water

1¼ cups raw brown rice

2 tablespoons canola oil, divided

8 links soy "sausage"

1 large onion, chopped

3 to 4 cloves garlic, minced

4 celery stalks, diced

1 medium green or red bell
   pepper, diced

1 28-ounce can diced tomatoes

1 teaspoon each: paprika, dried
   oregano, dried basil

½ teaspoon dried thyme

Cayenne pepper to taste

Salt to taste

Bring the water to a simmer in a saucepan. Stir in the rice; cover and cook at a gentle, steady simmer, covered, until the water is absorbed, about 35 minutes.

Heat just enough of the oil to lightly coat the bottom of a large, nonstick skillet. When hot, arrange the "sausage" links in the skillet and cook over medium-high heat, gently turning them until all sides are golden brown. Remove from the heat and set aside until needed.

Heat the remaining oil in the same skillet. Add the onion and sauté over medium heat until translucent. Add the garlic, celery, and bell pepper, and continue to sauté until all the vegetables are lightly browned.

Add the remaining ingredients except the salt. Bring to a simmer, then cover and simmer gently for 15 to 20 minutes.

Cut the "sausage" links into 1/2-inch-thick pieces. Add to the skillet and simmer briefly, just until they are heated through.

Combine the skillet mixture with the hot cooked rice in a large serving bowl and toss together thoroughly. Season to taste with salt (and a bit more cayenne if you'd like) and serve at once.

Calories: 173	Total fat: 5 g	Protein: 7 g
Carbohydrates: 24 g	Cholesterol: 0 g	Sodium: 215 mg

Note: Soy "sausage" links are available in many supermarkets, either in the produce section near the tofu products, or in the frozen foods section. They are also easy to find in natural foods stores.

CAJUN DIRTY RICE

6 to 8 servings

Truth be told, I wasn't really looking forward to attempting to adapt this Cajun classic. After all, the original is made "dirty" with gizzards and various other items that are, to say the least, unpalatable to a vegetarian. However, after I bit the bullet and tried it ("dirtying" my version with mushrooms and baked tofu or soy "sausage"), I was sold. Boldly seasoned the Cajun way, this is a marvelously hearty main dish, great for everyday meals.

3 cups water

1 vegetable bouillon cube

1 cup raw brown rice

2 tablespoons canola oil

1 large onion, chopped

2 cloves garlic, minced

2 celery stalks, diced

1 medium green bell pepper, finely diced

6 ounces white mushrooms, finely chopped

2 large firm, ripe tomatoes, diced

3 to 4 scallions, chopped

4 to 6 ounces baked tofu or 4 to 5 links soy "sausage" (see note), finely chopped

1 teaspoon paprika

½ teaspoon each: dried oregano and thyme

Cayenne pepper to taste

Bring the water to a boil with the bouillon cube in a medium saucepan. Stir in the rice, and simmer gently, covered, until the water is absorbed, about 35 minutes.

In the meantime, heat the oil in a large skillet. Add the onion, garlic, and celery and sauté over medium-low heat until golden. Add the bell pepper and mushrooms and sauté, covered, until the bell pepper has softened and the mushrooms are wilted. Add the tomatoes and scallions, and cook, covered, for another 3 to 4 minutes. Remove from the heat.

Preheat the oven to 350 degrees.

When the rice is done, combine it with the vegetable mixture, baked tofu or soy "sausage," and seasonings in a lightly oiled shallow 2-quart casserole dish and stir well to combine. Bake for 30 to 35 minutes, or until the top begins to get slightly crusty. Serve at once.

Note: See the note for the previous recipe for information on soy "sausage." Baked tofu comes in cellophane-wrapped 8-ounce packages and is available in natural foods stores and in some well-stocked supermarkets.

Calories: 162	Total fat: 6 g	Protein: 4 g
Carbohydrates: 24 g	Cholesterol: 0 g	Sodium: 59 mg

CREOLE ORANGE RICE

6 servings

A light and lilting side dish, abounding with citrus notes.

2 tablespoons whipped butter or
    natural canola margarine
1 large onion, finely chopped
2 large celery stalks, diced
1⅓ cups white or Texmati rice
2 cups homemade vegetable
    stock, or 1 15-ounce can
1 cup fresh orange juice
1 teaspoon grated orange zest,
    optional
¼ teaspoon dried thyme
Salt and freshly ground pepper
Minced parsley for garnish
Peeled and sectioned clementine
    or other small seedless oranges
    for garnish, optional

Heat the butter in a large saucepan. Add the onion and celery and sauté over medium heat until the onion is golden. Add the rice, stock, orange juice, optional orange zest, and thyme. Bring to a simmer, then simmer gently, covered, until the water is absorbed, about 20 minutes.

If the rice is not tender enough for your taste, add another ½ cup water and simmer until it is absorbed. Season to taste with salt and pepper. Serve at once. Garnish each serving with a little minced parsley and if desired, a few clementine sections.

Calories: 145   Total fat: 3 g   Protein: 2 g
Carbohydrates: 26 g   Cholesterol: 8 g   Sodium: 112 mg

New Orleans food is as delicious as the less criminal forms of sin.

—Mark Twain (1835-1910)

GREEN RICE

6 to 8 servings

This traditional Southern rice casserole, full of fresh parsley, makes a lovely buffet dish.

1 tablespoon canola oil
1 large onion, finely chopped
1 large celery stalk, finely
   chopped
2 eggs, beaten
½ cup low-fat milk
4 cups cooked brown rice (about
   1⅓ cups raw)
1½ cups grated sharp Cheddar
   cheese, reduced-fat if desired
2 tablespoons whipped butter or
   natural canola margarine,
   melted
1 cup finely chopped fresh
   parsley
1 tablespoon minced fresh basil,
   or 1 teaspoon dried
Salt and freshly ground black
   pepper

Preheat the oven to 350 degrees.

Heat the oil in a small skillet. Add the onion and celery and sauté over low heat until they are lightly browned. Transfer to a large mixing bowl and add all the remaining ingredients. Mix thoroughly, then pat the mixture into an oiled shallow 2-quart baking dish. Bake for 35 to 40 minutes, or until the top of the casserole is lightly browned and the cheese is bubbly.

Calories: 288   Total fat: 12 g   Protein: 13 g
Carbohydrates: 32 g   Cholesterol: 86 g   Sodium: 208 mg

HOPPIN'-JOHN
(Black-Eyed Peas and Rice)

4 to 6 servings

This is a famous deep South dish, which in its original form is always cooked with a piece of salt pork. It was traditionally eaten as a "good luck" dish on New Year's Day. My adaptation of this simple but delicious recipe is close to the Creole-influenced variety using tomatoes and herbs, which add enough flavor to make up for the absence of meat.

1½ tablespoons canola or
    olive oil
2 large onions, chopped
1 clove garlic, minced
2 cups diced ripe tomatoes with ¼
    cup water, or 1 14- to 16-
    ounce can diced tomatoes
1 teaspoon dried basil
¼ teaspoon dried thyme
3 cups cooked brown rice
2 cups cooked black-eyed peas
    (about ¾ cups raw), or 1
    1-pound can, drained and
    rinsed
Salt and freshly ground black
    pepper

Heat the oil in a soup pot or stir-fry pan. Add the onions and sauté over medium heat until translucent. Add the garlic and continue to sauté until the onions are golden. Add the tomatoes and herbs and cook until the tomatoes have softened a bit, about 5 minutes.

Add the rice and black-eyed peas, and season to taste with salt and lots of pepper. Stir together well and simmer over low heat for 10 to 15 minutes. Add a bit of water or cooking liquid from the peas to keep the mixture moist. Serve at once.

Calories: 290	Total fat: 6 g	Protein: 9 g
Carbohydrates: 52	Cholesterol: 0 g	Sodium: 10 mg

Now Hopping-John was F. Jasmine's very favorite food. She had always warned them to wave a pile of rice and peas before her nose when she was in her coffin, to make certain there was no mistake; for if a breath of life was left in her, she would sit up and eat, but if she smelled the Hopping-John, and did not stir, then they could nail down the coffin and be certain she was truly dead.

—Carson McCullers
  A Member of the Wedding, 1946

SOUTHERN LIMA BEANS

6 to 8 servings as a side dish; 4 to 6 servings as a main dish

Lima beans have long been, and are still, more widely used in the South than elsewhere. They're often called "butter beans" (though in other regions, "butter beans" are, I've been told, a different type of bean and not interchangeable with limas), and combining them with tomatoes, as in this Creole-influenced recipe, is a common way of preparing them.

1½ tablespoons canola oil
1 medium onion, finely chopped
2 cloves garlic, minced
2 teaspoons unbleached white
   flour
1 medium green bell pepper,
   finely chopped
2 cups diced ripe tomatoes with
   ¼ cup water, or 1 14- to 16-
   ounce can diced tomatoes
4 cups (2 10-ounce packages)
   thawed frozen baby lima
   beans
¼ cup chopped fresh parsley
½ teaspoon dried thyme
A few grains of cayenne pepper
Salt and freshly ground black
   pepper
Hot cooked rice, optional

Heat the oil in a large skillet. Add the onion and sauté over medium-low heat until it is translucent. Add the garlic and continue to sauté until the onion is golden. Sprinkle in the flour and stir until it blends in.

Add the bell pepper and tomatoes with water, and cook, covered, until the tomatoes have softened but aren't mushy, about 8 to 10 minutes. Stir in the remaining ingredients. Cover and cook over very low heat for 15 minutes, stirring once or twice. Serve on its own as a side dish or over rice as a main dish.

Calories: 158	Total fat: 3 g	Protein: 7 g
Carbohydrates: 25 g	Cholesterol: 0 g	Sodium: 35 mg

The frost lies heavy on the palings, and tips with silver the tops of the butter-bean poles.

—George Bagby
The Old Virginia Gentleman, 1866

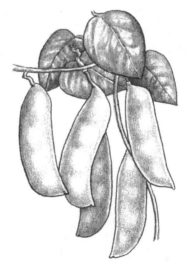

COWPEAS WITH CORN AND RICE

4 to 6 servings

Cowpeas are small, brown, and tasty, with small dark spots on their sides much like those on black-eyed peas. Perhaps more closely related to the field pea, this little legume is known almost exclusively in the South, though I've had some success finding them in dried form here in the northeast, where I live. This recipe comes from an old Louisiana family cookbook.

¾ cup raw cowpeas
2 tablespoons canola oil
1 large onion, chopped
2 cloves garlic, minced
1 small green bell pepper, diced
2 cups chopped ripe tomatoes
   with ¼ cup water, or 1 14-
   ounce can diced tomatoes, with
   liquid
1 cup cooked fresh or thawed
   frozen corn kernels
¼ cup chopped fresh parsley
¼ teaspoon dried thyme
⅛ teaspoon cayenne pepper,
   or to taste
Salt and freshly ground black
   pepper
Hot cooked rice

Rinse and sort the peas and soak them overnight. Drain and rinse them and place them in a deep saucepan with plenty of fresh water. Cook until tender, about 1 to 1½ hours. Drain and set aside.

Heat the oil in a large skillet. Add the onion and sauté over medium-low heat until translucent. Add the garlic and continue to sauté until the onion is lightly golden. Add the bell pepper and sauté for another minute or so. Add the cowpeas and all the remaining ingredients except the rice. Simmer over low heat, covered, for 15 to 20 minutes. Serve at once over rice.

Note: Substitute black-eyed peas if you can't find cowpeas.

With 1/2 cup rice per serving:
Calories: 304   Total fat: 6 g   Protein: 9 g
Carbohydrates: 52 g   Cholesterol: 0 g   Sodium: 12 mg

KEY WEST BLACK BEANS AND RICE

6 servings

This dish has come to be known as a regional standard in Florida due to the popularization of black beans by the Cuban-American community. Once you have your cooked beans on hand, this preparation requires a minimum of effort.

2 tablespoons olive oil, divided
1 cup finely chopped onion
3 to 4 cloves garlic, minced
4 cups cooked black beans
    (about 1⅓ cups raw), or 2
    1-pound cans, drained and
    rinsed
2½ tablespoons apple cider
    vinegar
Salt and freshly ground black
    pepper
A few grains of cayenne pepper
½ cup cooking liquid from beans
2 small green bell peppers, or 1
    green and 1 red bell pepper,
    cut into narrow strips
Hot cooked rice
1 small onion, finely chopped,
    optional

Heat 1½ tablespoons of the oil in a large skillet. Add the onion and sauté over medium-low heat until translucent. Add the garlic and continue to sauté until the onion is golden. Add the beans, vinegar, and seasonings (be generous with the black pepper) along with the cooking liquid. Simmer over very low heat, covered, for 15 minutes. With the back of a wooden spoon or a mashing implement, mash about ½ cup of the beans and stir well into the mixture. Make sure there is enough liquid to keep everything nice and moist but not soupy. Simmer gently, covered, for another 10 to 15 minutes.

Heat the remaining oil in a small skillet. Sauté the bell peppers until they are tender crisp and just beginning to be touched with brown.

Serve the black beans over a bed of cooked rice, topping each serving with some of the sautéed pepper strips and a sprinkling of the chopped raw onion, if desired.

Calories: 322   Total fat: 6 g   Protein: 12 g
Carbohydrates: 56 g   Cholesterol: 0 g   Sodium: 3 mg

RICE CROQUETTES

Makes about 16 croquettes

Rice, a major crop in Louisiana for over two hundred years, has long been a daily fixture on the Creole table. Even with the proliferation of outside cultural influences in New Orleans, the importance of rice in the local cuisine has not, to this day, been much diminished. These croquettes, from an old Louisiana recipe, make a great way to use up leftover cooked rice.

2½ cups cold cooked brown rice
    (about ¾ cups raw)
2 eggs, well beaten
2 tablespoons low-fat milk
    or soymilk
¼ cup minced celery
1 tablespoon grated onion
2 tablespoons minced fresh
    parsley
1 tablespoon minced fresh basil,
    or 1 teaspoon dried
⅓ cup fine whole-grain bread
    crumbs
Salt and freshly ground black
    pepper
A few grains cayenne pepper
Cornmeal for dredging
Canola oil for frying

Combine all but the last 2 ingredients in a mixing bowl and stir until thoroughly combined. Carefully shape into small, palm-sized croquettes, as the batter is rather loose, and dredge in cornmeal. Heat just enough oil to coat a nonstick griddle or skillet. Fry the croquettes until golden brown on both sides.

Per croquette:
Calories: 50
Carbohydrates: 8 g

Total fat: 0 g
Cholesterol: 27 g

Protein: 2 g
Sodium: 17 mg

BAKED RICE WITH CHEESE AND GREEN CHILES

4 to 6 servings

In this Southwestern casserole, chiles and cilantro lend a marvelous flavor to a simple casserole. The more chiles, the better, but of course, tailor the amount and heat level to your taste.

1 tablespoon olive oil
1 medium onion, chopped
4 cups cooked brown rice (about 1⅓ cups raw)
½ pound grated Monterey Jack cheese
½ cup reduced-fat sour cream
½ cup non-fat buttermilk
1 or 2 4-ounce cans chopped mild green chiles
¼ cup minced fresh cilantro
½ teaspoon chili powder
Salt and freshly ground black pepper

Preheat the oven to 350 degrees.

Heat the oil in a small skillet. Add the onion and sauté over medium-low heat until lightly browned.

In a mixing bowl, combine the onion with the rice and all the remaining ingredients. Stir together thoroughly. Pat the mixture into an oiled 1½-quart baking casserole. Bake for 35 minutes, or until the top is golden brown and bubbly.

Calories: 443	Total fat: 19 g	Protein: 19 g
Carbohydrates: 46 g	Cholesterol: 43 g	Sodium: 271 mg

[The Indians] place their canoes close to the bunches of rice, in such position as to receive the grain when it falls.

—Jonathan Carver
Travels Through Interior Parts of North America, 1778

MEXICAN RICE

6 servings

Mexican Rice is a traditional accompaniment to tortilla specialties of the Southwest. The secret of this savory rice is that it is sautéed before the cooking water is added.

2 tablespoons olive oil, divided
1 large onion, finely chopped
2 cloves garlic, minced
1 small green bell pepper, finely
    chopped
1 heaping cup diced ripe
    tomatoes, or diced canned
    tomatoes, drained
1 teaspoon dried oregano
1 teaspoon ground cumin
¼ teaspoon dried red pepper
    flakes, or to taste
Salt, to taste
1½ cups raw brown rice
3½ cups water

Heat half of the oil in a medium skillet. Add the onion and garlic and sauté over medium-low heat until the onion is translucent. Add the bell pepper, tomatoes, and seasonings and sauté until the tomatoes have softened. Remove from heat and cover.

Heat the remaining oil in a large skillet or stir-fry pan. Add the rice and sauté, stirring frequently, for 5 minutes. Add the sautéed vegetable mixture and the water. Stir together and cover tightly. Simmer over very low heat until the water is absorbed, about 40 minutes. Don't lift the lid during this time.

At the end, check to see if the rice is adequately done. If so, toss the mixture together, as the vegetables will have risen to the top. If not, add another ½ cup of water and simmer uncovered until it is absorbed.

Calories: 211   Total fat: 5 g   Protein: 4 g
Carbohydrates: 37 g   Cholesterol: 0 g   Sodium: 4 mg

APPLE-WALNUT WILD RICE PILAF

6 to 8 servings as a side dish

Here, earthy wild rice is tempered with brown rice and teamed with some classic companions—apples, walnuts, and celery.

4 cups water
1 vegetable bouillon cube
¾ cup wild rice
½ cup brown rice
¼ teaspoon dried thyme
1 tablespoon canola oil
1 medium red onion, chopped
2 stalks celery, diced
1 heaping cup diced unpeeled
    red apple
2 to 3 tablespoons finely
    chopped walnuts
¼ cup chopped fresh parsley
Salt and freshly ground black
    pepper

Combine the water and bouillon cube in a medium-sized saucepan and bring to a simmer. Stir to dissolve the bouillon cube, then stir in the wild rice, brown rice, and thyme. Simmer gently covered, until the water is absorbed, about 35 minutes.

In the meantime, heat the oil in a medium skillet. Add the onion and sauté over medium heat until translucent. Add the celery and continue to sauté until the onion is very lightly browned. Stir in the apple and walnuts and sauté for 2 minutes or so, stirring frequently, just until the apple is heated through, but don't let it soften.

When the rice is done, transfer it to a serving container and combine with the mixture from the skillet. Add the parsley and toss together. Season to taste with salt and pepper (taste first—you may not need very much salt, if at all, having used the bouillon cube). Serve at once or cover and keep warm until needed.

Calories: 170   Total fat: 4 g   Protein: 3 g
Carbohydrates: 29 g   Cholesterol: 0 g   Sodium: 95 mg

WILD RICE STUFFING WITH DRIED CRANBERRIES

6 or more servings

There's something so homey and satisfying about bread stuffing. Wild rice adds a wonderful texture, and the dried cranberries make it simply delicious.

2½ cups water or vegetable stock
⅔ cup raw wild rice
1½ tablespoons canola oil
1 medium red onion, chopped
2 large celery stalks, diced
3 cups whole-grain bread crumbs
⅓ cup dried cranberries
2 tablespoons finely chopped
    walnuts
½ teaspoon seasoned salt,
    or to taste
¼ teaspoon dried thyme
Freshly ground pepper to taste
½ cup apple juice

Bring the water to a simmer in a small saucepan. Stir in the wild rice, bring to a simmer, then cover and simmer gently until the water is absorbed, about 35 minutes. Once done, preheat the oven to 350 degrees.

Heat the oil in a medium skillet. Add the onion and celery and sauté over medium heat until both are golden. Combine the onion-celery mixture with the cooked wild rice and all the remaining ingredients except the apple juice in a mixing bowl. Stir well to combine. Drizzle the apple juice in slowly, stirring constantly, until the mixture is evenly moistened.

Transfer the mixture to a lightly oiled shallow 2-quart baking dish and bake for 25 to 30 minutes, or until the top begins to get slightly crusty. Keep warm until serving.

Calories: 197   Total fat: 6 g   Protein: 4 g
Carbohydrates: 30 g   Cholesterol: 2 g   Sodium: 404 mg

Chapter 7

CORN, THE ALL-AMERICAN CROP

Most of the Inhabitants of America live solely on this corn, because it is very healthful and nourishing. For this reason they use it for baking and cooking, indeed for all things.

—William Byrd
Natural History of Virginia, 1737

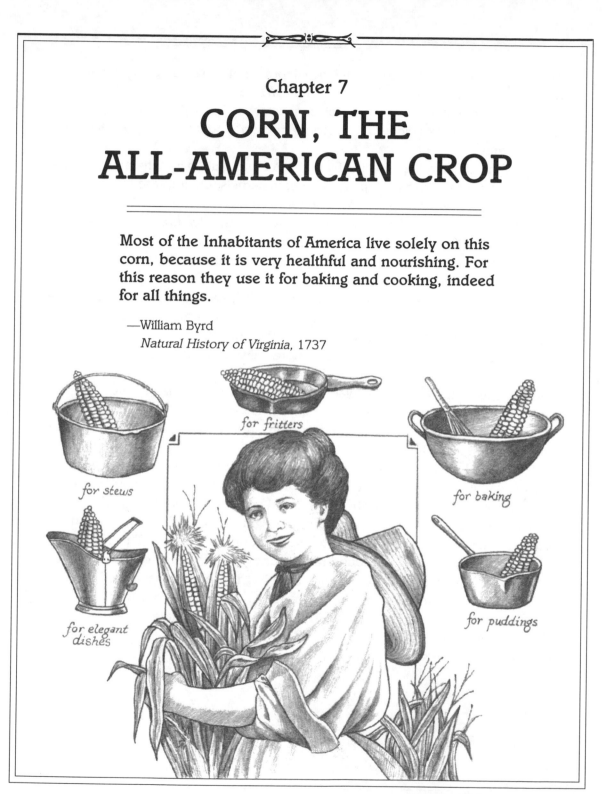

for stews

for fritters

for baking

for elegant dishes

for puddings

The pivotal role played by corn in the development of American cookery has been mentioned several times in this book, and can't be underestimated. Many of the recipes included here for the use of corn evolved from those that the Native Americans taught the colonists. It is still the most abundant crop by weight in the United States.

One of the pleasurable aspects of this chapter was getting into the habit of using fresh corn kernels. When a recipe calls for corn kernels, the impulse is to reach for the convenient frozen variety. And while frozen corn is a useful, good-quality product, it just doesn't have the same impact in recipes that feature corn as the main event. While the thought of cooking fresh ears of corn and then scraping the kernels off may at first seem like a hassle, it's really an easier task than it may seem. I think the effort is worthwhile, and hope you'll try it.

After learning of the hardiness of corn as a crop, early Americans soon came to appreciate its versatility in the kitchen. Used as a vegetable, it could be transformed into puddings, cooked in stews, stuffed into vegetables, scalloped with flavorful bread crumbs, and so much more. Almost every region has its own brand of succotash, from which I chose three amazingly varied and far more interesting examples than the plain corn-and-lima bean mixture we've grown accustomed to seeing in our supermarket's frozen food section. And as the colonists learned, corn could also be used in other, equally versatile forms—as cornmeal, grits, and hominy.

Hominy results from soaking corn kernels until their hulls come off. Once a widely used item in colonial times, today it is mainly used in the Southwest in a dish known as Posole. When the inner corn kernel has been dried and coarsely ground, the result is hominy grits. Somehow, grits have suffered from an image problem, having become known as a sort of "poor man's food." There is a lot of evidence to the contrary, as I found recipes using grits in many of the nineteenth century's most widely used cookbooks, including those aimed at a more affluent audience. These recipes underscore the versatility of grits, demonstrating their use in breads, muffins, puddings, and as a supper dish to substitute for rice.

The imagination of the cooks of days gone by made building a chapter around this great American staple a real pleasure.

CORN-STUFFED PEPPERS

6 servings

This attractive recipe is quite common in old Southern cookbooks. I suggest making it in late summer, when the evenings begin getting cool enough to allow baking. Using fresh sweet corn and a combination of both green and red bell peppers, this colorful preparation is an enticing dish for company.

6 green or red bell peppers,
  or 3 of each
1 tablespoon canola oil
1 medium onion, chopped
2 teaspoons unbleached white
  flour
1 teaspoon paprika
¼ teaspoon dried thyme
A few grains cayenne pepper
⅔ cup low-fat milk or soymilk
3 cups cooked fresh corn kernels
2 to 3 tablespoons chopped fresh
  parsley
½ cup fine whole-grain bread
  crumbs
Salt and freshly ground black
  pepper
Additional bread crumbs and
  paprika for topping

Preheat the oven to 350 degrees.

Prepare the bell peppers by cutting off the stems and slicing them in half lengthwise. Remove the seeds and white membranes and arrange the halves cut side up in one or two oiled shallow baking pans.

Heat the oil in a deep saucepan. Add the onion and sauté over medium-low heat until it is golden. Sprinkle in the flour, paprika, thyme, and cayenne and stir in until smoothly blended. Cook, stirring continuously, until the mixture begins to brown lightly. Pour in the milk, a little at a time, whisking it in carefully to ensure smoothness. Allow the mixture to simmer gently until it thickens, about 5 to 7 minutes.

Stir in the corn, parsley, and bread crumbs. Season to taste with salt and pepper and remove from the heat. Distribute the stuffing evenly among the peppers. Top each one with a small amount of additional bread crumbs and a dusting of paprika.

Bake, covered, for 20 minutes, then uncover and bake another 10 to 15 minutes, or until the peppers are done to your liking.

Calories: 140   Total fat: 3 g   Protein: 4 g
Carbohydrates: 24 g   Cholesterol: 1 g   Sodium: 45 mg

SCALLOPED CORN

4 to 6 servings

Scalloped corn is more of a general than a regional American recipe. I can imagine this simple, delicious dish being served on the family tables of the Great Plains around the turn of the century.

1 tablespoon canola oil

1 large onion, chopped

1 large green bell pepper, finely diced

2 medium firm ripe tomatoes, chopped

1½ tablespoons unbleached white flour

¼ teaspoon paprika

A few grains cayenne pepper

1 cup low-fat milk or soymilk

3 cups cooked fresh corn kernels (from 3 to 4 ears)

Salt and freshly ground black pepper

1 tablespoon whipped butter or natural canola margarine, melted

1 cup soft whole grain bread crumbs

Preheat the oven to 350 degrees.

Heat the oil in a large skillet. Add the onion and sauté over medium-low heat until golden. Add the bell pepper and tomatoes and continue to sauté just until they soften. Sprinkle in the flour, paprika, and cayenne, stirring until well blended. Pour the milk in slowly, stirring continuously. Bring to a simmer, then stir in the corn and simmer for another minute or so. Season to taste with salt and pepper.

Pour the mixture into an oiled shallow 9-by 13-inch baking pan. Quickly toss the melted butter with the bread crumbs until they are evenly coated and distribute the crumbs over the corn mixture. Bake for 25 minutes, or until the crumbs begin to turn crusty. Serve at once.

Calories: 197
Carbohydrates: 32 g
Total fat: 5 g
Cholesterol: 7 g
Protein: 5 g
Sodium: 81 mg

CORN PUDDING

6 to 8 servings

Here is another classic American recipe, still very common in the South (but also known as an old New England recipe), that requires the freshest, sweetest corn for optimal flavor. I like using the sweet white corn of midsummer for this delicate, custard-like treat.

3 heaping cups cooked fresh corn kernels (from 4 medium ears)

3 eggs, well beaten

3 tablespoons unbleached white flour

1 teaspoon salt, or to taste

1 cup low-fat milk or soymilk

2 tablespoons whipped butter or natural canola margarine, melted

Preheat the oven to 325 degrees.

Take care not to overcook the corn. It should be just done. When cool enough to handle, scrape the kernels off with a sharp knife and place them in a mixing bowl. Add the eggs and sprinkle in the flour, stirring to blend. Add the salt, milk, and melted butter and mix together thoroughly.

Pour the mixture into an oiled 1½-quart baking casserole. Bake for about 1 hour, or until the top is golden brown and the pudding is set.

Calories: 140	Total fat: 6 g	Protein: 6 g
Carbohydrates: 17 g	Cholesterol: 100 g	Sodium: 355 mg

I don't believe corn pudding was a unique delicacy, but I never seem to have eaten it anywhere except at Grandmother's, and I have rarely heard of it since her day.

—Edith Holton
Yankees Were Like This, 1944

CORN OYSTERS

Makes about 20 to 22

Corn Oysters, or as they were sometimes called, Mock Oysters, were thought to be so named because they fooled the unaware into thinking that they were real fried oysters. This is likely just a tall tale, as these look and taste of nothing but fresh sweet corn. This common, old recipe of probable New England origins calls for fresh uncooked corn, minced as finely as possible. The simplicity of the recipe allows the sweet flavor of the corn to shine through.

4 large ears fresh corn, cooked until just tender

2 eggs, well beaten

2 tablespoons low-fat milk or soymilk

2 tablespoons unbleached white flour

Salt and freshly ground black pepper

Canola oil for frying

Cut the whole corn kernels off the cobs with a sharp knife. Process them in a food processor, pulsing on and off, until the kernels are finely minced, but don't puree.

Combine the minced corn with the beaten egg and the milk in a mixing bowl. Sprinkle in the flour and season to taste with salt and pepper.

Heat just enough oil to coat the bottom of a nonstick skillet or griddle. When it's hot enough to make a drop of water sizzle, drop the corn mixture onto the surface by the heaping tablespoon. Cook over medium heat on both sides until nicely browned and crisp. Drain on paper towels and serve at once.

Calories: 31   Total fat: 0 g   Protein: 2 g
Carbohydrates: 4 g   Cholesterol: 21 g   Sodium: 19 mg

It is not elegant to gnaw Indian corn. The kernels should be scored with a knife, scraped off into the plate, and then eaten with a fork. Ladies should be particularly careful how they manage so ticklish a dainty, lest the exhibition rub off a little desirable romance.

—Charles Day
Hints on Etiquette, 1844

PENNSYLVANIA DUTCH CORN NOODLES

6 servings

Broad egg noodles are a staple in Pennsylvania Dutch cookery. Teamed with fresh corn and ripe tomatoes, this traditional treat makes a wonderful summer supper dish. The simple preparation will get you in and out of the kitchen quickly. For a non-traditional variation, pass around some freshly grated Parmesan cheese to top each serving.

12-ounce package broad egg noodles, preferably yolk-free
2 tablespoons canola oil
1 large onion, chopped
3 heaping cups diced ripe tomatoes
¼ cup water
2 to 3 cups cooked fresh corn kernels (from 3 to 4 medium ears)
¼ cup chopped fresh parsley
Salt and freshly ground black pepper
Grated fresh Parmesan cheese for topping, optional

Bring plenty of water to a boil in a large pot. Cook the noodles according to package directions until they are just tender, then drain.

In the meantime, heat the oil in a large skillet. Add the onion and sauté over medium-low heat until lightly browned. Add the tomatoes and water and cook just until they soften a bit, about 3 to 4 minutes. Add the corn and parsley and cook just until everything is heated through.

Combine the skillet mixture with the cooked noodles in a large serving bowl. Season to taste with salt and lots of freshly ground black pepper. Serve at once, topping each serving with some grated Parmesan cheese if you'd like.

Calories: 194	Total fat: 6 g	Protein: 4 g
Carbohydrates: 31 g	Cholesterol: 18 g	Sodium: 13 mg

Variation: Often, traditional recipes call for a cooked, diced potato or two to be added. It may sound odd to combine noodles with potatoes, but it works—try it!

DUTCH SUCCOTASH

6 to 8 servings

The Pennsylvania Dutch variety of succotash typifies their cooking style—filling and simply seasoned, but not bland, with a pleasant combination of flavorful vegetables.

1½ tablespoons canola oil
1 large onion, chopped
1 medium green bell pepper, diced
2 medium potatoes, cooked in their skin, peeled and diced
2 cups cooked fresh corn kernels (from 3 medium ears)
1 10-ounce package thawed frozen baby lima beans
2 heaping cups chopped ripe tomatoes
1 teaspoon paprika
Salt and freshly ground black pepper

Heat the oil in a large heavy saucepan. Add the onion and sauté over medium-low heat until translucent. Add the bell pepper and continue to sauté until the onion is golden. Add all the remaining ingredients and simmer, covered, for 20 to 25 minutes over very low heat, stirring occasionally. Serve at once.

Calories: 160
Carbohydrates: 28 g
Total fat: 3 g
Cholesterol: 0 g
Protein: 4 g
Sodium: 21 mg

SOUTHERN SUCCOTASH

6 to 8 servings

It should come as no surprise that okra is the characteristic ingredient in this Southern variation on succotash.

1 tablespoon canola oil
1 medium onion, chopped
½ medium green or red bell pepper, finely diced
2 cups small, fresh okra, stemmed and sliced ½ inch thick, or 1 10-ounce package frozen sliced okra, thawed
2 cups chopped ripe, juicy tomatoes
⅓ cup water
2 tablespoons cider vinegar
3 cups cooked fresh corn kernels (from 4 medium ears)
2 to 3 tablespoons chopped fresh parsley
Salt and freshly ground black pepper
Dash of ground nutmeg

Heat the oil in a deep saucepan. Add the onion and sauté over medium-low heat until translucent. Add the bell pepper and okra, and sauté, stirring frequently, for 5 minutes. Add the tomatoes, water, and vinegar. Cover and simmer for about 10 to 12 minutes, until the tomatoes are reduced to a loose sauce.

Stir in the cooked corn kernels and parsley. Season to taste with salt, pepper and nutmeg. Cover and cook over very low heat for another 5 minutes. Make sure there is just enough liquid to keep everything moist; add a bit more water if necessary.

Calories: 105   Total fat: 2 g   Protein: 2 g
Carbohydrates: 19 g   Cholesterol: 0 g   Sodium: 11 mg

And those who came were resolved
    to be Englishmen
Gone to the World's end,
    but English every one,
And they ate the white corn-kernels
    parched in the sun,
And they knew it not,
    but they'd not be English again.

—Stephen Vincent Benet
"*Western Star,*" 1943

COLACHE
(Southwestern Summer Succotash)

6 or more servings

In this Southwestern variation of succotash, the bright mélange of the freshest corn and vegetables makes for a wonderful celebration of the summer harvest.

1½ cups green beans, trimmed
    and cut into 1-inch pieces
1½ tablespoons olive oil
1 large onion, chopped
2 cloves garlic, minced
3 cups fresh uncooked corn
    kernels (from 4 medium ears)
1 heaping cup chopped ripe
    tomatoes
⅓ cup water
2 small yellow summer
    squashes, diced
1 small hot green chile, seeded
    and minced,
    or 1 4-ounce can chopped
    mild green chiles
1 tablespoon apple cider vinegar
Salt and freshly ground black
    pepper

Steam the green beans until they are tender-crisp. Refresh under cold water until they stop steaming and set aside until needed.

Heat the olive oil in a deep saucepan or stir-fry pan. Add the onion and garlic and sauté over medium-low heat until the onion is translucent. Add all the remaining ingredients except the green beans and stir together well. Cover and simmer gently for about 20 minutes, or until the corn and squash are just done. Add the green beans and simmer for another 3 to 5 minutes. Serve at once.

Calories: 140	Total fat: 3 g	Protein: 3 g
Carbohydrates: 24 g	Cholesterol: 0 g	Sodium: 11 mg

Spring and early summer brought an abundance of tender young pumpkins, green beans, sweet corn, which were flavored with onion, tomatoes and chilies. The m'sickquatash (succotash) of the American Indian improved by stewing in olive oil and seasoning, became the colache of old California. It was the traditional dish for the season.

—Ana Bégué de Packman
Early California Hospitality, 1938

RIO CORN PIE

4 to 6 servings

This is a recipe of special savor adapted from Phyllis Hughes' Pueblo Indian Cookbook. *It is a perfect example of a dish of native ingredients, influenced by Spanish seasonings. This is a terrific vegetarian main dish for Thanksgiving.*

1 tablespoon olive oil
1 medium onion, chopped
2 cloves garlic, minced
1 medium green or red bell
    pepper, diced
1 cup cooked fresh corn kernels
    (from 1 large ear)
2 cups cooked pinto beans
2 cups chopped, ripe tomatoes or
    1 14- to 16-ounce can diced
    tomatoes, lightly drained
2 teaspoons chili powder, or to
    taste, or ¼ teaspoon dried hot
    red pepper flakes
1 teaspoon dried oregano
½ teaspoon ground cumin
Salt
4 cups water
1 cup cornmeal
¾ cup grated Monterey Jack
    cheese, optional

Preheat the oven to 375 degrees.

Heat the oil in a large skillet. Add the onion and sauté over medium-low heat until translucent. Add the garlic and bell pepper and sauté until the onion is golden brown. Add the corn kernels, pinto beans, tomatoes, and seasonings. Season with salt to taste. Stir well and simmer for 10 to 15 minutes. Remove from the heat.

Bring the water to a simmer in a deep non-stick saucepan. Sprinkle the cornmeal in slowly, stirring constantly to avoid lumping. Cover and cook over very low heat for 20 minutes, stirring occasionally, or until thick.

Oil a shallow 1½-quart round or square baking pan and pour in half of the cooked cornmeal. Pour the mixture from the skillet over it, then sprinkle with the optional grated cheese. Top with the remaining cornmeal, patting it in smoothly. Bake for 45 to 50 minutes, or until the cornmeal is golden brown and crusty. Let stand for 5 to 10 minutes, then cut into wedges or squares to serve.

Calories: 273	Total fat: 3 g	Protein: 8 g
Carbohydrates: 51 g	Cholesterol: 0 g	Sodium: 10 mg

CREOLE CORN MAQUE CHOUX

Serves 6

This wonderful side dish was adapted by Creole cooks from a dish made by the Native Americans who populated southwest Louisiana.

1½ tablespoons canola oil
1 large onion, chopped
3 medium stalks celery, diced
1 medium red bell pepper, diced
½ medium green bell pepper, diced
4 cups cooked fresh corn kernels (from 4 large or 5 medium ears)
2 medium diced ripe tomatoes
¾ cup low-fat milk or soymilk
1 teaspoon sugar
1 tablespoon unbleached white flour
Salt to taste
Pinch of cayenne pepper, or to taste

Heat the oil in a large skillet. Add the onion and sauté over medium-low heat until golden. Add the celery and bell peppers and continue to sauté until all the vegetables are just tender, stirring occasionally, about 8 minutes.

Add the cooked corn kernels, tomatoes, milk, and sugar to the skillet. Bring to a simmer, then simmer gently, uncovered, about 5 to 7 minutes, or until everything is well heated through and the tomatoes have softened a bit.

Dissolve the flour in just enough water to make it smooth and flowing. Stir it into the skillet and stir until the liquid in the skillet thickens. Season to taste with salt and cayenne pepper. Remove from the heat and serve at once.

Calories: 167   Total fat: 3 g   Protein: 4 g
Carbohydrates: 29 g   Cholesterol: 1 g   Sodium: 45 mg

Mustn't pluck one's corn before it's ripe.

—Creole Proverb

SKILLET CORNBREAD AND "SAUSAGE" STUFFING

6 or more servings

Cornbread is only as good as it is fresh. Here's a great way to use cornbread that is a day or two old.

1½ tablespoons canola oil

1 medium onion, chopped

2 medium celery stalks, diced

4 links soy "sausage," sliced
    ½ inch thick (see note,
    page 137)

½ recipe leftover cornbread (any
    of those on pages 49 to 52,
    or other)

1 cup cooked fresh corn kernels
    (from 1 large ear)

¾ to 1 cup homemade or canned
    vegetable stock

1 teaspoon Mrs. Dash or other
    salt-free herb-and-spice
    seasoning mix

2 scallions, chopped

¼ cup chopped fresh parsley

Salt and freshly ground black
    pepper

Heat the oil in a large skillet. Add the onion, celery, and "sausage" and sauté over medium heat for 10 to 15 minutes, stirring gently and frequently, until the mixture is golden brown.

Add the remaining ingredients and stir together gently. Cook without stirring for several minutes, or until the underside begins to brown, then stir again, and cook until the underside browns once more. Remove from the heat and serve.

Calories: 210   Total fat: 7 g   Protein: 6 g
Carbohydrates: 31 g   Cholesterol: 1 g   Sodium: 316 mg

Since ancient times, corn has been the most esteemed crop of the Native Americans, and has long been the subject of a series of corn dances, which are performed on Pueblos even today. The dances address the growth of the corn, prayers for rain, and thanks for the harvest. The performance of these dances, often open to the public, is usually the culmination of rituals that are held for several days prior.

BAKED CHEESE GRITS

6 to 8 servings

This is a deep South recipe of utmost simplicity, yet it is as elegant and satisfying as a soufflé.

4 cups water
1 cup uncooked grits, regular or
    quick-cooking
1 teaspoon salt
2 tablespoons whipped butter or
    natural canola margarine
2 eggs, well beaten
2 tablespoons low-fat milk or
    soymilk
1½ cups firmly packed grated
    cheddar cheese, reduced-fat if
    desired
Freshly ground black pepper

Pray let me, an American, inform the gentleman, who seems ignorant of the matter, that Indian corn, take it all in all, is one of the most agreeable and wholesome grains in the world; that its green leaves roasted are a delicacy beyond expression; that samp, hominy, succatash and nokehock, made of it, are so many pleasing varieties; and that johny or hoecake, hot from the fire, is better than a Yorkshire muffin.

—Benjamin Franklin, in a 1765 letter

Preheat the oven to 375 degrees.

Bring the water to a gentle simmer in a deep nonstick saucepan. Sprinkle the grits in slowly, stirring continuously to avoid lumping. Turn the heat down to very low, then cook, stirring, for a minute or two. Add the salt, then cover and cook until thick (25 to 30 minutes for regular grits or 5 minutes for quick-cooking grits), stirring occasionally. Remove from the heat.

Stir the butter into the grits until it melts. Add the eggs, milk, cheese, and a few grindings of pepper. Mix together thoroughly and pour into an oiled 1½-quart, medium-deep square or round baking dish.

Bake for 45 to 50 minutes, or until the mixture is puffed and the top is golden and crusty.

Calories: 237   Total fat: 10 g   Protein: 13 g
Carbohydrates: 23 g   Cholesterol: 88 g   Sodium: 533 mg

SOUTHERN-STYLE "FRANKS" WITH GRITS CRUST

6 servings

This tasty casserole usually calls for a cooked cornmeal crust, but you can put it together faster with quick grits. This is an all-American shepherd's pie, of sorts.

1 tablespoon canola oil

1 medium onion, chopped

1 medium green bell pepper, diced

1 medium zucchini, quartered lengthwise and sliced

1 cup cooked fresh or thawed frozen corn kernels

1 14- to 16-ounce can diced tomatoes

8 links fat-free or low-fat tofu hot dogs, sliced ¼ inch thick (see note)

½ teaspoon dried oregano

¼ teaspoon dried thyme

Grits crust:

3¾ cup water

1 cup quick-cooking grits

1 teaspoon salt

2 tablespoons whipped butter or natural canola margarine

Preheat the oven to 400 degrees.

Heat the oil in a large skillet. Add the onion and sauté over medium heat until translucent. Add the bell pepper and continue to sauté until the onion is lightly golden. Add the zucchini, corn, tomatoes, tofu hot dogs, oregano, and thyme. Cook, covered, until the zucchini is just tender, about 4 to 5 minutes. Pour the mixture into a 2-quart shallow rectangular or round baking dish.

Bring water to a gentle simmer in a deep nonstick saucepan. Sprinkle the grits in slowly, stirring constantly to avoid lumping. Cook over very low heat for 3 to 4 minutes, or until thick and smooth, stirring frequently. Remove from the heat and stir in the salt and butter. Pour the grits over the vegetable mixture and smooth it out evenly over them with a wooden spoon.

Bake for 25 to 30 minutes, or until the grits topping is crusty. Let the casserole stand for 5 minutes, then cut into squares or wedges to serve.

Calories: 235	Total fat: 5 g	Protein: 14 g
Carbohydrates: 31 g	Cholesterol: 8 g	Sodium: 751 mg

Note: Tofu-based imitation "hot dogs" are commonly available in the produce section of well-stocked supermarkets, as well as in natural foods stores.

GRITS WITH FRESH CORN AND TOMATOES

4 to 6 servings

This is an inviting late-summer supper dish suffused with the flavors of the Southwest. Stone-ground grits are more flavorful than those available in supermarkets; they are available in natural foods stores and through natural-foods mail-order outlets.

3 cups water

¾ cup uncooked yellow grits, regular or quick-cooking, preferably stone-ground

1½ tablespoons olive oil

1 medium onion, chopped

1 small green bell pepper, diced

1 pound ripe tomatoes, chopped

1 small fresh hot green chile, seeded and minced, optional

2 cups cooked fresh corn kernels (from 3 medium ears)

½ teaspoon each dried oregano and ground cumin

Salt and freshly ground pepper, to taste

1 cup grated cheddar cheese, reduced-fat if desired

Bring 3 cups of water to a gentle simmer in a deep nonstick saucepan. Sprinkle the grits in slowly, stirring constantly to avoid lumping. Cook over low heat until smooth and thick (25 to 30 minutes for regular grits and 5 minutes for quick-cooking), stirring frequently.

Heat the oil in a large skillet. Add the onion and sauté over medium heat until translucent. Add the bell pepper and continue to sauté until the onion is golden. Add the tomatoes and optional chile and sauté until the tomatoes have softened, about 5 to 7 minutes. Stir in the cooked corn kernels and seasonings. When the grits are done, stir them into the skillet. Sprinkle in the cheddar cheese and cook until it melts. Serve at once.

Calories: 282	Total fat: 9 g	Protein: 10 g
Carbohydrates: 39 g	Cholesterol: 16 g	Sodium: 174 mg

POSOLE Y FRIJOLES
(Hominy with Pink Beans)

6 servings

A Native American recipe embellished by Spanish seasonings, posole usually consists of the hominy stewed with meat or beans in a spicy base. Here, of course, pink beans are used, resulting in a quick, easy, and very tasty stew. Canned hominy is available in Spanish groceries and increasingly in supermarkets, shelved near canned corn kernels. Serve with warm flour tortillas.

1 tablespoon olive oil
1 large onion, chopped
1 large clove garlic, minced
1 large green bell pepper, diced
1 14- to 16-ounce can diced
  tomatoes
2 1-pound cans whole hominy,
  drained
1 1-pound can pinto beans,
  drained and rinsed
1 small fresh hot chile, seeded
  and minced, or 1 4-ounce can
  chopped mild green chiles
1 teaspoon ground cumin
½ teaspoon dried oregano
¼ cup minced fresh cilantro or
  parsley

Heat the olive oil in a large saucepan. Add the onion and sauté over medium-low heat until translucent. Add the garlic and bell pepper and continue to sauté until the onion is golden.

Add the remaining ingredients except the cilantro, stir together, and bring to a simmer. Cover and simmer gently for 20 to 25 minutes. Stir in the cilantro and serve at once in shallow bowls.

Calories: 175 Total fat: 2 g Protein: 4 g
Carbohydrates: 34 g Cholesterol: 0 g Sodium: 16 mg

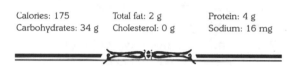

Homminy is an American dish, made of Indian corn, freed from the husks, boiled whole...until it becomes almost a pulp.

—John F. D. Smyth
 Tour in the United States of America, 1784

CREAMY HOMINY WITH CHEESE AND GREEN CHILE

6 to 8 servings

This old Southwestern classic is an easy and delicious way to use hominy. See the previous recipe for more information on canned hominy.

1 cup low-fat milk

2 tablespoons unbleached
  white flour

1 cup grated cheddar cheese,
  reduced-fat if desired

2 1-pound cans hominy (white or
  golden, or 1 can of each),
  drained

1 4-ounce can mild or hot
  chopped green chiles

½ teaspoon ground cumin

Preheat the oven to 375 degrees.

Heat the milk in a small saucepan. Dissolve the flour in just enough water to make it smooth and flowing. When the milk is hot, slowly pour the dissolved flour into it, stirring constantly. Simmer gently until it has thickened.

Combine the thickened milk with the remaining ingredients in a mixing bowl and stir together. Transfer to a lightly oiled shallow 9- by 13-inch baking dish. Bake for 30 minutes, or until the top begins to turn golden. Serve hot.

Calories: 186 Total fat: 3 g Protein: 9 g
Carbohydrates: 29 g Cholesterol: 13 g Sodium: 141 mg

Chapter 8

VEGETABLES

We proceed to Roots and Vegetables—and the best cook cannot alter the first quality, they must be good, or the cook will be disappointed.

—Amelia Simmons
  American Cookery, 1796

The advice given to cooks by Amelia Simmons, the author of the first American cookbook, could not be more on target, especially in today's world of processing, packaging, and importing. Most of the vegetable recipes I encountered from earlier days were not fancy or fussy, most likely because they relied on the good, basic flavor of the fresh produce. The majority of these recipes were developed in times when produce came straight from the kitchen garden, or at the very least, fresh from a local market.

Colonial Virginia, from all accounts, was a veritable paradise of vegetables in quantity and variety, which are today difficult to imagine. Of great influence in introducing and promoting all manner of produce, and in elevating the home garden to an art form, was Thomas Jefferson. In the introduction to this book, I elaborated on the lavish variety of vegetables commonly known in the early South. It seems safe to say, oddly, that nothing much happened (except perhaps a lot of regression) to the state of produce in America until the 1970s, when a resurgence of interest in fresh vegetables seems to have been spurred by the popularity of ethnic cuisines.

When starting this project, I probably knew my way around Oriental groceries blindfolded, but I had never used a traditional crop like okra, and couldn't tell a cymling from a mirliton. As far as I was concerned, parsnips were only for laughing at, and collard greens just looked like—well, too much trouble. Not that all the vegetables I encountered as typically American were this odd to me—most were the old familiar standbys: White and sweet potatoes, cabbage, beets, eggplant, and several varieties of squash.

My sense of discovery lay not only in new ways of preparation, but more importantly, in gaining an awareness of a multitude of great winter vegetable recipes, many of which highlight the aforementioned items in hearty, satisfying ways. This should be especially cheering to those of us who miss the bright variety of summer and fall harvest goods, but still want to use what is truly seasonal—and not just imported—during the cold weather months.

The wide range of regional styles represented in this chapter reflects the knowledge and creativity of our earlier cooks. From the simple dishes of the frugal Pennsylvania Dutch to the lavishly seasoned creations of the Creoles, American vegetables could not have been in better hands.

BEETS PIQUANT

6 servings

One of America's earliest cookbook writers, Mary Randolph, said in her 1824 book that beets "are not so much used as they deserve to be." I agree with this observation. I will grant, though, that they are not terribly versatile, they take a long time to cook, and that you and your kitchen may be splattered with magenta by the time you're finished. Barring these minor obstacles, I was happy to learn two new and delicious ways of preparing beets. The following recipe is adapted from an old New Orleans cookbook.

6 medium beets
2 tablespoons whipped butter or
   natural canola margarine
2 tablespoons unbleached
   white flour
¾ cup hot water
¼ cup low-fat milk
3 tablespoons apple cider vinegar
2 tablespoons dry white or
   red wine
1½ teaspoons honey
¼ teaspoon salt
Freshly ground black pepper
A few grains cayenne pepper

Remove the green tops from the beets, leaving about ¼ inch of the stalks on the beets (save the greens for later use; cooked or steamed, they can be used like spinach and are very nutritious). Rinse the beets to remove loose dirt but take care not to break the fibers.

Bring a deep pot of water to a boil and gently drop the beets in. Cook over medium-low heat until they are just tender. This will take anywhere from 45 minutes to 1½ hours, depending on the size and age of the beets.

Drain the cooked beets and rinse them briefly in cold water. Trim the roots and tops and slip off the skins. Slice them ¼ inch thick.

Heat the butter in a large saucepan until it melts. Sprinkle in the flour and stir until smoothly blended. Continue to cook over low heat until the mixture just begins to brown. Mix the hot water and milk and slowly pour it into the saucepan, stirring constantly to avoid lumping. Bring to a simmer, then add the remaining ingredients and simmer gently for 5 minutes. Stir in the sliced beets and simmer over very low heat for 10 to 15 minutes. Serve at once.

Calories: 68   Total fat: 3 g   Protein: 1 g
Carbohydrates: 7 g   Cholesterol: 8 g   Sodium: 119 mg

HARVARD BEETS

4 to 6 servings

Harvard Beets is a standard New England recipe, quite commonplace in the nineteenth century. I have modified the recipe by replacing the usual sugar and water mixture with orange juice, which enhances the natural flavor of beets without overpowering it.

6 medium beets
2 tablespoons whipped butter or
  natural canola margarine
2 teaspoons arrowroot or
  cornstarch
3 tablespoons apple cider
  vinegar
⅔ cup fresh orange juice
2 teaspoons honey
¼ teaspoon salt
⅛ teaspoon freshly ground black
  pepper

Follow the directions for washing and cooking the beets given in the previous recipe. When they are done, slip off the skins and cut them into ½-inch dice. Set aside.

Heat the butter in a large saucepan until it melts. Sprinkle in the arrowroot and stir until it is well blended. Stir in the vinegar, then slowly add the orange juice, stirring carefully to avoid lumps. Add the honey, salt, and pepper. Add the diced beets and stir together thoroughly. Cook over very low heat for 20 minutes, then serve.

Calories: 84	Total fat: 3 g	Protein: 1 g
Carbohydrates: 12 g	Cholesterol: 10 g	Sodium: 137 mg

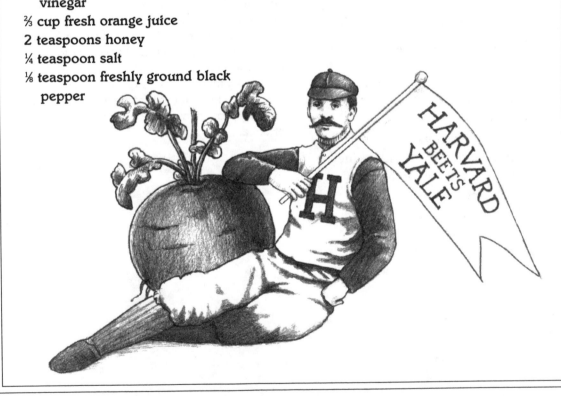

CREOLE OKRA AND TOMATOES

6 servings

Okra is a vegetable that arguably requires an acquired taste. I learned to appreciate it pickled or fried while traveling through the South, as well as when it is combined with tomatoes, as in this classic Creole recipe. The acidity of the tomatoes seems to temper that unusual texture that we Yankees are so wary of.

1 tablespoon canola oil

2 cloves garlic, minced

1 pound fresh tender okra, stemmed and sliced ½ inch thick

1 pound ripe juicy tomatoes

2 scallions, white and green parts, thinly sliced

2 tablespoons apple cider vinegar

1 tablespoon minced fresh basil, or ½ teaspoon dried

¼ teaspoon dried thyme

Pinch of allspice or nutmeg

Salt and freshly ground black pepper

Hot cooked rice, optional

Heat the oil in a large skillet. Add the garlic and sauté over low heat until lightly golden, a minute or so. Add the okra and sauté, stirring frequently, for 5 minutes. Add the remaining ingredients. then cover and simmer gently for 15 to 20 minutes, stirring occasionally, until the tomatoes are reduced to a loose sauce. If the mixture becomes too watery, simmer, uncovered, just until it thickens up a bit. Serve at once as a side dish or over hot cooked rice.

Calories: 65	Total fat: 2 g	Protein: 2 g
Carbohydrates: 9 g	Cholesterol: 0 g	Sodium: 13 mg

Never plant okra while standing. Always stoop and the plant will bear while still low.

—Louisiana husbandry folk-belief

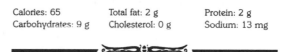

CREOLE EGGPLANT SOUFFLÉ

4 to 6 servings

Eggplant is presumed to have arrived in colonial Virginia as part of the slave trade. Thomas Jefferson was an early proponent of eggplant, though it has not been integrated to any great extent in any American cuisine, save for the Creole. Since eggplant grew abundantly in the area of New Orleans, and was sold in the famous French Market, Creole cooks developed some wonderful ways to use it.

2 tablespoons canola oil
1 medium onion, finely chopped
1 medium celery stalk, finely diced
2 cloves garlic, minced
1 tablespoon unbleached white flour
2 tablespoons minced fresh parsley
1 tablespoon minced fresh basil, or
 ½ teaspoon dried
½ teaspoon dried thyme
½ cup low-fat milk or soymilk
1 large eggplant (about 1½ pounds),
 peeled and diced
½ cup fresh soft whole-grain bread
 crumbs
1 cup firmly packed grated mild
 white cheese of your choice
Salt and freshly ground black
 pepper
A few grains cayenne pepper
3 eggs, separated, at room
 temperature

Preheat the oven to 350 degrees.

Heat the oil in a large skillet. Add the onion, celery, and garlic and sauté over medium-low heat until the onion is translucent. Sprinkle in the flour, stirring until well blended. Add the herbs and sauté, stirring until the mixture just begins to brown. Add the milk and eggplant. Cover and cook over low heat, stirring occasionally, until the eggplant is quite tender. Add small amounts of water as needed to keep the bottom of the skillet moist. When done, remove from the heat.

Transfer the mixture to a mixing bowl. Add the bread crumbs, cheese, salt and pepper to taste, cayenne, and egg yolks and stir together.

Beat the egg whites until they form stiff peaks, then fold them gently into the eggplant mixture. Pour the mixture into a well-oiled 1½-quart baking dish or soufflé pan. Bake for 40 to 45 minutes, or until puffed and golden brown. Let the soufflé stand for 5 minutes, then serve.

Calories: 258　　Total fat: 15 g　　Protein: 12 g
Carbohydrates: 16 g　　Cholesterol: 149 g　　Sodium: 214mg

CREOLE STUFFED EGGPLANT

4 servings

This dish is occasionally seen on contemporary restaurant menus in New Orleans but almost invariably contains some shellfish. Older recipes are nearly equally divided between the seafood version and those close to this completely vegetarian version.

2 tablespoons canola oil

1 large onion, finely chopped

1 large celery stalk, finely diced

2 cloves garlic, minced

1 small green bell pepper, finely chopped

2 medium eggplants (about 1 pound each)

1 heaping cup chopped ripe juicy tomatoes or canned diced tomatoes, lightly drained

¼ cup chopped fresh parsley

1 tablespoon chopped fresh basil or ½ teaspoon dried

½ teaspoon dried thyme

Salt and freshly ground black pepper

Cayenne pepper to taste

½ cup dry whole-grain bread crumbs

Preheat the oven to 375 degrees.

Heat the oil in a large skillet. Add the onion, celery, and garlic and sauté over medium-low heat until the onion is translucent. Add the bell pepper and continue to sauté until the onion is golden.

In the meantime, stem the eggplants and cut them in half lengthwise. With a sharp knife, score each half several times lengthwise and across. Then, carefully remove the pulp, leaving a sturdy ½-inch-thick shell all around.

Chop the eggplant pulp and add it to the skillet mixture along with all the remaining ingredients except the bread crumbs. Add a bit of water, just enough to keep the mixture moist. Cook, covered, until the eggplant is tender, stirring occasionally. Stir in the bread crumbs.

Set the eggplant shells in an oiled shallow baking dish in which they will be securely propped up against one another. Divide the stuffing evenly among the shells. Bake for 30 to 40 minutes, or until the eggplant shells are tender but not collapsed.

Calories: 163   Total fat: 7 g   Protein: 2 g
Carbohydrates: 22 g   Cholesterol: 0 g   Sodium: 49 mg

SCALLOPED CAULIFLOWER

6 servings

Maria Parloa, one of America's best late-nineteenth-century cookbook authors, said of cauliflower in the 1887 edition of Miss Parloa's Kitchen Companion, *"This is a handsome and delicate vegetable. It is a pity that more people do not know how to cook it properly." A commonplace way of preparing vegetables in such old general American cookbooks as Miss Parloa's, scalloping comes close to being a culinary cliché, saved by the fact that it makes certain vegetables taste so good. This recipe is inspired by Miss Parloa's.*

1 large head cauliflower

2 tablespoons whipped butter or natural canola margarine

2½ tablespoons unbleached white flour

1¼ cups low-fat milk or soymilk

½ teaspoon salt

Freshly ground black pepper

½ cup firmly packed grated mild white cheese, any variety, optional

2 scallions, minced

1 cup soft whole-grain bread crumbs

Paprika for topping

Preheat the oven to 350 degrees.

Break the cauliflower into smallish pieces and florets, a bit larger than bite-sized. Steam until tender-crisp, about 8 to 10 minutes, then refresh immediately under cold water until it stops steaming. Drain well, then arrange the cauliflower pieces in a lightly oiled shallow 9- by 13-inch baking pan.

Heat the butter in a small saucepan. Sprinkle in the flour, a little at a time, stirring until well blended. Add the milk, about ¼ cup at a time, stirring it in carefully to avoid lumping. Add the salt and a few grindings of pepper. Simmer gently over low heat until the sauce thickens.

Pour the sauce over the cauliflower, then sprinkle on the optional grated cheese, followed by the scallions. Top with the bread crumbs and garnish with a dusting of paprika.

Bake for 20 to 25 minutes, or until the crumbs are lightly browned. Serve at once.

Calories: 136	Total fat: 6 g	Protein: 6 g
Carbohydrates: 12 g	Cholesterol: 19 g	Sodium: 314 mg

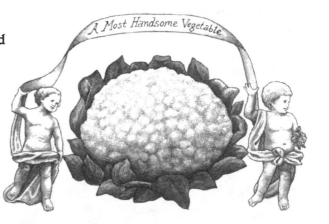
A Most Handsome Vegetable

SCALLOPED TOMATOES

6 to 8 servings

A great way to use late-summer's bumper crop of garden-fresh tomatoes.

1 tablespoon canola oil
1 large onion, chopped
2 cups fine dry bread crumbs
½ teaspoon each: dried basil, salt
1 teaspoon minced fresh thyme,
  or ¼ teaspoon dried thyme
Freshly ground pepper
2 pounds firm ripe tomatoes,
  sliced
2 tablespoons minced fresh
  parsley

Preheat the oven to 350 degrees

Heat the oil in a small skillet. Add the onion and sauté over medium heat until it is golden.

In a small mixing bowl, combine the bread crumbs with the basil, salt, and thyme. Add a few grindings of pepper and stir together.

In a lightly oiled round 1½-quart or 9- by 13-inch baking dish, layer as follows: A fine layer of the seasoned bread crumbs, half of the tomatoes (overlapped if necessary), the sautéed onion, another fine layer of bread crumbs, the remaining tomatoes, then the remaining bread crumbs. Finish by sprinkling the parsley over the top.

Bake for about 20 to 25 minutes, or until the tomatoes are cooked but not mushy. Serve at once.

Calories: 162   Total fat: 4 g   Protein. 5 g
Carbohydrates: 27 g   Cholesterol: 1 g   Sodium: 221 mg

RED WINE CABBAGE

6 servings

Cabbage was brought to the New World by the European settlers and, due to its hardiness, was especially valued in the colder climates. In New England, and in the heartland settled by the German immigrants (better known as the Pennsylvania Dutch), cabbage was a highly esteemed staple vegetable. This invitingly aromatic side dish is adapted from a Pennsylvania Dutch recipe, although versions of it appear in New England cookbooks as well.

1 tablespoon canola oil
1 large onion, cut in half and
    thinly sliced
5 heaping cups coarsely chopped
    red cabbage
1 large sweet apple, peeled,
    cored, quartered, and thinly
    sliced
½ cup dry red wine
2 tablespoons apple cider vinegar
1 tablespoon honey
½ teaspoon salt
Freshly ground black pepper
1 tablespoon unbleached white
    flour

Heat the oil in a large saucepan. Add the onion and sauté over medium heat until translucent. Add the cabbage and all the remaining ingredients except the flour. Stir together and cook over very low heat, covered, for 25 to 30 minutes, stirring occasionally, or until the cabbage is tender but still has a bit of crunch.

Sprinkle in the flour and stir it in completely. Simmer for another few minutes, uncovered, until the liquid in the pot has thickened a bit. Serve at once.

Calories: 106   Total fat: 2 g   Protein: 1 g
Carbohydrates: 15 g   Cholesterol: 0 g   Sodium: 187 mg

Cabbage: A familiar kitchen-garden vegetable about as large and as wise as a man's head.

—Ambrose Bierce
The Devil's Dictionary, 1906

FARMER'S CABBAGE

4 to 6 servings

This old New England recipe is a pleasant, old-fashioned way of preparing cabbage. It's reminiscent of a hot cole slaw.

2 tablespoons unbleached white flour

1 cup low-fat milk or soymilk

2 teaspoons apple cider vinegar

½ teaspoon salt

Freshly ground black pepper, to taste

5 cups firmly packed finely shredded white cabbage

1 small onion, grated

3 tablespoons minced fresh parsley

1 tablespoon whipped butter or natural canola margarine

½ cup soft whole grain bread crumbs

Paprika for topping

Preheat the oven to 350 degrees.

Use just enough of the milk to dissolve the flour in a small bowl, then combine the dissolved flour with the remaining milk in a small saucepan. Heat the mixture slowly, then add the vinegar, salt and pepper. Simmer gently over low heat until it thickens, about 10 minutes.

Combine the cabbage, onion, and parsley in a mixing bowl. Pour the sauce over them and toss until thoroughly combined. Transfer the mixture to a lightly oiled shallow 1½-quart baking dish.

Melt the butter in a small skillet and stir the bread crumbs in until they are evenly moistened. Top the cabbage mixture with the crumbs and sprinkle with paprika. Bake for 35 to 40 minutes, or until the cabbage is just tender and the crumbs are golden brown. Let the casserole stand for 5 minutes before serving.

Calories: 83
Carbohydrates: 12 g
Total fat: 3 g
Cholesterol: 7 g
Protein: 3 g
Sodium: 487 mg

BAKED HONEY-GLAZED ONIONS

8 servings

Slow-baking onions gives them a mellow sweetness. Try this with naturally sweet Vidalia onions.

1 cup homemade or canned
    vegetable stock
¼ cup honey
2 teaspoons whipped butter or
    natural canola margarine
Pinch each: dried rosemary and
    thyme, and ground nutmeg
4 large Vidalia or white onions
Wheat germ for topping

The cook who can do without onions has yet to be born.

—The Up-To-Date Cookbook, 1910

Preheat the oven to 375 degrees.

Combine all the ingredients except the last 2 in a small sauce pan. Heat gently, stirring, until the butter and honey are smoothly blended. Remove from the heat.

Peel the outer skin from the onions and cut them in half crosswise. Cut a thin sliver from the bottom of each onion half, so that they will stand steadily in a baking dish. Arrange the onion halves in a shallow baking dish and pour the mixture from the saucepan evenly over them.

Cover and bake for 45 minutes to 1 hour, or until the onions are tender when pierced with a fork. Once or twice during this time, spoon some of the liquid from the bottom of the baking dish over the onions.

Sprinkle the onions with wheat germ and bake, uncovered, for an additional 10 to 15 minutes, or until most of the liquid has been absorbed. Serve at once or keep warm until needed.

Calories: 95   Total fat: 0 g   Protein: 2 g
Carbohydrates: 20 g   Cholesterol: 2 g   Sodium: 41 mg

PARSNIP CROQUETTES

Makes about 16

This recipe is further proof of the wonders worked with winter vegetables by the Pennsylvania Dutch tradition.

1 pound parsnips, peeled and diced
1 egg, beaten
¼ cup unbleached white flour
1 tablespoon low-fat milk or water
1 tablespoon grated onion
Salt and freshly ground black pepper
Cornmeal for dredging
Whipped butter or natural canola margarine for frying

Steam the diced parsnips in a large saucepan with a small amount of water, covered, until they are tender, about 15 to 20 minutes. Drain them well in a colander, then transfer to a mixing bowl.

Mash the parsnips thoroughly, then add to them the beaten egg, flour, milk, onion, and salt and pepper to taste. Mix together well and allow the mixture to cool to room temperature. If time allows, cover and refrigerate.

With well-floured hands, shape the parsnip mixture into palm-sized croquettes. Dredge both sides in cornmeal. Heat just enough butter to coat the bottom of a nonstick skillet or griddle. Cook the croquettes over medium heat on both sides until golden brown.

Calories: 35　　Total fat: 0 g　　Protein: 1 g
Carbohydrates: 7 g　　Cholesterol: 13 g　　Sodium: 8 mg

There is little excuse for eating plain boiled parsnips, and fried parsnips are none too tempting, but parsnip croquettes are the ugly duckling become a swan.

—Marjorie Kinnan Rawlings
   Cross Creek Cookery, 1942

These toddlers once despised parsnips. But now that they've discovered parsnip croquettes, they actually fight over them.

ROASTED ROOT VEGETABLES

6 or more servings

Root vegetables are truly seasonal in late fall and winter, when they're fresh and abundant. To my mind, these hardy vegetables are under-used and somewhat misunderstood. Oven-roasting brings out the natural sweetness of any vegetable, and this is particularly true in the case of roots.

1 large sweet potato, peeled, cut in half lengthwise, and sliced

2 medium parsnips, peeled and sliced

1 large turnip, peeled, cut in half, and sliced

2 medium carrots, peeled and sliced

½ medium rutabaga, peeled and sliced

2 tablespoons canola oil

2 tablespoons light brown sugar or Sucanat

½ teaspoon salt

Pinch each: cinnamon and nutmeg

Preheat the oven to 400 degrees.

Prepare all the vegetables as directed, making sure to slice everything fairly evenly, about ¼ inch thick. Place in a large mixing bowl.

In a small bowl, combine the oil, brown sugar, and seasonings. Stir together, pour over the vegetables, and toss together.

Transfer the mixture to a lightly oiled large roasting pan (line it with foil first if you'd like). Bake for 20 to 25 minutes, stirring every 5 minutes or so. The vegetables should be tender on the inside and touched with golden brown on the outside. Serve warm.

Calories: 123   Total fat: 4 g   Protein: 1 g
Carbohydrates: 20 g   Cholesterol: 0 g   Sodium: 210 mg

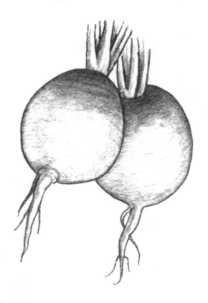

AMISH POTATOES WITH LIMA BEANS

6 servings

When it comes to vegetable dishes such as this one, the Amish dictum of "plain and simple" is well-taken.

6 large potatoes
2 tablespoons canola oil
1 large onion, chopped
1 10-ounce package frozen baby
  lima beans, thawed
Salt and freshly ground black
  pepper
Minced fresh parsley
Paprika

Nineteenth-century American folk-belief held potatoes in high esteem as cures for various ailments. Here are two examples:

• A potato, carried in the pocket, will cure or prevent rheumatism.
• A sore throat may be cured by wearing about the neck a stocking, in the toe of which a potato has been tied.

Bake or microwave the potatoes in their skins until tender but still firm. When cool enough to handle, peel them and cut into large dice.

Heat the oil in an extra-wide skillet or stir-fry pan. Add the onion and sauté over medium heat until golden. Add the potatoes and continue to sauté over medium heat for 10 minutes, stirring every 2 to 3 minutes.

Stir in the lima beans and continue to sauté for another 5 minutes or so, or until the potatoes are golden on most sides and the lima beans are tender. Season to taste with salt and pepper, then transfer to a serving container. Sprinkle the top with a little parsley and paprika and serve.

Calories: 238   Total fat: 4 g   Protein: 5 g
Carbohydrates: 44 g   Cholesterol: 0 g   Sodium: 23 mg

POTATO-BREAD STUFFING

6 servings

J. George Frederick, who in the 1930s wrote his recollections of growing up on a Pennsylvania Dutch farm, noted that "the Dutch are a potato-loving people, and why not, when they can cook them so well." It is perhaps in this tradition that the white potato gets more play than in any other regional style. This hearty stuffing recalls Thanksgivings of days gone by. You need not stuff it into anything, but simply enjoy it as a side dish.

5 or 6 medium potatoes, cooked
    or microwaved in their skins
1 cup low-fat milk or soymilk
4 average slices whole-grain
    bread
1½ tablespoons canola oil
1 cup chopped onion
1 cup chopped celery
¼ cup finely chopped fresh
    parsley
2 teaspoons Mrs. Dash or other
    salt-free herb-and-spice
    seasoning mix
Salt and freshly ground black
    pepper

Preheat the oven to 350 degrees.

Once the cooked potatoes are cool enough to handle, peel them and place them in a large mixing bowl. Coarsely mash the potatoes with ½ cup of the milk.

Cut the bread into ½-inch dice. Place them in a small mixing bowl and pour the remaining milk over them. Soak for several minutes.

In the meantime, heat the oil in a medium-sized skillet. Add the onion and celery and sauté over low heat until the onion is lightly browned and the celery is tender.

Combine the onion and celery mixture with the mashed potatoes in the large mixing bowl. Stir in the soaked bread, parsley, and seasoning mix. Season to taste with salt and lots of pepper. Pour the mixture into a well-oiled, 2-quart baking dish. Bake for 50 to 60 minutes, or until the top is a crusty golden brown.

Calories: 208   Total fat: 4 g   Protein: 5 g
Carbohydrates: 37 g   Cholesterol: 2 g   Sodium: 113 mg

ROASTED GARLIC MASHED POTATOES

6 servings

Mashed potatoes laced with smoky-flavored roasted garlic is a contemporary classic.

1 whole head garlic
6 large potatoes, peeled and
    diced
2 tablespoons whipped butter or
    natural canola margarine
¼ to ½ cup low-fat milk or
    soymilk
Salt and freshly ground black
    pepper
Thinly sliced scallion or minced
    chives for garnish

Mashed potatoes should be dipped out lightly into a hot covered dish and literally coaxed into a delicate mealy heap, instead of being stirred and patted and packed and cheesed into a shapely mass.

—The Buckeye Cookbook, 1883

Remove some of the papery outer layers from the garlic but keep the cloves intact. Place on a baking sheet and bake in a 350-degree oven or 375-degree toaster oven for 40 to 45 minutes, or until the cloves are soft.

When cool enough to handle, gently separate the cloves from the head of garlic and squeeze the soft pulp out of each clove into a small bowl and discard the outer skin.

In the meantime, cover the diced potatoes with plenty of water in a large saucepan and bring to a simmer. Simmer steadily but gently, covered, until the potatoes are very tender, about 20 to 25 minutes, then drain.

In a large, shallow bowl, combine the potatoes with the butter and stir until melted. Add ¼ cup of milk and the reserved garlic pulp and mash the potatoes until smooth and fluffy. If needed, add up to an additional ¼ cup of milk to loosen the consistency.

Season to taste with salt and pepper, then transfer to a serving container. Sprinkle some scallion over the top and serve at once, or keep warm until needed.

Calories: 154   Total fat: 3 g   Protein: 2 g
Carbohydrates: 29 g   Cholesterol: 9 g   Sodium: 15 mg

PARSLEY POTATO CROQUETTES

Makes about 20 croquettes

There's nothing especially "regional" about this recipe, but it's one that I noticed in several general nineteenth-century American cookbooks. These log-shape croquettes are visually appealing and make for an elegant side dish.

4 cups well-mashed potatoes
¼ cup low-fat milk or soymilk
3 tablespoons unbleached white
    flour
Salt and freshly ground black
    pepper
Pinch of nutmeg
⅓ cup minced fresh parsley
1 egg, well beaten
Fine dry bread crumbs
Canola oil for frying

In a mixing bowl, combine the mashed potatoes with the milk, flour, salt and pepper to taste, nutmeg, and parsley. Cover and refrigerate for an hour or two.

When ready to cook, shape the mashed potato mixture into oblong "logs," about 3 inches long.

Dip each croquette in the beaten egg, then roll it in the bread crumbs. Heat just enough oil to coat the bottom of a nonstick skillet or griddle. Cook the croquettes over medium-high heat, turning them on all sides until the outsides are browned and crisp. This has to be done patiently so that they keep their shape—using a pair of tongs is helpful. Replenish the oil as needed and drain the croquettes on paper towels. Arrange on a platter to serve.

Calories: 44
Carbohydrates: 9 g
Total fat: 0 g
Cholesterol: 11 g
Protein: 1 g
Sodium: 7 mg

POTATOES WITH COLLARD GREENS

4 to 6 servings

Most members of the family of greens are good sources of calcium and have a significant amount of protein. Greens have long been one of the pillars of Southern cookery and a prominent item in the soul food repertoire. Traveling around the South, I learned that greens are well liked and served often, but that it is almost unthinkable to cook them without the characteristic piece of salt pork or bacon. The owner of a diner in South Carolina and his two cooks had a good laugh when I asked them how a vegetarian could prepare greens without using the meat. Undaunted, I was determined to find a recipe for these nutritious vegetables that would be both meatless and tasty.

1 large bunch collard greens
   (about 1 pound)
3 medium potatoes, peeled and
   cut into ¼-inch dice
1 medium onion, finely chopped
1 tablespoon canola oil
½ cup water
½ pound fresh spinach, washed,
   stemmed, and chopped
2 tablespoons apple cider vinegar
Salt and freshly ground black
   pepper
A few grains cayenne pepper

Wash the collard greens well, and trim away the thick midribs. Chop the leaves coarsely and thinly slice the mid-ribs. Combine them with the potatoes, onion, oil, and water in a large soup pot. Cover and cook over medium heat, stirring occasionally, until the potatoes and greens are tender, about 20 to 30 minutes. Make sure that there is always just enough water to keep everything moist, but not soupy.

Add the spinach, then cover and steam until it is wilted. Stir in the vinegar, then season to taste with salt, pepper, and cayenne. Serve at once.

Calories: 133   Total fat: 3 g   Protein: 3 g
Carbohydrates: 23 g   Cholesterol: 0 g   Sodium: 66 mg

Only remember that, if a bushel of potatoes is shaken in a market-cart without springs to it, the small potatoes always get to the bottom.

—Oliver Wendell Holmes
   The Autocrat of the Breakfast Table, 1858

POTATOES WITH GREEN CHILE

4 to 6 servings

This tasty recipe is a fairly common one from the Southwest, and needs a minimal amount of attention as it cooks.

2 tablespoons olive oil
1 large onion, chopped
1 to 2 cloves garlic, minced
4 large or 5 to 6 medium
    potatoes, scrubbed
    and thinly sliced
½ cup water or vegetable stock
1 to 2 small fresh hot green
    chiles, seeded and minced,
    or 1 4-ounce can chopped
    mild chiles
½ teaspoon ground cumin
Salt to taste

Heat the olive oil in a large skillet. Add the onion and sauté over medium-low heat until it just begins to turn golden. Add the garlic and sauté for another minute, then add the potatoes and water. Cover and simmer until the potatoes are about half done, about 10 minutes.

Add the remaining ingredients, plus additional water or stock if necessary to keep the mixture moist. Simmer, covered, another 5 to 8 minutes, or until the potatoes are tender but still retain their shape.

Calories: 202	Total fat: 6 g	Protein: 2 g
Carbohydrates: 36 g	Cholesterol: 0 g	Sodium: 10 mg

SWEET POTATO PONE

6 servings

Sweet potatoes have long been a valued crop in the South, where their yield is plentiful even when grown in poor soil. The nutritious sweet potato has come to be best known for its use in such recipes as Candied Yams (see recipe that follows) and Southern Sweet Potato Pie (page 235), but in times past the preferred way of preparing them was simply to roast them in the ashes of the fire place and eat them piping hot. Sweet Potato Pone is an old deep South recipe. Pone comes from a Native American dialect, and means "a small oven loaf."

3 cups firmly packed finely grated
   raw, peeled sweet potato
½ cup fresh orange juice
1 teaspoon grated orange rind
2 to 3 tablespoons molasses,
   to taste
2 eggs, beaten
2 tablespoons whipped butter or
   natural canola margarine,
   melted
¼ teaspoon ground ginger
½ teaspoon salt
Cinnamon for topping

Preheat the oven to 350 degrees.

If you are using a food processor to grate the sweet potatoes, use a fine grating attachment, or else run the potato through twice; otherwise the grated potato will be too coarse and will take a long time to bake. Combine all the ingredients in a large mixing bowl and stir together until well mixed. Pour into an oiled, 1 ½-quart baking casserole.

Bake for 20 minutes, covered, then for another 35 to 40 minutes, uncovered, or until the outside begins to turn brown and crusty. Let it stand for 10 minutes before serving, then cut into squares.

Calories: 171	Total fat: 5 g	Protein: 3 g
Carbohydrates: 28 g	Cholesterol: 79 g	Sodium: 210 mg

CANDIED YAMS

8 or more servings

Here's a lightened version of the American holiday classic.

½ cup orange juice, preferably freshly-squeezed

½ cup light brown sugar or Sucanat

¼ teaspoon cinnamon

Pinch of nutmeg

2 tablespoons whipped butter or natural canola margarine, melted

3 pounds sweet potatoes, peeled and sliced ¼ inch thick

¼ cup finely chopped walnuts or pecans for topping, optional

Preheat the oven to 375 degrees.

Combine all the ingredients except the last two in a large mixing bowl. Stir until well combined. Add the sliced potatoes and stir well, then transfer to a shallow 1½-quart round or 9- by 13-inch baking dish.

Bake, covered, until the sweet potatoes are just tender, about 40 minutes. Stir once or twice during that time to distribute the liquid over the potatoes. If desired, sprinkle the nuts over the sweet potatoes at this time. Bake, uncovered, for an additional 10 to 15 minutes, or until the glaze thickens. Cover and keep warm until ready to serve.

Calories: 259	Total fat: 2 g	Protein: 2 g
Carbohydrates: 57 g	Cholesterol: 6 g	Sodium: 18 mg

A nineteenth-century traveler in Mississippi recorded that he "... had a [sweet] potato pie for dessert and roasted potatoes were offered to him as a side dish, drank sweet potato coffee and sweet potato home brew, had his horse fed on sweet potatoes and sweet potato vines, and when he retired he slept on a mattress stuffed with sweet potato vines and dreamed that he was a sweet potato that someone was digging up."

—Frank Owsley
Plain Folk of the Old South, 1944

BAKED SWEET POTATOES AND APPLES

4 to 6 servings

Though sweet potatoes have never been as favored in the North as in the South, this simple dish hails from old New England. A cheering winter recipe, and a great side dish for Thanksgiving, it is characteristically sweetened with maple syrup.

4 large sweet potatoes

2 tablespoons whipped butter
  or natural canola margarine,
  melted

½ cup maple syrup

2 large apples, peeled, cored,
  and thinly sliced

Cinnamon

Ground cloves

½ cup apple juice

Preheat the oven to 350 degrees.

Bake or microwave the sweet potatoes until done but still firm. When cool enough to handle, cut them into ½-inch-thick slices.

Oil a deep, 1½-quart baking casserole. Arrange half of the sweet potato slices on the bottom. Drizzle with half of the butter, then half of the maple syrup. Top with the apple slices. Sprinkle lightly with the cinnamon and cloves. Repeat the layers, then pour the apple juice over the top. Bake for 30 minutes, covered, then for another 10 minutes, uncovered. Serve at once or cover and keep warm until needed.

Calories: 299	Total fat: 3 g	Protein: 1 g
Carbohydrates: 65 g	Cholesterol: 10 g	Sodium: 14 mg

QUELITES (Greens with Pinto Beans)

4 to 6 servings

Originally, the Pueblo Indians of the Southwest made this dish with wild greens. More contemporary recipes call for spinach or chard instead. The dark greens look very appealing with the pink beans, and the more garlicky you make it, the better.

1 pound spinach or Swiss chard
1½ tablespoons olive oil
2 or 3 cloves garlic, minced
3 scallions, white and green
    parts, finely chopped
1 to 1½ cups cooked or canned
    pinto beans
1 teaspoon chili powder
Salt and freshly ground black
    pepper

Stem and wash the greens and coarsely chop the leaves. If you're using chard, trim away the thicker midribs from the leaves and thinly slice them. Steam with a very small amount of water in a large, tightly covered soup pot until wilted. The spinach will be done as soon as it wilts, but the chard needs to steam a bit longer. It will be done when it turns a deep green. Drain the greens and finely chop them.

Heat the oil in a large skillet. Add the garlic and sauté over low heat until it just begins to turn golden. Add the scallions and sauté just until they soften a bit. Stir in the greens, beans, and seasonings. Cook, covered, over low heat for 5 minutes, or just until everything is heated through.

Calories: 103   Total fat: 4 g   Protein: 4 g
Carbohydrates: 12 g   Cholesterol: 0 g   Sodium: 72 mg

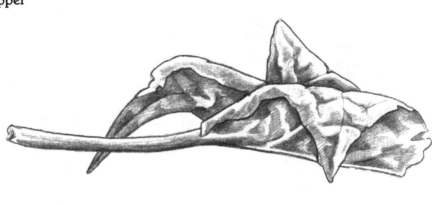

STEAMED GREENS WITH TOMATOES

6 servings

Using bags of pre-cut and washed greens is a tremendous time-saver. I recommend giving those a quick rinse, though, just to make absolutely sure there's no remaining grit in the leaves. I think that steaming the greens in vegetable broth rather than plain water gives them a nice flavor boost.

1 medium bunch kale or collard
   greens (10 to 12 ounces)
1 teaspoon canola oil
1 clove garlic, cut in half
½ to ¾ cup homemade or canned
   vegetable stock
2 large or 3 medium ripe
   tomatoes, diced
Juice of ½ lemon or lime
Salt and freshly ground black
   pepper

Wash the greens well and cut the leaves away from the thick mid-ribs. Chop the leaves coarsely and slice the mid-ribs thinly on the diagonal.

Heat the oil in an extra-wide skillet or stir-fry pan. Add the garlic and sauté for a minute or 2 over low heat. Add the greens and ½ cup of the stock. Cover and steam until the greens are tender but not overdone, stirring occasionally, about 20 to 25 minutes. If the mixture gets dry, add small amounts of additional stock, as needed.

Stir in the tomatoes and lemon juice. Cook, uncovered, until the tomatoes have softened a bit, about 4 to 5 minutes. Season to taste with salt and pepper and serve at once.

Calories: 45   Total fat: 0 g   Protein: 2 g
Carbohydrates: 7 g   Cholesterol: 0 g   Sodium: 28 mg

PECAN-STUFFED SQUASH

Serves 4 as a main dish or 8 as a side dish

Squash and pecans, two favorite Southern staples, make for a memorable dish when combined in this Louisiana recipe. The savory nut, bread, and rice stuffing, contrasted with the smooth sweetness of the butternut squash, is a sure cure for the winter vegetable doldrums.

2 medium butternut squashes
   (about 2 pounds each)
1 tablespoon canola oil
1 large onion, finely chopped
1½ cups soft whole grain bread
   crumbs
1 cup cooked brown rice
⅓ cup finely chopped pecans
⅓ cup fresh orange juice, or as
   needed
2 teaspoons honey
¼ teaspoon each: dried thyme,
   dried summer savory
Salt and freshly ground black
   pepper
Pinch of nutmeg

Preheat the oven to 375 degrees.

Cut each squash in half lengthwise and remove the seeds and fibers. Cover with aluminum foil and place the halves, cut side up, in foil-lined shallow baking dishes. Bake for 40 to 50 minutes, depending on the size of the squashes, or until the pulp can be easily pierced with a knife but is not overly soft.

In the meantime, heat the oil in a small skillet. Add the onion and sauté until golden brown. Combine the sautéed onion in a mixing bowl with the bread crumbs, cooked rice, and pecans.

When the squash is done and cool enough to handle, scoop out the pulp, leaving a sturdy, ½-inch shell all around. Add the pulp to the pecan mixture along with the remaining butter, stirring it in to melt. Add the orange juice, more or less as needed to moisten the mixture, the honey, and dried herbs. Season to taste with salt, pepper, and nutmeg, mix thoroughly, and divide the stuffing evenly among the squash shells. Bake for 20 minutes.

Serve each squash half as a hearty main dish; or cut each half across to serve 8 as a side dish.

Per main-dish serving:

Calories: 428	Total fat: 10 g	Protein: 8 g
Carbohydrates: 75 g	Cholesterol: 0 g	Sodium: 144 mg

STUFFED SQUASH WITH MASHED POTATOES, CARROTS, AND PEAS

4 servings

This makes a great alternative main dish for Thanksgiving, but it's a welcome treat at any time during fall harvest season. Double the recipe to feed a bigger crowd.

2 medium butternut or carnival squashes (about 1½ to 2 pounds each)

6 medium potatoes, peeled and diced

1 tablespoon canola oil

1 large onion, chopped

1 large carrot, cut into thick 2-inch-long matchsticks

¼ cup low-fat milk or soymilk

1 cup frozen petite green peas, thawed

½ teaspoon ground ginger

Pinch of nutmeg

Salt and freshly ground black pepper

Preheat the oven to 400 degrees.

Cut the squash in half lengthwise and remove the seeds and fibers. Cover with aluminum foil and place the halves, cut side up, in a foil-lined shallow baking pan. Bake for 40 to 50 minutes, or until easily pierced with a knife but still firm. When cool enough to handle, scoop out the pulp, leaving a firm ¼- to ½-inch-thick shell all around. Mash the pulp and set aside until needed.

In the meantime, combine the potatoes with enough water to cover in a large saucepan. Bring to a simmer, then simmer steadily, covered, until the potatoes are tender, about 10 to 15 minutes.

Heat the oil in a medium skillet. Add the onion and carrot and sauté over medium heat until the onion is golden and the carrot is tender-crisp. Remove from the heat.

When the potatoes are done, drain them and transfer to a mixing bowl. Add the milk and mash until smooth. Stir in the onion-carrot mixture, followed by the peas, ginger, and nutmeg. Add the reserved squash pulp, and stir gently until the mashed potato and squash are well integrated. Season to taste with salt and pepper.

Divide the mixture evenly among the four squash shells. Bake for 15 minutes, until well heated through, then serve.

Calories: 448   Total fat: 3 g   Protein: 8 g
Carbohydrates: 95 g   Cholesterol: 1 g   Sodium: 44 mg

BUTTERNUT SQUASH SOUFFLÉ

6 servings

Most of the squashes we know today were developed by ancient South Americans and were already long in use by the Native Americans by the time the white settlers arrived. This abundant crop came to be especially favored in the South. This soufflé, naturally sweet with the flavor of butternut squash, is a simple but elegant way to use this hardy vegetable.

1 medium butternut squash
   (about 2 pounds)
4 eggs, separated and at room
   temperature
½ cup low-fat milk or soymilk
½ teaspoon salt
¼ teaspoon cinnamon
⅛ teaspoon nutmeg or allspice
2 tablespoons whipped butter or
   natural canola margarine,
   melted

Preheat the oven to 375 degrees.

Cut the squash in half lengthwise and remove the seeds and fibers. Cover with aluminum foil and place the halves, cut side up, in a foil-lined shallow baking pan. Bake for 45 to 55 minutes, or until quite tender when tested with a knife. Remove the squash and reduce the oven temperature to 325 degrees.

When the squash is cool enough to handle, scoop out all the pulp and place it in a food processor fitted with the steel blade, along with the egg yolks and milk. Process until smoothly pureed, then transfer to a mixing bowl and stir in the salt, spices, and half of the melted butter.

In another bowl, beat the egg whites until they form stiff peaks. Gently fold them into the squash puree, then pour the mixture into an oiled 1½-quart baking dish or soufflé pan. Drizzle the remaining melted butter over the top. Bake for 30 to 40 minutes, or until puffed and lightly browned. Serve at once.

Calories: 107   Total fat: 3 g   Protein: 4 g
Carbohydrates: 15 g   Cholesterol: 9 g   Sodium: 227 mg

"THREE SISTERS" STEW

6 servings

In Native American mythology, squash, corn, and beans are known as the "three sisters." They are also, in some legends, the daughters of the Earth Mother.

1 small sugar pumpkin or 1 large butternut or carnival squash (about 2 pounds)
1 tablespoon olive oil
1 medium onion, chopped
2 cloves garlic, minced
½ medium green or red bell pepper, cut into short, narrow strips
1 14- to 16-ounce can diced tomatoes,
2 cups cooked pinto beans (about ¾ cup raw), or 1 1-pound can, drained and rinsed
2 cups corn kernels (from 2 large or 3 medium ears)
1 cup homemade or canned vegetable stock, or water
1 or 2 small fresh hot chiles, seeded and minced,
  or 1 4-ounce can chopped mild green chiles
1 teaspoon each: ground cumin, dried oregano
Salt and freshly ground black pepper
¼ cup minced fresh cilantro

Preheat the oven to 400 degrees.

Cut the pumpkin in half lengthwise and remove the seeds and fibers. Cover with aluminum foil and place the halves, cut side up, in a foil-lined shallow baking pan. Bake for 40 to 50 minutes, or until easily pierced with a knife but still firm (if using squash, prepare the same way). When cool enough to handle, scoop out the pulp, and cut into large dice. Set aside until needed.

Heat the oil in a soup pot. Add the onion and sauté over medium-low heat until translucent. Add the garlic and continue to sauté until the onion is golden.

Add the pumpkin and all the remaining ingredients except the last 2 and bring to a simmer. Simmer gently, covered, until all the vegetables are tender, about 20 to 25 minutes. Season to taste with salt and pepper.

If time allows, let the stew stand for 1 to 2 hours before serving, then heat through as needed. Just before serving, stir in the cilantro. The stew should be thick and very moist but not soupy; add additional stock or water if needed. Serve in shallow bowls.

Calories: 236   Total fat: 2 g   Protein: 8 g
Carbohydrates: 45 g   Cholesterol: 0 g   Sodium: 66 mg

CALAVACITAS (Summer Squash with Corn and Green Chiles)

4 to 6 servings

This is a traditional summer dish from the Southwest. The combination of fresh squash and corn, flavored with garlic and chiles, is simply delicious.

2 tablespoons olive oil
1 medium onion, finely chopped
2 cloves garlic, minced
1½ pounds yellow summer
   squash, quartered lengthwise
   and sliced
1 or 2 small fresh hot green
   chiles, seeded and minced,
   or 1 4-ounce can chopped
   mild green chiles
1½ cups cooked fresh corn
   kernels (from 2 medium ears)
1 medium ripe tomato, diced
2 tablespoons chopped fresh
   cilantro
Salt and freshly ground black
   pepper

Heat the oil in a large skillet. Add the onion and sauté over medium-low heat until translucent. Add the garlic and continue to sauté until the onion is golden. Add the squash and chiles and sauté, stirring frequently, until the squash is tender-crisp, about 5 to 8 minutes. Stir in the cooked corn kernels, tomato, and cilantro. Season to taste with salt and pepper. Sauté for another minute or two, then serve.

Calories: 135	Total fat: 6 g	Protein: 2 g
Carbohydrates: 18 g	Cholesterol: 0 g	Sodium: 6 mg

STUFFED MIRLITON

4 servings

The mirliton is a small green pear-shaped squash that's known by various names, depending on geography. In the Southwest it is called chayote, while in other areas you might run across it as a "vegetable pear." In Creole cookery, this pretty squash is well known as mirliton. This slightly modified version of a classic recipe (it usually contains seafood) was contributed by Amina DaDa (who, when I met her in the mid-1980s, was the owner and chef of I & I Creole Vegetarian restaurant in New Orleans).

4 medium mirliton squashes
1 tablespoon canola oil
1 large onion, finely chopped
2 cloves garlic, minced
½ medium green bell pepper,
**   finely diced**
1 small bay leaf
2 tablespoons minced parsley
1 teaspoon dried basil
¼ teaspoon dried thyme
1 cup fresh whole-grain bread
**   crumbs**
Salt and freshly ground black
**   pepper**

Bring water to a rolling boil in a large soup pot. Drop the mirlitons in whole, then cover and simmer until they are easily pierced with a knife. This will take from 35 to 50 minutes, depending on their size. Once they are done, remove them from the water and set aside.

Preheat the oven to 350 degrees.

Heat the oil in a medium-sized skillet. Add the onion and sauté over medium-low heat until translucent. Add the garlic and bell pepper and continue to sauté until the onion is golden. Stir in the bay leaf and herbs, then remove from the heat and cover.

Cut each mirliton in half lengthwise and remove the seeds. Scoop out the pulp, leaving a ¼-inch-thick shell all around. Finely chop the pulp and add it to the mixture in the skillet. Return to low heat, stir in half the bread crumbs, and season to taste with salt and pepper. Sauté the mixture just until the squash cooks down a bit so that it's not too watery. Remove the bay leaf.

Arrange the squash shells in a shallow baking pan and divide the stuffing equally among them. Sprinkle the tops with the remaining bread crumbs. Bake for 25 to 20 minutes, or until the crumbs turn golden, then serve.

| Calories: 115 | Total fat: 3 g | Protein: 4 g |
| Carbohydrates: 15 g | Cholesterol: 0 g | Sodium: 66 mg |

SIMPLE CYMLING RECIPES

The cymling, often called pattypan squash, is, I believe, one of the most underused treasures of the American harvest, though its use has been documented since the early 1700s. It bears closest resemblance to the zucchini in that it is quick-cooking and has a similar texture, and yet its flavor is at the same time more delicate and yet tastier.

The first time I asked my husband to buy these squashes for me at a local farmers market, I described them as pale-green "flying saucers" with scalloped edges. He had no trouble finding them. Making fussy recipes with the cymling would overshadow its subtle flavor, so I am presenting three very simple preparations. There's no need to peel them, but scrub well.

I'll break that empty cymlin' of a head of yourn.

—Charles E. Craddock
(a.k.a. Mary N. Murfree)
In the Tennessee Mountains, 1884

CYMLING FRITTERS

4 servings as a side dish

Cut 2 cymlings into ½-inch dice. Steam them until tender, about 10 minutes. Mash them well in a mixing bowl and stir in a well-beaten egg and 3 tablespoons of milk. Season to taste with salt and pepper. Drop by heaping tablespoonsful onto a very lightly oiled nonstick skillet or griddle. Cook on both sides over medium heat until golden brown.

Calories: 46	Total fat: 2 g	Protein: 3 g
Carbohydrates: 4 g	Cholesterol: 54 g	Sodium: 25 mg

BREADED CYMLING

4 servings as a side dish

Cut 2 cymlings into ¼-inch-thick slices. Dip the slices first into 1 well-beaten egg, then dredge in fine dry bread crumbs lightly seasoned with salt and pepper. Cook on a very lightly oiled nonstick skillet over medium heat until golden brown on both sides.

Calories: 90	Total fat: 3 g	Protein: 4 g
Carbohydrates: 13 g	Cholesterol: 54 g	Sodium: 111 mg

SAUTÉED CYMLING

4 servings as a side dish

This may seem too simple to even be considered a recipe, but it is perhaps the best way of all to appreciate the delicate flavor of cymling. Use 2 cymlings, as desired. Cut into ¼-inch-thick strips. Simply sauté them in a nonstick skillet that has been very lightly coated with whipped butter or natural canola margarine, stirring frequently over medium heat, until the squash begins to brown lightly. Season to taste with salt and pepper.

Calories: 21	Total fat: 1 g	Protein: 1 g
Carbohydrates: 4 g	Cholesterol: 0 g	Sodium: 2 mg

EJOTES (Piquant Green Beans)

4 to 6 servings

This nippy preparation of string beans is adapted from the fascinating book on early Mission cooking of the Southwest, Early California Hospitality *(1938). Use the most tender fresh green beans for best results.*

2 tablespoons olive oil
1 medium onion, finely chopped
2 cloves garlic, minced
1½ pounds green beans, trimmed and snapped or cut in half
3 medium ripe juicy tomatoes, chopped
1 or 2 jalapeño peppers, seeded and minced
¼ cup water
1 tablespoon apple cider vinegar
Salt and freshly ground black pepper

Heat the oil in a large skillet or saucepan. Add the onion and sauté over medium-low heat until translucent. Add the garlic and green beans and sauté, stirring frequently, for 5 minutes. Add the remaining ingredients and simmer, covered, until the green beans are tender. This will take approximately 10 to 20 minutes, depending on their size and thickness. Serve at once.

Calories: 116
Carbohydrates: 14 g
Total fat: 6 g
Cholesterol: 0 g
Protein: 3 g
Sodium: 52 mg

SIMPLE GREEN BEAN RECIPES

Green beans, also known as string beans or snap beans, have been a favorite Southern garden vegetable for a very long time. The traditional way to cook them is in a big pot with a piece of salt pork—for hours. Although this method is still being used regularly both by home and restaurant cooks, some contemporary cooks are devising lighter ways to prepare this ever-popular vegetable.

Here are two ideas gleaned while traveling in the South. Of utmost importance is the quality of the green beans. Use them early in their season, since no amount of effort will salvage the tough variety that seem to be on the market for the better part of the year.

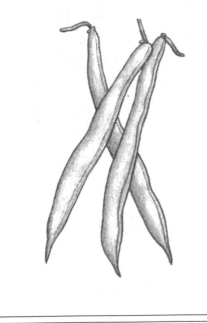

LEMON-GARLIC GREEN BEANS

4 to 6 servings as a side dish

Trim 1 pound of green beans and cut or snap them in half. Steam them until tender- crisp. In a large skillet, heat 1 tablespoon of canola or olive oil and sauté 1 or 2 cloves of minced garlic over low heat until golden. Add the steamed string beans and sauté, stirring continuously, for just a minute or so. Remove from the heat, squeeze on as much fresh lemon juice as you'd like and add a few grindings of black pepper.

Calories: 54	Total fat: 3 g	Protein: 1 g
Carbohydrates: 6 g	Cholesterol: 0 g	Sodium: 5 mg

TOMATO-BASIL GREEN BEANS

4 to 6 servings as a side dish

This preparation may seem rather Italian, but tomatoes and basil are a Creole combination as well. Trim 1 pound of green beans and cut or snap them in half. Steam them until tender-crisp. Heat 1 tablespoon of canola or olive oil in a large skillet. Add 2 large very ripe chopped tomatoes and sauté them for a minute or so over low heat. Add chopped fresh basil to taste, and cook until the tomatoes are soft. Add the string beans, a pinch of salt, and a few grindings of black pepper. Simmer over low heat for another 2 minutes.

Calories: 62	Total fat: 3 g	Protein: 2 g
Carbohydrates: 8 g	Cholesterol: 0 g	Sodium: 9 mg

SIMPLE TURNIP RECIPES

Turnips were a major Southern crop for many decades and were as much valued for their nutritious green tops as for the root, if not more so. Turnips still show up on many a Southern menu, often cooked with their greens plus the ubiquitous piece of salt pork. I think turnips are an underused winter vegetable, lending themselves better to simple preparations rather than to more elaborate ones. Here are three very basic ideas adapted from the Southern tradition.

MASHED TURNIPS

4 servings as a side dish

Pare and dice 4 to 6 medium turnips and steam them until tender. Mash them well. Heat a nonstick skillet and lightly coat with whipped butter or natural canola margarine. Cook the mashed turnips over medium heat until their liquid evaporates, stirring frequently (mashed turnips tend to be a bit watery otherwise, unlike mashed potatoes). Season to taste with salt and pepper. This is also delicious topped with rings of well-sautéed onion.

Calories: 28   Total fat: 1 g   Protein: 1 g
Carbohydrates: 7 g   Cholesterol: 0 g   Sodium: 78 mg

FRIED TURNIPS

4 servings as a side dish

Pare 4 to 6 medium turnips and slice them into 1/4-inch-thick rounds. Heat a nonstick skillet and lightly coat with whipped butter or natural canola margarine. Sauté on both sides over medium heat until golden brown. This preparation gives the turnips a pleasant, slightly sweet flavor.

Calories: 28   Total fat: 1 g   Protein: 1 g
Carbohydrates: 7 g   Cholesterol: 0 g   Sodium: 78 mg

TURNIPS WITH GREENS

4 servings as a side dish

Use 4 to 6 medium turnips. Trim away and discard the stems and thick mid-ribs from the turnip greens. Wash the greens well and coarsely chop them. Steam in a covered saucepan until tender, about 10 minutes, then drain and finely chop them.

Pare the turnips and cut them into 1/2-inch dice. Heat a nonstick skillet and lightly coat with whipped butter or natural canola margarine. Sauté the turnip dice, stirring frequently, until they are golden brown on all sides. Stir in the greens and add about 1 teaspoon of cider vinegar per turnip used. Season to taste with salt and pepper.

Calories: 58   Total fat: 1 g   Protein: 2 g
Carbohydrates: 12 g   Cholesterol: 0 g   Sodium: 120 mg

"BEEFY" VEGETABLE STEW

6 to 8 servings

In this delicious vegetarian version of a classic heartland dish, I call for seitan, a product made of high-protein wheat gluten. It's available ready made in natural foods stores, or make it yourself with Arrowhead Mills' Seitan Quick Mix.

2 tablespoons canola or olive oil, divided
1 cup chopped onion
2 cloves garlic, minced
3 large potatoes, peeled and diced
3 large carrots, peeled and sliced
2 cups water
1 vegetable bouillon cube
1 teaspoon Mrs. Dash or other salt-free herb-and-spice seasoning mix
1 to 1½ cups trimmed fresh or thawed frozen green beans, cut into 1-inch lengths
1½ pounds fresh seitan, cut into bite-sized pieces
Salt and freshly ground pepper to taste

Heat half of the oil in a large soup pot. Add the onion and garlic and sauté over medium-low heat until the onion is golden. Add the potatoes, carrots, water, bouillon cube, and seasoning mix. Bring to a simmer, then simmer gently, covered, for 10 minutes.

Add the green beans and continue to simmer for about 15 to 20 minutes more, or until the vegetables are tender. If the potato has not begun to break up on its own, use the back of a wooden spoon to mash enough of the potatoes to thicken the base of the stew.

In the meantime, heat the remaining oil in a wide skillet. Add the seitan pieces and sauté over medium-high heat, stirring frequently, until most sides are nicely browned and crisp. Add the sautéed seitan to the stew. Add a bit more water if necessary. The consistency should be thick and moist, but not soupy. Season to taste with salt and pepper (use salt sparingly, if at all, since the bouillon cube and seitan add a salty flavor). Serve in shallow bowls.

Calories: 268	Total fat: 4 g	Protein: 34 g
Carbohydrates: 00 g	Cholesterol: 0 g	Sodium: 15 mg

Chapter 9
SOUTHWESTERN TORTILLA SPECIALTIES

Tortillas were made by the Aztecs, long before Hernando
Cortes looked down on the walls of Tenochtitlan...The
whole corn is first soaked in lime water and then boiled.
The wet grains are crushed laboriously by pounding
them with a stone on a *métate*—a rock mortar. The mash
is then baked.

—Green Peyton
  San Antonio: City in the Sun, 1946

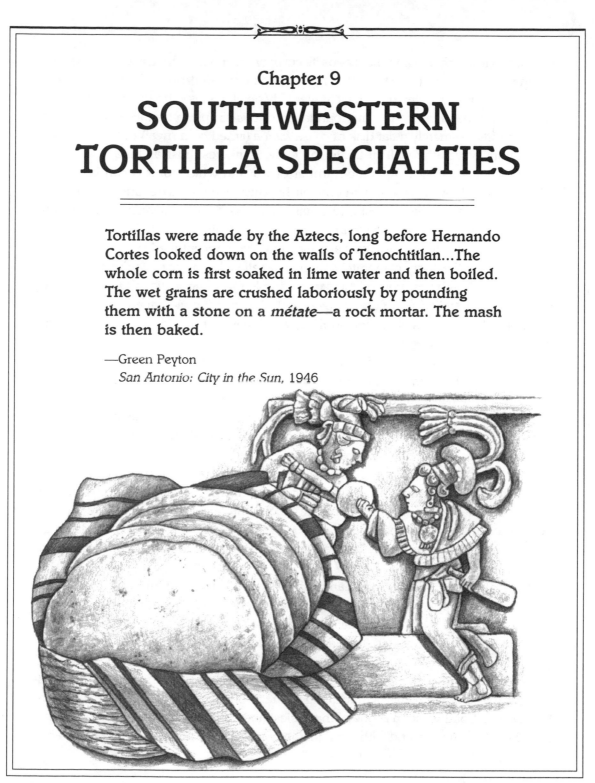

It's hard to imagine a region that keeps its culinary traditions more alive than does the Southwest. Even more fortunately, the restaurant cooking seems closer to home cooking than in any other area I have visited. My opinion was echoed by several chefs and home cooks I spoke to. The foundation of this simple yet exotic cuisine is the humble tortilla—merely a flat disk of *masa harina* (limed corn meal) or wheat flour.

The tortilla was the staff of life in the early Southwest, just as bread was elsewhere. What is astonishing is the number of ways in which tortillas can be rolled, folded, stacked, and shaped, with embellishments inside, outside, and on top. The best known, and perhaps most traditional, are the *enchilada* (meaning, descriptively, "filled with chile") and the *burrito* (meaning, cryptically, "little donkey"), from which all the variations seem to have evolved. I've concentrated mainly on these, rather than on the more elaborately shaped varieties that involve deep frying. But if you visit the Southwest you might like to sample these innovations, which include *flautas* (tortillas rolled into flute shapes) and *chalupas* (bowl-shaped tortillas). You might also look for blue cornmeal tortillas, which have a nutty, distinct flavor and an unusual slate blue–gray color.

One aspect of tortilla-based recipes that I particularly enjoy is the fact that most everything can be made ahead of time and then assembled at the last minute. This is very useful when cooking for company. Most sauces, fillings, and relishes can be made in advance and stored until needed. Baking time, if any, is minimal—usually just long enough to warm the dish or melt the cheese, so there's little guesswork as to when to put the food in the oven.

Corn tortillas available in supermarkets are not as good as the ones freshly made for Southwestern restaurants. However, it seems to me that they've gotten a little better over the years—they are not quite as dry and tasteless as they were when I bemoaned their quality in the first edition of this book. Flour tortillas available in supermarkets are even better. They are now lard-free, and in fact often fat-free, and come in several sizes.

Proof of the burgeoning popularity of north-and-south-of-the-border cuisines is nowhere more apparent than in supermarkets everywhere. In the mid-1980s, when I wrote and researched the first edition of this book, fresh chiles were a rare find outside the southwestern states, as were cilantro and fresh tomatillos (in that edition, my recipe for tomatillo salsa called for canned tomatillos, which were just somewhat easier to find than fresh, which were nearly impossible). Now, these and other items intrinsic to this region's cuisine (including canned hominy and fresh jícama) are widely available. Southwestern is one of the easiest and most satisfying of cuisines for the home cook to master; and with the right ingredients, a bounty of great meals awaits.

STACKED CHEESE ENCHILADAS

4 to 6 servings

Few preparations are as basic to Southwestern cuisine as enchiladas, and as such, they have spawned countless variations and embellishments. Ana Bégué de Packman, in Early California Hospitality (1938), explains that enchiladas, along with tamales, were the traditional foods of the native Mexicans. The Spanish colonists came along and improved them with their own special seasonings, as is the case with much of the food of the region. She also claims that the true enchilada is meatless. The word enchilada literally means "filled with chile," and so it is supposed to be drenched in pure, red chile. I've modified the recipe to use the tomato-based enchilada sauce, since cooking with pure, red chiles is not something that cooks outside the Southwest are likely to attempt. This simple and hearty dish is traditionally enhanced by a helping of Frijoles Refritos (page 129) and Mexican Rice (page 147) on the side.

12 corn tortillas, as fresh as possible
1 recipe Cooked Enchilada Sauce (page 224)
½ cup finely minced raw onion
2 cups grated Monterey Jack or cheddar cheese, reduced-fat if desired
Shredded lettuce for garnish
Black olives for garnish

Preheat the oven to 350 degrees.

Allow 2 tortillas per person if you're preparing 6 servings, or 3 tortillas for each of 4 servings. Place one tortilla on each of 4 or 6 ovenproof plates. Pour a bit of sauce over it, then sprinkle with the minced onion and grated cheese. Top with another tortilla and repeat the layers, once more for a 2-tortilla enchilada and twice for a 3-tortilla enchilada. Place the plates in the oven for 10 minutes, or just until the cheese melts. Allow the plates to cool a bit, then garnish with shredded lettuce and black olives.

Calories: 378   Total fat: 16 g   Protein: 19 g
Carbohydrates: 39 g   Cholesterol: 32 g   Sodium: 483 mg

STACKED SQUASH AND BELL PEPPER ENCHILADAS

6 servings

A vegetable-filled variation of the traditional stacked enchilada.

1 tablespoon olive oil

2 tablespoons water

1 medium yellow summer squash, halved lengthwise and thinly sliced

1 medium zucchini, cut as above

1 medium green bell pepper, cut into short, narrow strips

1 medium red bell pepper, cut as above

2 to 3 tablespoons chopped fresh cilantro

12 corn tortillas

1 recipe Cooked Enchilada Sauce (page 224)

1½ cups grated Monterey Jack or cheddar cheese, reduced-fat if desired

Heat the oil and water in a large skillet. Add the squashes and bell peppers and cook, covered, until just tender, stirring occasionally, about 8 minutes. Stir in the cilantro.

Preheat the oven to 375 degrees.

Line a large baking sheet with foil and oil lightly. Arrange 6 tortillas on it in a single layer, or as many as will fit, and layer them as follows: A small amount of the sauce, a layer of the vegetables, a sprinkling of cheese, another tortilla, more sauce, and another sprinkling of cheese. Bake for 10 to 12 minutes, or until the cheese is melted and the enchiladas are hot. Transfer the enchiladas to plates and serve at once.

Calories: 315   Total fat: 13 g   Protein: 13 g
Carbohydrates: 34 g   Cholesterol: 20 g   Sodium: 336 mg

When strolling through the southwest's older cities, the sight of ristras of chiles drying in the sun is a familiar one.

GREEN CHILE ENCHILADAS

6 servings

This creamy, casserole-like preparation of enchiladas highlights the penchant for pure green chiles as both seasoning and substance in New Mexican cookery. Adding the zucchini is an unusual touch recommended by a friend from the region.

Filling:
1 tablespoon olive oil
1 small onion, chopped
1 clove garlic, minced
2 cups grated zucchini
2 4-ounce cans chopped mild green chiles
2 tablespoons minced fresh cilantro
½ teaspoon dried oregano

Sauce:
1¼ cups low-fat milk
1 tablespoon whipped butter or natural canola margarine
¼ teaspoon salt
2 tablespoons unbleached white flour

12 corn tortillas
1 heaping cup grated Monterey Jack or cheddar cheese, reduced-fat if desired
1 scallion, thinly sliced

Diced tomatoes and black olives for garnish

Preheat the oven to 400 degrees.

Heat the oil in a medium skillet. Add the onion and sauté over medium-low heat until translucent. Add the garlic and continue to sauté until the onion is golden. Stir in the remaining filling ingredients and sauté, stirring frequently, until the zucchini is tender but not overdone. Transfer the mixture from the skillet to a bowl, draining off any excess liquid.

In a small saucepan, heat the milk, butter, and salt to a gentle simmer. Dissolve the flour in just enough water to make a smooth, flowing paste. Whisk it into the saucepan in a steady stream. Allow the sauce to simmer gently until thickened, about 8 minutes, then remove from the heat.

In the meantime, reheat the skillet. Briefly heat each tortilla until softened. If the tortillas seem inflexible, sprinkle each with a few drops of water before heating. Place a small amount of the filling down the center of each tortilla, roll them up, and place them seam side down in a 9- by 13-inch baking pan.

Pour the white sauce evenly over the tortillas, then sprinkle with the grated cheese, and top with the scallions. Bake for 15 minutes, or until the cheese is bubbly.

Calories: 282	Total fat: 10 g	Protein: 13
Carbohydrates: 35 g	Cholesterol: 20 g	Sodium: 256 m

CHEESE ENCHILADAS WITH SALSA VERDE

4 to 6 servings

Made with distinctively flavored green tomatillo sauce (salsa verde), these simple enchiladas need little other embellishment.

12 corn tortillas
1½ cups sautéed chopped mushrooms, green and/or red bell pepper, yellow summer squash, or a combination
2 cups grated Monterey Jack cheese
1 recipe Salsa Verde (page 226)

Garnish:
Shredded lettuce
Chopped tomatoes
Black olives

Preheat the oven to 400 degrees.

Briefly heat each tortilla on a medium-hot dry skillet until softened. If the tortillas seem inflexible, sprinkle each with a few drops of water before heating.

Spoon a small amount of the sautéed vegetables down the center of each tortilla, followed by a light sprinkling of the cheese. Roll them up and place them seam side down in a lightly oiled 9- by 13-inch baking pan. Repeat with the remaining tortillas. Spoon the sauce evenly over them and top with any remaining grated cheese. Bake for 10 to 15 minutes, or until the cheese is bubbly.

Arrange 2 or 3 enchiladas on each plate and garnish with the lettuce, tomatoes, and olives. Serve at once.

Calories: 421   Total fat: 21 g   Protein: 19 g
Carbohydrates: 38 g   Cholesterol: 41 g   Sodium: 473 mg

Full stomach, happy heart.

—Southwestern Spanish proverb

GUACAMOLE ENCHILADAS

6 servings

I encountered these enchiladas quite frequently on my travels. It's easy to see why this rich, sensuous standard is so popular. Save this dish for special occasions—it's not for calorie-counters!

12 corn tortillas
1 recipe Guacamole (page 110)
Cooked Enchilada Sauce (page 224), or Green Chile Sauce (page 227)
1 cup grated cheddar cheese, reduced-fat if desired

Garnishes:
Shredded lettuce
Diced ripe tomatoes
Reduced-fat sour cream

Preheat the oven to 400 degrees.

Briefly heat each tortilla on a medium-hot dry skillet until softened. If the tortillas seem inflexible, sprinkle each with a few drops of water before heating. Spoon some guacamole down the center of each tortilla, roll them up, and place them seam side down in an oiled 9-by 13-inch baking pan. Spoon any leftover guacamole over them, followed by the sauce of your choice. Sprinkle with the cheese.

Bake for 10 to 15 minutes, or until the cheese is melted. Garnish with lettuce and tomatoes, and pass around the sour cream to spoon over the enchiladas, if you'd like.

Calories: 370   Total fat: 16 g   Protein: 12 g
Carbohydrates: 40 g   Cholesterol: 14 g   Sodium: 273 mg

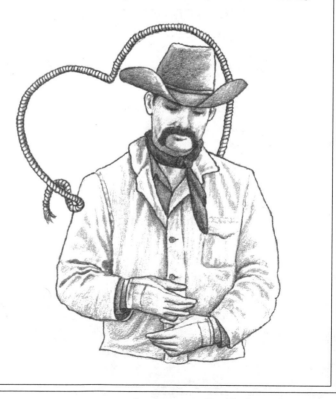

BLACK BEAN TOSTADAS

4 to 6 servings

Tostadas are crisp corn tortillas layered with a variety of tasty things. I still haven't figured out how to eat one in polite company, but it's easiest to just pick up the whole thing, as you would a slice of pizza. If you're willing to forgo table decorum and propriety, you will have a sensuously good time.

1½ tablespoons olive oil

1 medium onion, chopped

2 cloves garlic, crushed or minced

2 cups cooked black beans (about ¾ cup raw), or 1 1-pound can, drained and rinsed

¼ cup cooking liquid from the beans, or water

1 teaspoon each: dried oregano and ground cumin

Salt to taste

6 to 8 corn tortillas

1 recipe Green Chile Sauce (page 227)

Grated cheddar cheese, reduced-fat if desired, optional

Shredded lettuce

1 or 2 medium ripe tomatoes, finely diced

1 cup reduced-fat sour cream

Heat the oil in a large skillet. Add the onion and sauté over medium-low heat until translucent. Add the garlic and continue to sauté until the onion is golden. Add the beans, liquid, oregano, cumin, and salt and simmer, covered, over low heat for 20 to 25 minutes. Mash a few of the beans with a fork. Stir occasionally and make sure that there is always enough liquid to keep everything moist and bubbling.

In the meantime, toast each tortilla in a dry skillet over medium-high heat until crisp.

Place one tortilla on each dinner plate. Spread some of the black-bean mixture over each, followed by a spoonful or two of the Green Chile Sauce. Sprinkle on some grated cheese, if using, then some chopped lettuce and tomatoes. Finally, top everything with a dollop of sour cream. Serve at once.

Calories: 351
Carbohydrates: 48 g

Total fat: 11 g
Cholesterol: 11 g

Protein: 11 g
Sodium: 224 mg

If a yankee eats a tostado, he must hold a large plate beneath it, to protect his clothes.

CHILAQUILES (Tortilla Casserole)

Serves 6

In classic American cookery, nothing has ever been wasted. In the Southwestern tradition, for instance, stale tortillas go into making tasty specialties such as Migas (page 120) or this unusual casserole, which I think of as a sort of Mexican lasagna.

2 tablespoons olive oil

1 large onion, chopped

2 cloves garlic, minced

1 28-ounce can diced tomatoes

1 or 2 small hot green chiles, seeded and minced, or 1 4-ounce can chopped mild green chiles

2 to 3 tablespoons minced fresh cilantro

1 teaspoon each: dried oregano and ground cumin

12 corn tortillas

2 cups grated Monterey Jack or cheddar cheese, reduced-fat if desired

Salsa Ranchera (page 225) or store-bought salsa for topping

Reduced-fat sour cream for topping, optional

Preheat the oven to 400 degrees.

Heat the oil in a heavy saucepan. Add the onion and garlic and sauté over low heat until the onion is golden. Add the tomatoes, chiles, and seasonings. Simmer gently over low heat, covered, for 10 minutes.

In the meantime, tear each tortilla into several large pieces.

Oil a shallow 1½-quart round or 9- by 13-inch baking dish. Pile in half the tortilla pieces, then pour half the sauce over them. Sprinkle with half the grated cheese. Repeat the layers.

Bake for 20 to 25 minutes, or until the cheese is bubbly. Let stand for 5 minutes, then cut into squares or wedges to serve. Top each serving with salsa and, if desired, a small dollop of sour cream.

Calories: 330	Total fat: 14 g	Protein: 16 g
Carbohydrates: 33 g	Cholesterol: 27 g	Sodium: 285 mg

BEAN BURRITOS

4 servings

Burritos, literally meaning "little donkeys," are a staple of basic Southwestern cookery; they and their variations are characterized by the use of flour tortillas.

Filling:

1 tablespoon olive oil

1 small onion, chopped

1 clove garlic, minced

½ medium green bell pepper, finely diced

2½ cups well-cooked pinto beans (about 1 cup raw), or 1 20-ounce can, drained and rinsed

1 4-ounce can chopped mild green chiles

2 tablespoons minced fresh cilantro

1 teaspoon ground cumin

Salt to taste

Cooking liquid from the beans, or water, as needed

8 burrito-size (10- to 12-inch) flour tortillas

1 cup firmly packed grated Monterey Jack or cheddar cheese, reduced-fat if desired, optional

Salsa Ranchera (page 225)

Shredded lettuce for garnish

Black olives for garnish

Heat the oil in a medium skillet. Add the onion and sauté over medium-low heat until translucent. Add the garlic and sauté for another minute before adding the green pepper. Continue to sauté until the onion is lightly golden. Add the pinto beans along with the remaining filling ingredients and enough liquid to keep the mixture moist. Simmer, covered, for 10 minutes.

With a mashing implement, mash about half of the beans. Make sure there is enough liquid in the mixture to form a thick, saucy base. Cook, covered, for another 5 minutes.

Spoon some the bean mixture onto the centers of each flour tortilla. Sprinkle with some grated cheese, if desired, and top with a spoonful or so of salsa. Fold the burritos as directed in the illustration below.

Arrange 2 burritos on each dinner plate. Garnish with shredded lettuce and black olives. Pass around extra salsa. Serve at once.

Calories: 463	Total fat: 11 g	Protein: 16 g
Carbohydrates: 73 g	Cholesterol: 0 g	Sodium: 412 mg

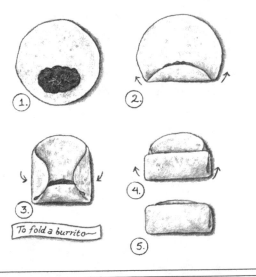

To fold a burrito—

YELLOW RICE AND BLACK BEAN BURRITOS

Makes 8 large burritos

Often, rice is served alongside burritos, but the combination of rice and beans wrapped inside the tortilla is quite satisfying.

2¼ cups water
1 vegetable bouillon cube
¾ cup brown rice
½ teaspoon each: ground cumin and turmeric

1 tablespoon olive oil
1 medium onion, chopped
1 to 2 cloves garlic, minced
½ medium green bell pepper, finely diced
1 small fresh hot chile, seeded and minced, or 1 4-ounce can chopped mild green chiles
2 cups cooked black beans (about ¾ cup raw), or 1 1-pound can black beans, drained and rinsed
1 medium tomato, diced
½ teaspoon each: dried oregano, ground cumin

8 10-inch (burrito-sized) flour tortillas, warmed
Salsa Ranchera (page 225) or store-bought salsa

Bring the water and bouillon cube to a boil in a medium saucepan. Stir in the rice, cumin, and turmeric and simmer gently, covered, until the water is absorbed, about 35 minutes.

Heat the oil in a large skillet. Add the onion and sauté until translucent. Add the garlic and bell pepper and sauté until the onion is golden. Add the chile, beans, tomato, and seasonings. Cook over medium heat until the mixture is heated through and the tomato has softened, about 8 minutes.

To assemble, place a small amount each of the cooked rice and black bean mixture in the center of each tortilla. Add a stripe of salsa. Fold as shown in the illustration on page 214. Repeat with the remaining tortillas and serve at once.

Calories: 275   Total fat: 6 g   Protein: 9 g
Carbohydrates: 46 g   Cholesterol: 0 g   Sodium: 207 mg

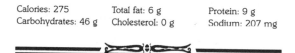

Que vivan, que vivan
Los burritos para las bonitas!

Long live, long live
The little donkeys for the little beauties!

—Old California vendors' street cry
Early California Hospitality, 1938

VEGETABLE BURRITOS

Makes 8 burritos

Many Southwestern-style restaurants offer vegetable burritos as a meatless option, and they are a nice change of pace from bean burritos. Some restaurants serve them with refried beans on the side, and some with the refried beans in the burrito, as they are in my version. The advantage to doing so is that the refried beans help hold everything together. They also make these burritos more filling and substantial. Feel free to substitute vegetables other than those suggested here.

1 tablespoon olive oil

1 large onion, quartered and
    thinly sliced

2 cups small broccoli florets

1 medium red bell pepper, cut
    into 2-inch strips

1 small zucchini, sliced

1 cup sliced white mushrooms

1 large tomato, diced

1 4-ounce can chopped mild
    green chiles

½ teaspoon each: chili powder
    and ground cumin

8 burrito-sized (10-inch) flour
    tortillas

Frijoles Refritos (page 129),
    about ½ recipe (see note)

1 cup grated cheddar cheese,
    reduced-fat if desired, optional

Garnishes:

**Salsa Ranchera (page 225), Salsa Verde
    (page 226), or store-bought salsa**

**Reduced-fat sour cream or plain low-fat
    yogurt, optional**

Preheat the oven to 250 degrees.

Heat the oil in a large skillet. Add the onion and sauté over medium heat until translucent. Layer the broccoli florets and red pepper strips over the onion and without stirring, cover and cook for 5 minutes more.

Add the zucchini, mushrooms, tomatoes, chiles, and seasonings and stir well. Cover and cook another 5 to 8 minutes, or until the vegetables are just tender. Drain off any liquid that has formed.

In the meantime, wrap the tortillas in foil and place in the oven until needed. Heat the refried beans in a small saucepan until just heated through.

To assemble, spoon a small amount of the refried beans down the center of each warmed tortilla, followed by some of the vegetable mixture and a bit of cheese, if desired. Roll up and place seam side down on a plate.

Serve at once, passing around the garnishes to be used as desired. These large moist burritos are best eaten with knife and fork rather than out of hand.

Calories: 260	Total fat: 8 g	Protein: 9 g
Carbohydrates: 37 g	Cholesterol: 3 g	Sodium: 367 m

Note: For a shortcut version, substitute a 1-pound can of fat-free refried beans for the Frijoles Refritos. Warm them up in a small saucepan, adding about ¼ cup water to loosen their consistency.

SIZZLING SOY FAJITAS

6 servings

What I like about serving fajitas is that everyone participates in creating their own meal—and no one seems to mind!

1½ pounds extra-firm tofu

Marinade:
Juice of 1 lime or ½ large lemon
¼ cup dry white wine
1 teaspoon canola oil
1 teaspoon chili powder
1 teaspoon salt

1 medium green bell pepper, cut into 2-inch strips
1 medium red bell pepper, cut as above
12 fajita-sized (8-inch) flour tortillas

Garnishes:
Diced fresh tomatoes
Shredded lettuce
Store-bought salsa or picante sauce
Reduced-fat sour cream
Grated cheddar cheese, reduced-fat if desired, optional

Preheat the oven's broiler.

Cut the tofu into ½-inch-thick slices. Blot well between layers of paper towel or clean tea towels. Then, cut the slices into ½-inch-thick strips.

In a small bowl, combine the marinade ingredients and stir together. Place the tofu strips in a bowl, pour the marinade over them and toss gently.

Lightly oil a foil-lined baking sheet. Arrange the tofu strips and bell pepper strips on it. Broil until golden, about 5 to 8 minutes, then carefully stir and broil for another 5 to 8 minutes, until the mixture is lightly browned. Transfer to a serving platter and cover to keep the mixture warm until needed.

Wrap the tortillas in foil and warm them in the hot oven for no longer than 5 minutes.

Place the tomatoes, lettuce, salsa, sour cream, and optional cheddar cheese in separate serving bowls. Distribute two warmed flour tortillas to everyone. To assemble the fajitas, have everyone place a few strips of the tofu and peppers in the center of their tortillas and garnish them as they wish with any or all of the garnishes. Then roll up the fajitas and eat them out of hand.

Calories: 233   Total fat: 7 g   Protein: 9 g
Carbohydrates: 31 g   Cholesterol: 0 g   Sodium: 581 mg

CHIMICHANGAS (Fried Burritos)

4 servings

Chimichanga is a nonsense word very much akin to "thingamajig," and that's how this popular variation of burritos has come to be known. I've modified the procedure from the traditional deep-frying to shallow frying with little oil.

Leftover Frijoles Refritos (page 129; about ½ recipe is needed)
8 burrito-size (10-inch) flour tortillas
Canola oil for frying

Garnishes (choose any combination):
Guacamole (page 110)
Salsa Ranchera (page 225)
Shredded lettuce
Diced tomatoes

Divide the *frijoles* among the tortillas, placing a small amount in the center of each. Fold the tortillas as directed in the illustration on page 214, as for burritos.

Heat just enough oil to coat the bottom of a heavy skillet. Fry each chimichanga on both sides until golden brown and crisp.

Arrange two chimichangas on each serving plate. Serve at once with garnishes of your choice.

Calories: 433   Total fat: 12 g   Protein: 16 g
Carbohydrates: 64 g   Cholesterol: 6 g   Sodium: 715 mg

Legend has it that Calamity Jane was awfully fond of burritos and chimichangas.

AVOCADO QUESADILLAS

6 servings

This is one of the popular flour tortilla concoctions that I picked up while in New Mexico. Serve this grilled turnover as an appetizer or a light main dish.

6 soft taco–size (8-inch) flour tortillas

1 large firm ripe avocado, finely diced

2 to 3 scallions, minced

1 cup grated Monterey Jack cheese

Salsa Ranchera (page 225) or Black Bean Salsa (page 223)

Reduced-fat sour cream, optional

Shredded lettuce for garnish

Arrange the avocado, grated cheese, and scallions on one half of each tortilla, leaving about a ½-inch border near the edges. Fold each tortilla over to make a half-circle.

On a hot dry griddle, cook the quesadillas on both sides until nicely golden brown (flip them carefully!). Arrange one quesadilla on each serving plate and cut in half with a sharp knife to make two wedges. Top with a bit of the salsa and if desired, a small dollop of sour cream. Garnish with the lettuce.

Calories: 209 Total fat: 11 g Protein: 8 g
Carbohydrates: 18 g Cholesterol: 17 g Sodium: 215 mg

BLACK BEAN, CORN, AND RED PEPPER QUESADILLAS

Makes 8, 1 or 2 per serving

Since these are chock-full, I've included an option for heating them in the oven.

Filling:

- 2 cups cooked black beans (about ¾ cup raw), or 1 1-pound can, drained and rinsed
- 1 cup cooked fresh or thawed frozen corn kernels
- 1 6-ounce jar roasted red peppers, drained
- 2 to 3 tablespoons minced fresh cilantro
- 1 scallion, thinly sliced
- 1 teaspoon ground cumin
- 1 or 2 fresh jalapeño peppers, seeded and minced, or 1 4-ounce can mild or hot chopped green chiles
- 8 soft taco–size (8-inch) flour tortillas
- 1 cup grated cheddar cheese, reduced-fat if desired

Salsa Ranchera (page 225) or store-bought salsa
Reduced-fat sour cream, optional

Heat a large non-stick griddle, or preheat the oven to 400 degrees.

Combine the filling ingredients in a mixing bowl and stir together. Arrange the filling on one half of each tortilla, leaving about a ½-inch border near the edges. Sprinkle each with a little of the cheese. Fold each tortilla over to make a half-circle.

If heating on a griddle, cook the quesadillas on both sides until nicely golden brown (flip them carefully!). If using the oven, bake for 15 minutes at 400 degrees, or until the quesadillas are hot and beginning to turn light golden brown.

Arrange one quesadilla on each serving plate and cut in half with a sharp knife to make two wedges. Top with a bit of the salsa and if desired, a small dollop of sour cream.

Calories: 210	Total fat: 5 g	Protein: 10 g
Carbohydrates: 31 g	Cholesterol: 10 g	Sodium: 215 mg

NACHOS WITH CHILE CON QUESO

Serves 8 or more as an appetizer

A Southwestern appetizer that's become popular everywhere, this is an enticingly rich dish of melted cheese and chiles enveloping crisp tortilla wedges. Though customarily made with jalapeños, you can substitute mild green chiles if you prefer a tamer flavor.

12 corn tortillas
2 teaspoons canola oil
1 small onion, minced
1 clove garlic, minced
1 medium ripe tomato, finely
 chopped
1 to 2 jalapeño peppers, to taste,
 seeded and thinly sliced,
 or 1 4-ounce can chopped
 mild green chiles
1 tablespoon unbleached white
 flour
3 tablespoons low-fat milk
8 ounces cheddar cheese, diced,
 or 8 ounces grated reduced-fat
 cheddar cheese

Preheat the oven to 375 degrees.

Cut the tortillas into six wedges each (kitchen shears are perfect for doing so) and spread them on 1 or 2 large baking sheets. Bake for 15 to 20 minutes, or until they are dry and crisp. Remove and allow to cool.

Heat the oil in a large saucepan. Add the onion and garlic and sauté over low heat until golden. Add the tomatoes and jalapeños and simmer until the tomato softens. Sprinkle in the flour and stir until it is well blended, then stir in the milk. Add the cheese and cook, stirring, until it is smoothly melted. Remove from the heat. Spread the tortilla wedges on a large serving platter. Pour the cheese sauce over them and serve at once.

Calories: 211   Total fat: 8 g   Protein: 12 g
Carbohydrates: 21 g   Cholesterol: 21 g   Sodium: 240 mg

INDIVIDUAL TORTILLA PIZZAS

6 servings

These Southwestern-flavored "pizzas" are contemporary innovations. They can be part of a satisfying meal served with a bean chili (such as those on pages 133 and 134) or a bean salad (such as Pinto Bean Salad, page 105). Otherwise, they make a nice appetizer.

6 soft taco-size (8-inch) flour tortillas

½ red bell pepper, cut into very thin strips

½ green bell pepper, cut as above

1 cup cooked fresh or thawed frozen corn kernels

1 cup finely diced firm, ripe tomatoes

1 4-ounce can chopped mild green chiles

2 scallions, thinly sliced

1½ cups grated Monterey Jack or cheddar cheese, reduced-fat if desired

Dried oregano

Preheat the oven to 400 degrees.

Spread the tortillas in a single layer on two nonstick baking sheets (you may have to bake them in batches if they don't all fit).

Divide the ingredients evenly over the tortillas in the order listed, ending each with the grated cheese and a sprinkling of oregano.

Bake for 10 minutes, or until the cheese is bubbly. Cut each tortilla into 4 wedges to serve.

Calories: 211
Carbohydrates: 23 g
Total fat: 7 g
Cholesterol: 20 g
Protein: 11 g
Sodium: 318 mg

The origins of chile peppers are often credited to ancient South Americans, whose agricultural techniques were adopted by Native Americans of the Southwest. Chiles have since become big business—according to a report in the *Taos News*, chile peppers are New Mexico's major vegetable crop, with nearly 15,000 acres cultivated. This makes red and green chiles a multi-million dollar industry—that's a lot of hot stuff!

BLACK BEAN SALSA

Makes about 2 cups

This chunky salsa is a good companion for tortilla specialties that don't themselves contain beans, such as Stacked Cheese Enchiladas (page 207), Vegetable Burritos (page 216), and others.

1 cup canned black beans,
    drained and rinsed
1 cup finely diced ripe tomatoes
1 small onion, minced
Juice of ½ to 1 lime, to taste
1 small hot fresh chile, seeded
    and minced, or 1 4-ounce can
    chopped mild green chiles
¼ cup finely chopped fresh
    cilantro
¼ teaspoon each: ground cumin
    and dried oregano

Combine all the ingredients in a serving container and mix well. Cover and refrigerate for at least an hour to allow the flavors to blend.

Per 1/4 cup:
Calories: 44
Carbohydrates: 8 g
Total fat: 0 g
Cholesterol: 0 g
Protein: 2 g
Sodium: 4 mg

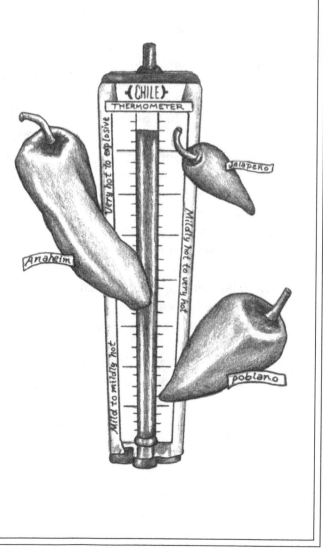

COOKED ENCHILADA SAUCE

Makes about 2 cups

Cooked tomato-based sauces such as this one are more common in some parts of the Southwest than in others. It's a good bet for those who are wary of super-hot chile sauces—it's milder and has a more familiar flavor. This is flavored with what are known as the "Spanish seasonings."

1½ tablespoons olive oil

1 small onion, finely chopped

1 clove garlic, minced

½ medium green bell pepper, minced

2 cups chopped ripe juicy tomatoes, or 1 14- to 16-ounce can diced tomatoes, lightly drained

½ cup thick tomato sauce

1 to 2 tablespoons minced fresh cilantro

1 small jalapeño pepper, seeded and minced, optional

1 teaspoon chili powder, or to taste

½ teaspoon each: salt, dried oregano, and ground cumin

Heat the oil in a deep saucepan. Add the onion and garlic and sauté over medium-low heat until the onion is translucent. Add the bell pepper and continue to sauté for another minute or so. Add all the remaining ingredients and simmer over very low heat, covered, for 25 to 30 minutes.

per 1/3 cup:
Calories: 58   Total fat: 2 g   Protein: 1 g
Carbohydrates: 6 g   Cholesterol: 0 g   Sodium: 130 mg

Chile, or chilly, as the name of a sauce, and a very familiar word at this season, is in none of the dictionaries.

—*American Notes and Queries VII*, 1891

Not one of these dictionaries contains —
Chile sauce n.: a spiced tomato sauce orig. made with chilies.

SALSA RANCHERA (Raw Tomato Salsa)

Makes about 2 cups

The most basic relish of the Southwest—coarsely pureed raw tomatoes spiked with chile peppers— is sometimes known as salsa cruda. Commonly used as an appetizer dip for crisp tortilla chips or nachos, it's called for in several recipes throughout this book. Store-bought salsas are generally quite good, not to mention convenient, but there's nothing like the fresh, homemade kind.

2 cups chopped ripe tomatoes, or
    1 14- to 16-ounce can diced
    tomatoes, lightly drained
1 small onion, quartered
1 4-ounce can chopped mild
    green chiles
1 to 2 fresh jalapeño peppers,
    seeded and coarsely chopped,
    optional (see note)
Several sprigs fresh cilantro
1 tablespoon lemon juice
½ teaspoon cumin
¼ teaspoon salt, or to taste

To prepare in a food processor, simply combine all the ingredients in its container and pulse on and off until coarsely pureed. To prepare by hand, finely chop the tomatoes, onion, optional jalapeños, and cilantro. Stir in the remaining ingredients. Store in an airtight jar. This will keep for several days, but it's best fresh.

Per 1/4 cup:

Calories: 21	Total fat: 0 g	Protein: 1 g
Carbohydrates: 4 g	Cholesterol: 0 g	Sodium: 134 mg

Note: The use of one jalapeño will result in a hot salsa, while two will make this downright incendiary. Those with more experienced palates are free to use as many jalapeños as they'd like.

SALSA VERDE (Fresh Tomatillo Sauce)

Makes about 2 cups

Tomatillos are members of the berry family that resemble small green tomatoes. Their flavor is distinct, though not hot. This makes an exotic sauce for enchiladas or an offbeat dip for nachos. Look for them in specialty groceries and well-stocked supermarkets.

2 tablespoons olive oil

1 medium onion, chopped

2 cloves garlic, minced

1 pound fresh tomatillos, husked

1 fresh jalapeño pepper, seeded and minced, or 1 4-ounce can chopped mild green chiles

¼ cup chopped fresh cilantro

2 scallions, coarsely chopped

Juice of ½ lime

½ teaspoon salt

Heat the oil in a medium saucepan. Add the onion and garlic and sauté over medium-low heat until the onion is translucent. Transfer the mixture to a food processor along with the remaining ingredients. Process until coarsely pureed. Transfer back to the saucepan and bring to a simmer. Simmer gently, covered, for 15 minutes. Let cool to room temperature or chill before serving.

per 1/4 cup:

Calories: 55	Total fat: 2 g	Protein: 1 g
Carbohydrates: 5 g	Cholesterol: 0 g	Sodium: 139 mg

There are all sorts of chile peppers, ranging from the kind that scorch your throat a little to the kind that burst into white flame like an atomic bomb as they go down. The hottest you can buy is the *chile jalapeño*—Chile of Jalapa. Mexicans eat it raw, and claim that it's good for digestion. God help you if you try to do the same without a long tactical training period in Mexican cookery.

—Green Peyton
San Antonio: City in the Sun, 1946

GREEN CHILE SAUCE

Makes about 1 cup

No matter what time of day or night, the food I ate in New Mexico was, more often than not, liberally doused with this type of sauce. It's now far easier to find fresh Anaheim or Poblano chiles, and making the effort to use them results in a splendid sauce. Still, many cooks may prefer to use canned green chiles for convenience. Whether canned or fresh, green chiles are indispensable for giving Southwestern recipes an authentic flair.

2 to 3 good-sized fresh Anaheim
   or poblano chiles (see note)
1 tablespoon olive oil
1 medium onion, finely chopped
1 clove garlic, finely minced
1 tablespoon unbleached white
   flour
½ cup water
½ teaspoon salt

Preheat the oven to 450 degrees.

Place the chiles on a foil-lined baking sheet and roast, turning on all sides, until the skins are charred. Remove from the oven and place in a paper bag. Close the bag tightly and let stand for 10 minutes.

When cool enough to handle, slip the skins off of the chiles, then remove the stems and seeds and finely chop the chiles.

Heat the oil in a small heavy saucepan. Add the onion and sauté over medium-low heat until translucent. Add the garlic and continue to sauté until the onion is golden. Sprinkle in the flour and cook, stirring, until the mixture begins to brown lightly. Stir in the chopped chiles, water, and salt. Simmer over very low heat, covered, for 15 minutes. Remove from the heat and serve or use as an ingredient in other recipes.

Per 1/4 cup:

Calories: 72	Total fat: 2 g	Protein: 2 g
Carbohydrates: 8 g	Cholesterol: 0 g	Sodium: 272 mg

Note: For a shortcut version, use 2 4-ounce cans mild or hot chopped green chiles.

This chile sauce is excellent and much better and healthful than catsups.

—*Buckeye Cookery*, 1885 edition

Chapter 10
DESSERTS

When you are seated next to a lady, you should only be polite during the first course; you may be gallant in the second, but you must not be tender till the dessert.

—*The New York Mirror*, 1838

The task of choosing desserts to include in this collection was mindboggling. All the old menus and cookbooks I pored over, and the numerous dining establishments I visited on my travels, left no doubt that this is a land with a colossal, collective sweet tooth. The number of pies and puddings alone could fill volumes.

My goal was to choose desserts that have some intrinsically healthful quality, and as it turned out, this was easy to achieve, thanks to the great selection of classic fruit desserts. This allowed me to substantially reduce the amount of sugar used in the original recipes, often by as much as two thirds, and in some cases, eliminate it almost completely.

The South, as chronicled by Robert Beverly and William Byrd in the early 1700s, was a paradise of fruit and nut trees. Beverly would occasionally comment on the superiority of the native fruits over their European corollaries, saying, for example, that there were "many kinds of peaches, which have come from Europe, all of which are not nearly so good as the natural Native Indian ones, which are exceedingly good." He goes on to rhapsodize on the luscious, colorful berries and currants and provides a list of apple varieties that is unimaginably long. Nut trees are similarly enumerated by Byrd.

With the availability of such produce in the New Land, combined with the sophisticated dessert-making skills brought over by European women, it's no wonder that this arena of cookery gained so prominent a place in the annals of American food.

So many of us are trying to cut down on sugar, but still, most everyone occasionally wants to satisfy their sweet tooth. Many of these recipes will show that it's possible to do both, and that dessert can be delicious without having to be completely decadent!

BASIC PIE CRUST

Makes 1 9-inch single crust

Making pie crust is easy, once you get the hang of it. A food processor is especially handy for making the dough, but is not essential. Double this recipe for making two-crust pies or those that call for lattice strips on top. I experimented with using whipped butter or canola margarine in place of the standard butter or vegetable shortening used in pastry crusts. While fine pastry-makers may not approve of this unorthodox practice, I prefer pie crust that's not laden with the full caloric impact of regular butter or the unstable fats of supermarket margarine.

½ **cup unbleached white flour**
½ **teaspoon salt**
¼ **cup whipped butter or natural canola margarine**
4 to 5 tablespoons ice water

Combine the flour and salt. To make by hand, place the flour mixture in a mixing bowl with the butter. Work the butter into the flour with a pastry blender or with the tines of a fork until the mixture resembles a coarse meal. Work in the ice water, a tablespoon at a time, until the dough holds together. Shape the dough into a smooth round.

To make in a food processor, place the flour mixture in the workbowl fitted with the special plastic dough blade. Add the butter and pulse on and off several times until the mixture resembles a coarse meal. Add the water a tablespoon at a time through the feed tube and pulse on and off until the dough holds together. Remove and shape into a smooth round.

If time allows, cover the dough in plastic wrap and refrigerate for 30 minutes to an hour. On a well-floured board, roll the dough out evenly and uniformly until it is large enough to fit a 9-inch pie pan. Line the pan with the crust and trim the edges. Scallop the edges with your fingers if desired, for a decorative effect.

Per 1/8 of a crust:

Calories: 91	Total fat: 4 g	Protein: 2 g
Carbohydrates: 10 g	Cholesterol: 12 g	Sodium: 134 mg

None of them will speak to you, or if they do, they are as short as pie-crust.

—William K. Northall
Before and Behind the Curtain, 1851

PUMPKIN OR BUTTERNUT SQUASH PIE

Makes one 9-inch pie

After the all-American apple pie, nothing so typifies the American dessert as pumpkin pie, with its evocations of old-fashioned Thanksgivings. I chose to include this standard recipe mostly to show off its lesser-known but equally venerable counterpart, squash pie. which was also a colonial New England institution. You'll find that the smooth, sweet butternut puree tastes just as good as pumpkin—perhaps even better!

2 cups mashed, well-cooked
    sugar pumpkin or butternut
    squash
2 eggs
⅔ cup firmly packed light brown
    sugar or Sucanat
½ cup low-fat milk or soymilk
1 teaspoon cinnamon
¼ teaspoon each: ground ginger,
    nutmeg, and allspice
1 Basic Pie Crust (page 231)

Preheat the oven to 350 degrees.

Combine the pumpkin or squash pulp in a food processor with the eggs, sugar, milk, and spices. Process until velvety smooth. Pour the mixture into the crust. Bake for 40 to 45 minutes, or until the mixture is set and the crust is golden. Let the pie cool until just warm or to room temperature before serving.

Per 1/8 pie wedge:
Calories: 182
Carbohydrates: 27 g
Total fat: 7 g
Cholesterol: 66 g
Protein: 4 g
Sodium: 165 mg

Ah! On Thanksgiving day, when from
    East and from West,
From North and from South come the
    pilgrim and guest,
When the gray-haired
    New Englander sees round
    his board
The old broken links of affection
    restored,
When the care-wearied man seeks his
    mother once more,
And the worn matron smiles where the
    girl smiled before,
What moistens the lip and what
    brightens the eye?
What calls back the past, like the rich
    pumpkin pie?

—Anonymous
The New England Cookbook, 1936

BOSTON CRANBERRY PIE

Makes one 9-inch pie

This New England pie pleases the eye with its old-fashioned lattice strips, and offers the palate the contrasting flavors of tart berries and sweet raisins.

2 tablespoons cornstarch or
    arrowroot
⅔ cup firmly packed light brown
    sugar or Sucanat
1 cup boiling water
2 cups (1 8-ounce bag) fresh
    cranberries
1 cup dark raisins
Double recipe Basic Pie Crust
    (page 231), for bottom crust
    plus ½-inch-wide lattice strips

Preheat the oven to 400 degrees.

Combine the cornstarch and brown sugar in a heavy saucepan or the top of a double boiler. Over low heat, pour in ¼ cup of the boiling water and whisk in until smoothly dissolved. Stir in the remaining water and cook, allowing it to bubble gently, until thickened. Add the cranberries and raisins and cook over low heat for 10 minutes.

Let the mixture stand off the heat for 10 minutes, then pour it into the crust. Cover the top with lattice strips ½ inch wide, spaced about ½ inch apart. Bake for 35 to 40 minutes, or until the fruit is soft and the crust is golden. Allow the pie to cool until just warm or to room temperature before serving.

Per 1/8 pie wedge:

Calories: 298	Total fat: 10 g	Protein: 4 g
Carbohydrates: 49 g	Cholesterol: 24 g	Sodium: 277 mg

Cranberries grow in the low lands, and barren Sunken Grounds, upon low Bushes, like the Gooseberry, and are much the same size. They are of a lively Red, when ripe, and make very good Tarts.

—Robert Beverly
*The History and Present State
of Virginia,* 1705

BANANA CREAM PIE

Makes one 9-inch pie

Cream pies have been common since the early part of the nineteenth century, particularly in New England, but Banana Cream Pie is an early twentieth-century innovation. This pie is easy to make, but takes some time, due to cooling periods between the steps. Allow 1½ to 2 hours for the procedure, including baking time, plus additional time for final cooling.

1 recipe Basic Pie Crust
　(page 231)
½ cup granulated sugar or ¼ cup
　granular fructose, or to taste
2½ tablespoons unbleached
　white flour
1½ cups low-fat milk
1 teaspoon vanilla extract
Pinch of nutmeg
2 large bananas, thinly sliced
2 egg whites, at room
　temperature
1 tablespoon granulated sugar or
　1½ teaspoons granular fructose

Preheat the oven to 350 degrees.

Prick a few holes in the bottom of the pie crust with a fork. Bake the crust for 15 minutes, or until golden.

In the meantime, combine the sugar and flour in the top of a double boiler or heavy saucepan. Over very low heat, pour in the milk, a little at a time, stirring constantly to avoid lumping. Cook until the sugar and flour are smoothly dissolved, then stir in the vanilla and nutmeg. Cook for 10 to 15 minutes, stirring frequently, until thick and smooth.

Let the baked pie crust and the filling cool to room temperature. When nearly cooled, turn the oven temperature up to 425 degrees.

Spoon half the cooled filling into the crust. Arrange half the banana slices in concentric circles around the pie. Repeat the layers.

Beat the egg whites until they form stiff peaks. Sprinkle in the sugar and beat briefly again. Top the pie with the meringue and bake for 5 minutes in the hot oven, or until touched with golden brown. Allow the pie to cool once again before serving. Serve at room temperature or refrigerate and serve chilled.

Per 1/8 pie wedge:

Calories: 198	Total fat: 5 g	Protein: 5 g
Carbohydrates: 33 g	Cholesterol: 14 g	Sodium: 135 mg

Variation: For a Chocolate Banana Cream Pie, simply add a 1-ounce square of unsweetened chocolate to the milk-and-sugar mixture as it is cooking. Stir in until completely blended and continue cooking as directed.

SOUTHERN SWEET POTATO PIE

Makes one 9-inch pie

The product of an abundant regional crop, this classic dessert continues to be a tradition in many parts of the South.

2 cups (about 1 very large) cooked diced sweet potato

1 egg

⅔ cup light brown sugar or Sucanat

¼ cup low-fat milk or soymilk

2 tablespoons lemon juice, optional

1 teaspoon vanilla extract

1 teaspoon cinnamon

¼ teaspoon each: ground ginger, cloves, and nutmeg

1 Basic Pie Crust (page 231)

Preheat the oven to 350 degrees.

Combine the sweet potato with all the remaining ingredients (except, of course, the crust) in a food processor. Process until smoothly pureed. Pour into the pie crust and bake for 40 to 50 minutes, or until the crust is golden and the filling is set. Allow the pie to cool, then serve just warm or at room temperature.

Per 1/8 pie wedge:

Calories: 192	Total fat: 5 g	Protein: 3 g
Carbohydrates: 32 g	Cholesterol: .09 g	Sodium: 157 mg

There was no deficiency of custards, delicious sweet potato pies, and various wild fruits.

—Timothy Flint
George Mason, the Young Backwoodsman, 1829

PEANUT BUTTER PIE

Makes one 9-inch pie

Since peanut butter is a late-nine-teenth-century innovation, it's likely that this pie originated shortly thereafter. Most prevalent in the Midwest states, I first had this rich, full-flavored pie in the Wichita (Kansas) Art Museum's cafe, locally famous for its great American pies, baked fresh daily.

⅓ cup light brown sugar or Sucanat

¼ cup molasses

½ cup low-fat milk or soymilk

1 teaspoon vanilla extract

½ teaspoon cinnamon

¾ cup reduced-fat or natural-style peanut butter, at room temperature

2 egg whites

1 Basic Pie Crust (page 231)

¼ cup coarsely chopped peanuts, optional

Is it good? Sir, it is pie. It will bring to camp any idiot that sits in darkness anywhere.

—*North American Review*, 1901

Preheat the oven to 350 degrees.

In a large mixing bowl, combine the brown sugar with the molasses, milk, and vanilla. Whisk together until smoothly blended, then whisk in the peanut butter until smoothly blended.

Beat the egg whites until they form stiff peaks. Fold them gently into the peanut butter mixture. Pour the mixture into the pie crust and if desired, top with the chopped peanuts. Bake for 35 to 40 minutes, or until the mixture is set and the crust is golden. Allow the pie to cool, then serve just warm or at room temperature.

Per 1/8 pie wedge:

Calories: 293	Total fat: 13	Protein: 9 g
Carbohydrates: 36 g	Cholesterol: 13 g	Sodium: 282 mg

MOCK MINCE PIE

Makes one 9-inch pie

Another pie with roots in the Midwest states, Mock Mince Pie showed up in ladies' club cookbooks with as much regularity as did real mincemeat pies. It is chock-full of naturally sweet-and-spicy flavors and is best served slightly warm.

½ cup strong black coffee

¼ cup (scant) molasses

2 tablespoons apple cider vinegar

1 teaspoon vanilla extract

1 heaping cup raisins

2 medium sweet apples, peeled, cored, and finely chopped

¾ cup soft whole-grain bread crumbs

¼ cup finely chopped walnuts

1 teaspoon cinnamon

½ teaspoon ground allspice

¼ teaspoon ground cloves

Double recipe Basic Pie Crust (page 231) for bottom crust plus ½-inch-wide lattice strips

Preheat the oven to 375 degrees.

In a heavy saucepan, combine the coffee, molasses, and vinegar. Bring to a simmer, then add the vanilla, raisins, and apples. Simmer over low heat, covered, for 8 to 10 minutes.

In the meantime, combine the bread crumbs, walnuts, and spices in a mixing bowl. Pour the saucepan mixture over the dry mixture and stir together until completely combined.

Pour into the pie crust and top with ½-inch-wide lattice strips, arranged ½ inch apart. Bake for 30 to 35 minutes, or until the crust is golden. Allow the pie to cool, then serve just warm or at room temperature.

Calories: 311	Total fat: 10 g	Protein: 5 g
Carbohydrates: 50 g	Cholesterol: 24 g	Sodium: 325 mg

Pie was such a great part of the American menu that it worked its way into many common expressions. Mostly, it was used to describe anything that was the pinnacle of goodness or ease. "Easy as pie" and "as polite as pie" were ordinary phrases, as were variations of this:

He is as nice as pie this afternoon.

—G.B. McCutcheon
Green Fancy, 1917

SHOO-FLY PIE

Makes one 9-inch pie

This classic Pennsylvania Dutch pie didn't become widely known to the rest of America until the late nineteenth or early twentieth century. The prevalent and rather obvious explanation for its name is that the sweet, sticky filling of the pie attracts flies that must be shooed away. This distinctive pie will please you if you enjoy the robust flavor of molasses.

Crumb mixture:

1 cup unbleached white flour or whole wheat pastry flour, or half of each

⅓ cup firmly packed light brown sugar or Sucanat

1 teaspoon cinnamon

¼ teaspoon each: ground ginger and cloves, and salt

¼ cup whipped butter or natural canola margarine

Filling:

½ cup molasses

½ cup boiling water

½ teaspoon baking soda

1 Basic Pie Crust (page 231)

Preheat the oven to 375 degrees.

In a mixing bowl, combine the ingredients for the crumb mixture. Work in the butter with a fork until the mixture resembles a coarse meal.

In another bowl, dissolve the molasses in the boiling water. Sprinkle in the baking soda and stir until it dissolves. Add about two-thirds of the crumb mixture and stir together until the crumbs are moistened, but the mixture need not be smooth. Pour into the pie crust and top with the remaining crumbs. Bake for 35 to 40 minutes, or until the crust and crumbs are golden and the filling is set. Allow the pie to cool, then serve just warm or at room temperature.

Per 1/8 pie wedge:

Calories: 273	Total fat: 10 g	Protein: 3 g
Carbohydrates: 44 g	Cholesterol: 24 g	Sodium: 215 mg

Amish women have debated for generations on how to keep flies off of shoo-fly pie.

PECAN SQUARES

Makes one 9-inch cake, 12 servings

Pecans are the most popular nut in traditional Southern cookery. This dessert is not as common as others, but it makes a very nice cake to have with tea, and is equally good served with fresh fruit such as peaches or cantaloupe.

1 egg plus 1 egg white, well beaten

½ cup firmly packed light brown sugar or Sucanat

⅔ cup low-fat vanilla yogurt

1 cup whole wheat pastry flour or unbleached white flour, or half of each

1½ teaspoons baking powder

½ teaspoon each: baking soda and cinnamon

¼ teaspoon each: ground allspice and cloves, and salt

¾ cup finely chopped pecans

½ cup currants

Preheat the oven to 350 degrees.

In a small mixing bowl, combine the beaten eggs with the sugar and yogurt and stir until well mixed.

In another mixing bowl, combine the flours, baking powder, baking soda, spices, and salt. Add the wet mixture to the dry and stir together until smoothly blended. Fold in the pecans and currants. Pour the mixture into a lightly oiled 9- by 9-inch cake pan. Bake for 25 to 30 minutes, or until the top is golden and a knife inserted into the center tests clean. Allow to cool until just warm, then cut into 12 squares to serve.

Calories: 140	Total fat: 5 g	Protein: 4 g
Carbohydrates: 20 g	Cholesterol: 18 g	Sodium: 101 mg

About pecan shells...it is said that when they are hard, the winter is going to be cold.

—Alexander F. Sweet and John A. Knox
  On a Mexican Mustang, Through Texas,
  1883

SOUTHERN BLACK CAKE

Makes one 9-inch cake, 12 servings

Moist and dark with a spicy, complex flavor, this cake originated in Virginia and Maryland, then traveled widely in the nineteenth century. General cookbooks, whether Southern or not, often contained several versions of it.

¼ cup whipped butter or natural canola margarine, at room temperature

⅓ cup light brown sugar or Sucanat

2 eggs, well beaten

⅓ cup molasses

½ cup strong hot coffee

¼ cup low-fat milk or soymilk

1¾ cups whole wheat pastry flour or unbleached white flour, or a combination

1½ teaspoons baking powder

1 tablespoon dry unsweetened cocoa powder

1 teaspoon cinnamon

¼ teaspoon each: ground nutmeg, cloves, and allspice

¾ cup raisins

Preheat the oven to 350 degrees.

In a mixing bowl, cream the butter with the sugar. Add the beaten eggs and whisk together until smooth. Stir in the molasses, coffee, and milk and stir together until well blended.

In another bowl, combine the flours, baking powder, cocoa, and spices. Add the wet ingredients gradually to the dry and stir together until smoothly blended. Stir in the raisins.

Pour the batter into a lightly oiled 9- by 9-inch square or 9-inch round cake pan. Bake for 30 to 35 minutes, or until a knife inserted into the center tests clean. Allow to cool until just warm, then cut into squares or wedges to serve.

Calories: 174   Total fat: 3 g   Protein: 4 g
Carbohydrates: 30 g   Cholesterol: 44 g   Sodium: 31 mg

I hope before I'm through
To eat my cake and bake it, too.

—Margaret Fishback
Career Girl, 1940

HARWICH HERMITS

Makes one 9-inch cake, 12 servings

This New England spice cake is related to the somewhat more common "hermit cookie," whose ingredients are very similar. I enjoy the spicy flavors more in this form, and it's easier and quicker to make, too.

2 eggs, well beaten
⅓ cup firmly packed light brown
    sugar or Sucanat
1 8-ounce container low-fat
    vanilla yogurt
⅓ cup molasses
1¾ cups whole wheat pastry flour
    or unbleached white flour, or a
    combination
1 teaspoon each: baking powder,
    baking soda, and cinnamon
½ teaspoon ground cloves
¼ teaspoon ground nutmeg
¼ cup low-fat milk or soymilk,
    or as needed
⅔ cup raisins
⅓ cup finely chopped walnuts

Preheat the oven to 350 degrees.

Combine the beaten eggs with the sugar until it dissolves. Stir in the yogurt and molasses and stir together until completely combined.

Combine the flour, baking powder, baking soda, and spices in a mixing bowl and stir together. Add the wet ingredients gradually to the dry and stir together vigorously until smoothly blended. If the batter seems too dense, add a bit more milk as needed. Fold in the raisins and nuts.

Pour the batter into a lightly oiled 9- by 9-inch cake pan. Bake for 25 to 30 minutes, or until a knife inserted into the center tests clean and the top is golden. Allow to cool until just warm or at room temperature, then cut into squares to serve.

Calories: 178	Total fat: 4 g	Protein: 5 g
Carbohydrates: 32 g	Cholesterol: 37 g	Sodium: 112 mg

"Let all things be done decently and in order," and the first thing to put in order when you are going to bake is yourself. Secure the hair in a net or other covering, to prevent any from falling, and brush the shoulders and back to be sure none are lodged there that might blow off; make the hands and finger nails clean, roll the sleeves up above the elbows, and put on a large, clean apron.

—*The Buckeye Cookbook,* 1883

GUILT-FREE CHOCOLATE BROWNIE CAKE

Makes 1 9-inch cake, about 12 servings

Brownies can surely be classified as a quintessential American dessert. I devised these yogurt-based, cake-like brownies so that this treat can be enjoyed with a minimum of guilt.

1½ cups unbleached white flour
  or whole wheat pastry flour, or
  a combination
1¼ cups sweetened instant cocoa
  powder
½ teaspoon baking soda
¼ teaspoon salt
2 egg whites
1 6-ounce container (¾ cup) non-
  fat vanilla yogurt
2 tablespoons low-fat milk
1 teaspoon vanilla extract

Preheat the oven to 350 degrees.

Combine the flour, cocoa powder, baking soda, and salt in a mixing bowl. In another bowl, combine the egg whites with the yogurt, milk, and vanilla and stir until well blended.

Make a well in the center of the dry ingredients and pour in the wet mixture. Stir vigorously until thoroughly combined. Pour into a lightly oiled 9- by 9-inch cake pan. Bake for 30 minutes, or until the sides of the cake begin to pull away from the pan, and a knife inserted in the middle tests clean.

Calories: 109	Total fat: 2 g	Protein: 6 g
Carbohydrates: 18 g	Cholesterol: 1 g	Sodium: 105 mg

We can't eat our cake and have it, but we kin borrow money on a Ford and still drive it.

—Kin Hubbard,
Abe Martin's Almanack, 1911

APPLESAUCE SPICE CAKE

Makes 1 9-inch cake, about 12 servings

Applesauce cake was a fixture in early twentieth-century Ladies' Club cookbooks. It's appropriate for today's savvy bakers, knowing as we do that applesauce is a great fat substitute.

2 cups whole wheat pastry flour or unbleached flour, or half of each

2 teaspoons baking powder

½ teaspoon baking soda

1½ teaspoon cinnamon

¼ teaspoon each: ground ginger, nutmeg, and allspice

1 cup applesauce

¼ cup undiluted apple juice concentrate

¼ cup light brown sugar or Sucanat

1 cup raisins

¼ cup finely chopped walnuts

Preheat the oven to 350 degrees.

Combine the flour with the baking powder, baking soda, and spices in a large mixing bowl. In another bowl, combine the applesauce, apple juice concentrate, and sugar and stir until the sugar is dissolved.

Make a well in the center of the dry ingredients and pour in the wet mixture. Stir vigorously until well blended, then stir in the raisins and walnuts. Pour the mixture into a lightly oiled 9- by 9-inch square or 9-inch round cake pan.

Bake for 40 to 45 minutes, or until a knife inserted into the center tests clean. Allow to cool and cut into 12 squares or wedges to serve.

Calories: 149   Total fat: 1 g   Protein: 3 g
Carbohydrates: 30 g   Cholesterol: 0 g   Sodium: 42 mg

APPLE PANDOWDY

6 to 8 servings

This homey Old New England recipe became well known to the rest of the country early in the twentieth century, but has since become somewhat obscure. I think it's a perfect addition to a vegetarian collection, since it's such a wholesome dessert.

5 heaping cups thinly sliced
    peeled cooking apples (such
    as Cortland)
¼ cup maple syrup
¼ teaspoon each: ground cloves,
    nutmeg, and cinnamon

Batter:
1 cup whole wheat pastry flour
    or unbleached white flour, or
    half of each
1 teaspoon baking powder
½ teaspoon baking soda
1 egg, beaten
⅓ cup light brown sugar or
    Sucanat
⅔ cup non-fat vanilla yogurt
¼ cup finely chopped walnuts,
    optional

Low-fat vanilla ice cream or
    frozen yogurt, optional

Preheat the oven to 350 degrees.

Combine the apple slices, syrup, and spices in a bowl and stir together until the apples are coated. Arrange in a lightly oiled baking pan. Bake, covered, for 20 minutes.

Combine the flour, baking powder, and baking soda. In another bowl, mix the beaten egg with the sugar and yogurt until well blended. Stir the wet mixture into the dry and stir together until smooth.

Sprinkle the optional nuts over the apples, then pour the batter over them and pat it in. Bake, uncovered, for 25 to 30 minutes, or until golden. Serve fresh and warm on its own or over ice cream.

Calories: 201	Total fat: 1 g	Protein: 4 g
Carbohydrates: 42 g	Cholesterol: 32 g	Sodium: 89 mg

In the eighteenth and nineteenth centuries, Americans loved their apples. There must have been dozens and dozens, if not hundreds, of distinct varieties. Along with these also developed quite a number of "apple sayings." Here are just a few:

- Victorian girls with healthy coloring were referred to as "apple-cheeked."

- At the turn of the twentieth century, "go climb a sour apple tree" was a way of telling someone to go to the devil!

- In the roaring twenties, yes-men came to be known as "apple-polishers."

APPLE BROWN BETTY

6 servings

Another healthy apple dessert, this recipe has been known since colonial times. Alternatively called Apple Betty or Apple Crisp, the beauty of this recipe is that it's so naturally sweet. In old recipes, the crumbs are usually just plain bread crumbs, but I've updated the mixture by adding high-protein wheat germ and nuts.

Crumb mixture:

¾ cup soft whole-grain bread crumbs

½ cup wheat germ

¼ cup finely chopped pecans or walnuts

1 tablespoon light brown sugar or Sucanat

¼ teaspoon cinnamon

1 tablespoon whipped butter or natural canola margarine, melted

⅓ cup apple juice

1 teaspoon cinnamon

¼ teaspoon each: ground cloves and allspice or nutmeg

4 or 5 large sweet apples (such as Cortland), peeled, cored, and thinly sliced

½ cup raisins

Low-fat vanilla ice cream or frozen yogurt, optional

Preheat the oven to 350 degrees.

Combine the ingredients for the crumb mixture in a small bowl and stir together until evenly coated with the melted butter.

In another mixing bowl, combine the apple juice with the spices, then add the apple slices and raisins and stir until the apples are evenly coated.

Sprinkle the bottom of an oiled 9- by 9-inch cake pan with a light layer of the crumb mixture. Pour in half the apple mixture, followed by half the crumbs. Repeat.

Bake, covered, for 35 to 40 minutes, or until the apples are easily pierced with a fork. Uncover and bake for an additional 10 minutes. Serve warm on its own or over ice cream.

Calories: 212	Total fat: 6 g	Protein: 4 g
Carbohydrates: 36 g	Cholesterol: 4 g	Sodium: 34 mg

A classic "apple-polisher" with boss

BAKED INDIAN PUDDING

6 servings

This has got to be the grandmother of all American desserts, having been among the earliest of cornmeal recipes that the Native Americans taught the colonists. Amazingly, this pudding is still served in many fine New England restaurants. I was unsure about including this recipe, in fact, until I tried it while eating out. This is a culinary wonder, considering that it's basically made of milk, cornmeal, and molasses. Keep in mind that you need 2½ hours of baking time, but adventurous cooks will enjoy the experience! Vanilla ice cream or frozen yogurt, melting over this dark, moist pudding, is a must.

4 cups (1 quart) low-fat milk

1½ tablespoons whipped butter
 or natural canola margarine

⅛ teaspoon salt

⅓ cup cornmeal

⅓ cup molasses

1 large egg, well beaten

¼ cup light brown sugar or
 Sucanat

½ teaspoon cinnamon

½ teaspoon ground ginger

¼ cup raisins, optional

Low-fat vanilla ice cream or
 frozen yogurt

Preheat the oven to 300 degrees.

Bring 3 cups of the milk to a simmer in the top of a double boiler or in a heavy saucepan. Stir in the butter and salt. Slowly and carefully, sprinkle in the cornmeal, stirring continuously to avoid lumping. Stir in the molasses and cook over very low heat for 20 minutes, or until thickened and smooth. Remove from heat.

Combine the beaten egg with the brown sugar. Add the cinnamon, ginger, and optional raisins, then stir this mixture into the cornmeal mixture. Stir until thoroughly blended. Pour into an oiled 1½-quart baking dish.

Bake for 30 minutes, then pour the remaining cup of milk over the top of the pudding but do not stir it in. Bake for another 2 hours. Serve warm in bowls, topped by a scoop of ice cream.

Calories: 213
Carbohydrates: 35 g
Total fat: 5 g
Cholesterol: 48 g
Protein: 7 g
Sodium: 166 mg

Then again there was the Indian baked pudding made of ambrosia, milk, and eggs, with a trifle of Muscovado sugar or Portorique molasses. I can remember when I could eat near upon a six-quart pan of this delicious viand and then cry for more.

—Thomas Robinson Hazard
 *The Jonny-Cake Papers of
 "Shepherd Tom,"* 1915

BREAD PUDDING WITH WHISKEY SAUCE

6 servings

Originally devised as a way of using day-old bread, this sumptuous dessert is a New Orleans classic, still served in many good restaurants. I have made one modification in the recipe—a good amount of a heavy, butter-based sauce is usually poured over each serving; in this version, only a small amount of sauce is made and baked right into the pudding, making it considerably lighter.

1 good-sized loaf of French or
    Italian bread, 1 or 2 days old
2 cups low-fat milk
2 eggs, beaten
2 teaspoons vanilla extract
½ cup light brown sugar or
    Sucanat
¾ cup raisins

Sauce:
3 tablespoons whipped butter or
    natural canola margarine
2 tablespoons light brown sugar
    or Sucanat
¼ cup bourbon whiskey

Preheat the oven to 350 degrees.

Cut the bread into 1-inch cubes. Place them in a mixing bowl and pour the milk over them. With your hands, squeeze the milk through the bread cubes until they are soaked and all or most of the milk is absorbed. In a small bowl, beat the eggs with the vanilla, then stir in the sugar until it dissolves. Add this to the bread mixture and stir together quickly. Fold in the raisins.

Lightly oil a 1½-quart baking dish, pour the bread mixture in, and pat it in smoothly. Bake for 30 minutes. Melt the butter in a small saucepan. Add the sugar, stirring until it dissolves, then remove from the heat and stir in the whiskey. Spoon the sauce evenly over the pudding, then bake for another 10 minutes, or until the top is golden brown and the pudding is nicely puffed. Serve warm.

Calories: 418	Total fat: 9 g	Protein: 14 g
Carbohydrates: 63 g	Cholesterol: 85 g	Sodium: 374 mg

BERRY-TOPPED LIGHT CHEESECAKE

Serves 8

Incorporating silken tofu into this lightened cheesecake gives it a healthful spin.

1½ cups mixed fresh berries (use a combination of any two or more berries, including sliced strawberries or whole blueberries, blackberries, or raspberries)

1 tablespoon sugar

8 ounces light or Neufchâtel cream cheese

1 10-ounce package light silken tofu

½ cup granulated sugar, or ¼ cup granular fructose

1 teaspoon vanilla extract

1 9-inch store-bought graham-cracker crust

Preheat the oven to 350 degrees.

Combine the berries in a mixing bowl. Sprinkle with the sugar and refrigerate until needed.

Combine the cream cheese, tofu, sugar, and vanilla in a food processor. Process until completely smooth. Pour the mixture into the crust and bake for 45 to 50 minutes, or until set.

Let the pie cool completely, then chill for at least an hour. Just before serving, top with the berries.

Calories: 303   Total fat: 16 g   Protein: 6 g
Carbohydrates: 32 g   Cholesterol: 25 g   Sodium: 295 mg

Then, later, when the blackberries are in blossom, we have another cold spell that we call the blackberry winter.

—Clifton Johnson,
   Highways and Byways of the South, 1905

LIGHT LEMONY POUND CAKE

Makes 1 loaf, 10 to 12 servings

I've heard it said that pound cake is so named because it takes a pound of flour, a pound of sugar, a pound of butter, and a pound on the heart to get it beating again after all that butter. Not so with this much-lightened version, in which all the fat is replaced with non-fat lemon yogurt. This is delicious served with Mixed Berry Sauce, following.

1¾ cups cake flour or unbleached white flour

1 teaspoon baking soda

½ teaspoon baking powder

3 egg whites

⅓ cup lemon juice

1 8-ounce container (1 cup) low-fat lemon yogurt

¾ cup granulated sugar or ½ cup granular fructose

Preheat the oven to 350 degrees.

Combine the first 3 ingredients in a large mixing bowl and stir together. In a smaller mixing bowl, combine the egg whites with the remaining ingredients and whisk together until smooth. Pour the wet ingredients into the dry and stir vigorously until completely smooth.

Pour the batter into a lightly oiled non-stick 9- by 5- by 3-inch loaf pan. Bake for 45 to 50 minutes, or until the top is golden brown and a knife inserted into the center tests clean.

Let the loaf cool to room temperature, then cut into slices to serve. Serve with Mixed Berry Sauce (recipe follows) spooned over each slice, if desired.

Calories: 133	Total fat: 0 g	Protein: 4 g
Carbohydrates: 28 g	Cholesterol: 1g	Sodium: 142 mg

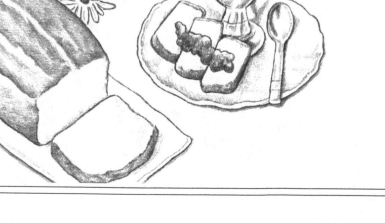

MIXED BERRY SAUCE

Serves 6 as a topping

A versatile topping for cake, pie, ice cream, or frozen yogurt.

2 cups mixed fresh berries (use any combination you wish of whole blueberries, strawberries, raspberries, etc.)

½ cup apple juice

2 teaspoons cornstarch or arrowroot

1 tablespoon light brown sugar or Sucanat, or to taste, optional

Wash the berries well. Use small berries such as blueberries or raspberries whole; remove hulls and chop strawberries into approximately ½-inch chunks.

Combine the berries in a medium-sized saucepan with the apple juice. Bring to a simmer, then cover and simmer gently for 5 to 10 minutes, or until all the berries have softened and burst.

Dissolve the cornstarch in a small amount of cold water. Stir slowly into the berry mixture and simmer for another minute or so, until it has thickened. If you'd like the sauce to be sweeter, stir in brown sugar to taste. Let cool to room temperature before serving.

Calories: 46   Total fat: 0 g   Protein: 0 g
Carbohydrates: 10 g   Cholesterol: 0 g   Sodium: 4 mg

Strawberries they have, as delicious as any in the world, and growing almost everywhere in the Woods and Fields. They are eaten by almost all Creatures; and yet they are so plentiful that very few Persons take care to transplant them, but can find enough to fill their Baskets, when they have a mind, in the deserted old fields.

—Robert Beverly
The History and Present State of Virginia, 1705

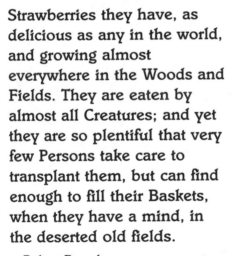

STRAWBERRY FLUMMERY

6 servings

Flummery is a nonsense word of Welsh and English origins that came to define a food made by coagulation. Here in the United States the name and the practice were continued with thickened milk usually served with sweetened fruit. This cornstarch-thickened version has come to be associated with the Shakers and has been included in several collections as "Sister Abigail's Strawberry Flummery." I have modified the original recipe by folding the berries into the thickened milk rather than setting them on top, thus significantly reducing the amount of sugar needed. This is a wonderful, elegant dessert that is, I think, even more delectable than strawberries with heavy cream.

2 cups low-fat milk
3 to 4 tablespoons granulated
   sugar or 1½ to 2 tablespoons
   granular fructose, to taste
¼ cup cornstarch or arrowroot
½ teaspoon vanilla extract
1 pint sweet, ripe strawberries,
   hulled and finely chopped
1 tablespoon lemon juice,
   optional

Bring 1½ cups of the milk to a simmer in the top of a double boiler or heavy saucepan.

In the meantime, combine the sugar and cornstarch in small bowl and moisten them slowly with the remaining ½ cup of milk. Stir until thoroughly dissolved, then pour slowly into the scalded milk. Add the vanilla and cook over very low heat for 10 to 15 minutes, or until smooth and thick. Remove from the heat.

Let the mixture cool for 10 minutes, then stir in the strawberries and the optional lemon juice, if you'd like a slight tang. Turn the mixture out into a 1-quart serving bowl or 6 individual dessert cups. Refrigerate until well chilled.

Calories. 95	Total fat: 1 g	Protein: 3g
Carbohydrates: 19 g	Cholesterol: 3 g	Sodium: 42 mg

All the woods, fields and gardens are full of strawberries, which grow excellently well in this beautiful and lovely land.

—William Byrd
Natural History of Virqinia, 1737

STRAWBERRY SHORTCAKE

Serves 6

There were many different types of shortcake in the annals of nineteenth-century baking, some like stacked pancakes to be eaten with sauce, and some that were almost like plain biscuits. This recipe, adapted from one of my favorite cooks of that century, Maria Parloa, is the old-fashioned predecessor of today's strawberry shortcake—simply crushed, sweetened fruit between two rounds of warm dough.

1½ cups whole wheat pastry flour or unbleached white flour, or half of each

1½ teaspoons baking powder

½ teaspoon salt

⅓ cup firmly packed light brown sugar or Sucanat

2 tablespoons whipped butter or natural canola margarine, melted

¾ cup low-fat milk

1 pint sweet, ripe strawberries, hulls removed and crushed

3 tablespoons granulated sugar or 1½ tablespoons granular fructose

Low-fat vanilla or lemon yogurt, optional

Preheat the oven to 400 degrees.

In a mixing bowl, combine the flour or flours, baking powder, and salt. In another bowl, combine the brown sugar with the melted butter. Stir in the milk, then combine the wet with the dry ingredients and work them together to form a soft dough.

Turn the dough out onto a well-floured board and knead for a minute or so. Divide the dough into 2 equal parts, form into smooth balls, and roll out to fit the bottom of a pie pan. Place the rounds of dough in 2 lightly oiled pie pans. Bake for 12 to 15 minutes, or until the dough is golden.

In the meantime, combine the crushed strawberries with the sugar in a small bowl. Set aside until ready to use.

Allow the baked dough to cool until it is just warm to the touch. Place one round on a serving plate, spread it with the berries, and top with the other round of dough. Cut into wedges to serve. This is best served fresh and warm. Top each serving with a dollop of yogurt, if you'd like.

Calories: 208	Total fat: 4 g	Protein: 5 g
Carbohydrates: 38 g	Cholesterol: 9 g	Sodium: 201 mg

BLACKBERRY OR BLUEBERRY COBBLER

6 servings

This classic dessert is delicious served warm on its own or with vanilla ice cream or frozen yogurt.

1 pint fresh blackberries or blueberries

⅓ to ½ cup light brown sugar or Sucanat, to taste

1 cup whole wheat pastry flour or unbleached white flour, or half of each

1½ teaspoons baking powder

¼ teaspoon salt

1 egg, well beaten

¾ cup low-fat milk or soymilk

2 tablespoons whipped butter or natural canola margarine, melted

Low-fat vanilla ice cream or frozen yogurt, optional

Preheat the oven to 400 degrees.

Wash the berries and make sure that they are thoroughly picked over. In a mixing bowl, toss them with about half the sugar. Place the berries in a lightly oiled 9- by 9-inch baking pan.

In the same mixing bowl, combine the flour, baking powder, and salt and stir together. In a small bowl, mix the remaining sugar with the beaten egg. Pour this mixture into the flour mixture, then slowly add the milk, followed by the melted butter. Stir until smoothly blended. Pour the batter evenly over the berries. Bake for 30 to 35 minutes, or until the berries are soft and the batter is golden brown. Serve warm on its own or with ice cream.

Calories: 185   Total fat: 4 g   Protein: 5 g
Carbohydrates: 31 g   Cholesterol: 44 g   Sodium: 126 mg

NEW ENGLAND BLUEBERRY CAKE

Makes 1 9-inch cake, about 12 servings

This easy and marvelously moist cake is great made with the smaller wild blueberries, which are available fresh from Maine in late June, or year-round in the frozen foods section in supermarkets.

¼ cup whipped butter or natural
    canola margarine
¾ cup granulated sugar or
    ½ cup granular fructose
1 egg, beaten
1 cup non-fat buttermilk
2 cups unbleached white flour or
    whole wheat pastry flour, or
    half of each
1 teaspoon baking soda
1 teaspoon baking powder
1 heaping cup (½ pint) wild
    blueberries

Preheat the oven to 325 degrees.

Cream together the butter and sugar in a medium-sized mixing bowl. Add the egg and buttermilk and whisk the mixture until smooth. Combine the flour, baking soda, and baking powder in a large mixing bowl and stir together. Add the wet ingredients to the dry and stir vigorously until completely mixed. Gently fold in the blueberries.

Pour the mixture into a lightly oiled 9- by 9-inch square or 9-inch round baking pan. Bake for 40 to 45 minutes, or until the top is golden and a knife inserted into the center tests clean. Allow to cool, then cut into wedges or squares to serve.

Calories: 161	Total fat: 3 g	Protein: 3 g
Carbohydrates: 28 g	Cholesterol: 27 g	Sodium: 85 mg

STEWED SPICED PEARS IN RED WINE

4 to 6 servings

Though the practice of stewing fruits in wine has a decidedly European background, it has become an American classic due to its early adoption by Southern cooks. An absolutely delicious and elegant way to present pears, this is especially nice in the winter when so few other fruits are available.

5 large firm, ripe Bosc pears
⅓ cup dry red wine
¼ cup undiluted apple juice
   concentrate
6 whole cloves
1 small cinnamon stick,
   broken in half
¼ teaspoon ground allspice
1 tablespoon arrowroot or
   cornstarch, dissolved in 3
   tablespoons water
Low-fat vanilla yogurt for topping,
   optional

Stem the pears and cut them into quarters lengthwise. Core them and divide the quarters in half again lengthwise.

In a deep saucepan, combine the wine, apple juice concentrate, cloves, cinnamon, and allspice. Bring the mixture to a gentle simmer. Slowly pour in the dissolved arrowroot, then stir in the pear slices. Cover and simmer over very low heat, about 25 to 35 minutes, depending on the size and ripeness of the pears, stirring occasionally. When the pears are done, they should be easily pierced with a fork, but still firm enough to retain their shape.

If there seems to be too much liquid in the saucepan once the pears are done, uncover and cook for 5 to 10 minutes until it is reduced. Served warm in shallow bowls, garnished with a dollop of yogurt if desired.

Calories: 147	Total fat: 0 g	Protein: 1 g
Carbohydrates: 30 g	Cholesterol: 0 g	Sodium: 6 mg

Pears and peaches ain't often found on the same tree, I tell you.

—Thomas C. Haliburton
The Attaché, or Sam Slick in England, 1843

UNBAKED PEACH CRISP

6 servings

The first thing I saw when driving into South Carolina for the first time was a giant peach on a pedestal that seemed to reach the sky. Peaches are one of the hallmark fruits of the South, and many of its classic recipes developed there. I decided to alter this standard a bit; I love peaches but dislike how they taste baked—they seem to lose all their flavor, and their juiciness turns to mush. I hope you'll agree that this modification does justice to the peach. The result is a healthy dessert that's very low in sugar.

2 tablespoons whipped butter or natural canola margarine, divided

5 or 6 good-sized sweet juicy peaches, thinly sliced

1 to 2 tablespoons light brown sugar or Sucanat, to taste

1 teaspoon cinnamon, divided

½ cup rolled oats

⅓ cup wheat germ

⅓ cup raisins

⅛ teaspoon ground cloves

Low-fat vanilla ice cream or frozen yogurt, optional

Heat half of the butter in a large skillet. Add the sliced peaches and sauté over low heat for 5 minutes. Stir the sugar in until it dissolves, then sprinkle in half the cinnamon. Transfer the peaches to a 9- by 9-inch cake pan.

Toast the oats in a dry skillet over medium heat, stirring frequently, until they are golden. Add the wheat germ and the remaining butter and stir until it is evenly melted throughout. Stir in the raisins, the remaining cinnamon, and the cloves. Sprinkle this mixture evenly over the peaches and pat it in. Allow to cool to room temperature. Serve plain or as a topping for ice cream.

Calories: 172	Total fat: 4 g	Protein: 4 g
Carbohydrates: 29 g	Cholesterol: 8 g	Sodium: 4 mg

MENUS

The following menus, built around seasons, regional themes, or special occasions, offer ideas on how to build meals with individual recipes. In all cases, dessert is entirely optional—I prefer having fruit after everyday meals, saving desserts for special occasions or company.

SUPPERS WITH REGIONAL THEMES

Southern Suppers for Spring

BAKED CHEESE GRITS (page 164)

POTATOES WITH COLLARD GREENS (page 187)

GREEN BEANS WITH TOMATOES AND BASIL (page 202)

Honeydew melon

HOPPIN'-JOHN (page 141)

BUTTERMILK CORN BREAD (page 49) or **HOMINY MUFFINS** (page 35)

NORTH CAROLINA RELISH SLAW (page 96)

GREEN BEANS WITH LEMON AND GARLIC (page 202)

BLACKBERRY COBBLER (page 253)

A Southern Supper for Fall or Winter

SOUTHERN LIMA BEANS (page 142)

RICE AND CORNMEAL SPOONBREAD (page 65)

Seasonal mixed salad

Baked butternut squash

APPLE BROWN BETTY (page 245)

A New England Supper for Summer

CORN PUDDING (page 155)

HARVARD BEETS (page 172)

PICNIC POTATO SALAD (page 98)

Sliced red bell pepper

BLUEBERRY COBBLER (page 253)

A New England Supper for Winter

FARMER'S CABBAGE (page 178)

BAKED SWEET POTATOES AND APPLES (page 191)

BAKED BARBECUE BEANS (page 132)

Simple green salad

BOSTON CRANBERRY PIE (page 233)

A Light Pennsylvania Dutch Supper for Fall or Winter
DUTCH SUCCOTASH (page 158)
RED WINE CABBAGE (page 177)
Sliced cucumbers with fresh dill in yogurt
SHOO-FLY PIE (page 238)

A Creole Supper for Summer, Fall, or Winter
CREOLE EGGPLANT SOUP (page 73)
RICE MUFFINS (page 34)
Seasonal mixed salad
STUFFED MIRLITON (page 199) for summer, or
PECAN-STUFFED SQUASH (page 194) for fall or winter
SOUTHERN BLACK CAKE (page 240) or fruit in season

A Late Spring or Early Summer Creole Supper for Company
BUTTERMILK BISCUITS (page 31)
CREOLE EGGPLANT SOUFFLÉ (page 173)
CREOLE OKRA AND TOMATOES (page 175)
Fresh green peas, steamed and minted
Simple green salad
BREAD PUDDING WITH WHISKEY SAUCE (page 247)

A Simple Creole Supper for Spring or Fall

(This is a good meal to make on a rainy Sunday, as both the beans and the beets are long-cooking dishes)

RED BEANS AND RICE (page 136)

BEETS PIQUANT (page 171)

Seasonal mixed salad

PECAN SQUARES (page 239) or fruit in season

Southwestern Suppers

(Since these meals tend to be filling, I suggest a light dessert of a cooling sherbet or a colorful fruit salad dressed in yogurt with a touch of honey)

BAKED RICE WITH CHEESE AND GREEN CHILES (page 146)

FRIJOLES BORRACHOS (page 130)

Sautéed chayote (vegetable pear) or zucchini

Diced tomatoes drizzled with olive oil

GREEN CHILE ENCHILADAS (page 209)

POSOLE Y FRIJOLES (page 167)

or **MEXICAN RICE** (page 147)

Seasonal mixed salad

CHILAQUILES (page 213)

BLACK BEAN SALSA (page 220)

CALAVACITAS (page 198)

Shredded lettuce and black olives

VEGETABLE BURRITOS (page 216)
or SIZZLING SOY FAJITAS (page 217)
Brown rice
JÍCAMA SALAD WITH ORANGES, CILANTRO, AND PUMPKIN SEEDS
(page 113)

SOUP AND SALAD SUPPERS

(I have a penchant for meals built around soup, salad, and a good bread. Here are a few suggestions. Dessert is, of course, optional, but a fruity dessert is a good bet.)

For Any Season

ZUCCHINI CHOWDER (page 83)
SOUTHWESTERN RICE SALAD (page 108)
ZUNI QUICK BREAD (page 58)

BLACK BEAN SOUP (page 72)
NORTH CAROLINA RELISH SLAW (page 96)
SHAKER CHEDDAR BREAD (page 61)

VIRGINIA PEANUT SOUP (page 92)
PENNSYLVANIA DUTCH CORN RELISH (page 99)
CAROLINA RICE AND WHEAT BREAD (page 55)

For Summer
COLD AVOCADO SOUP (page 85)

"TEXAS CAVIAR" (Marinated Black-Eyed Pea Salad, page 102**)**

BUTTERMILK CORN BREAD (page 49)

For Early Fall
SWEET POTATO SOUP (page 76)

JERUSALEM ARTICHOKE SALAD (page 112)

Sliced tomatoes and bell peppers

HOMINY MUFFINS (page 35)

SQUASH AND CORN CHOWDER (page 87)

CAULIFLOWER AND AVOCADO SALAD (page 109)

POTATO BISCUITS (page 32)

For Winter
RED BEAN SOUP (page 71)

CABBAGE AND PEPPER SLAW (page 95)

RICE MUFFINS (page 34)

SPECIAL BRUNCHES

Breakfast in New Orleans
EGGS NEW ORLEANS (page 125)

BUTTERMILK BISCUITS (page 31)

Cooked grits

PECAN SQUARES (page 239) and fresh fruit

An Elegant Brunch for Company

EGGS CREOLE (page 124)

PARSLEY POTATO CROQUETTES (page 186)

APPLE MUFFINS (page 36)

Mixed fruit salad with yogurt and honey

Three Southwestern Brunches

CALIFORNIA OMELET (page 123)

GREEN CHILE CORN BREAD (page 51)

Salad of greens, tomatoes, and avocado

BLACKBERRY OR BLUEBERRY COBBLER (page 253), in season

MEXICAN OMELET (page 118)

FRIJOLES REFRITOS (Refried Pinto Beans, page 129**)**

Warm flour tortillas

Cantaloupe and honeydew, or grapefruit and orange wedges

HUEVOS RANCHEROS (Ranch-Style Eggs, page 117**)**

POTATOES WITH GREEN CHILE (page 188)

Crisp raw fresh vegetables

UNBAKED PEACH CRISP (page 256), in season

MENUS FOR SPECIAL OCCASIONS

Two Vegetarian Thanksgivings

Menu #1
ANADAMA BREAD (page 53)
CABBAGE AND PEPPER SLAW (page 95)
POTATO-BREAD STUFFING (page 184)
"THREE SISTERS STEW" (page 197)
CRANBERRY-APPLE RELISH (page 114)
Steamed broccoli, zucchini, and carrots
PUMPKIN OR BUTTERNUT SQUASH PIE (page 232)
STEWED SPICED PEARS IN RED WINE (page 255)
Low-fat vanilla ice cream or frozen yogurt

Menu #2
JERUSALEM ARTICHOKE SALAD (page 112)
PINTO BEAN CORN BREAD (page 52)
BAKED HONEY-GLAZED ONIONS (page 180)
CANDIED YAMS (page 190)
**STUFFED SQUASH WITH MASHED POTATOES,
CARROTS, AND PEAS** (page 196)
CRANBERRY-APPLE RELISH (page 114)
MOCK MINCE PIE (page 237)

A Summer Picnic of Various Salads

PICNIC POTATO SALAD (page 98)

PENNSYLVANIA DUTCH CORN RELISH (page 99)

SUMMER SQUASH, GREEN BEAN, AND CHICKPEA SALAD (page 104)

ZUNI QUICK BREAD (page 58)

Cherry tomatoes

NEW ENGLAND BLUEBERRY CAKE (page 254)

Fresh fruits

An Outdoor Summer Supper

*(If you don't have a grill, you might simply wrap the vegetables in foil
and bake them in the oven at the same time as the beans.
Double any recipes as needed, depending on the number of eaters.)*

BAKED BARBECUE BEANS (page 132)

Grilled vegetables, including corn on the cob, green and red bell peppers,
onions, broccoli, cauliflower, and potatoes

GREEN CHILE CORN BREAD (page 51)

CREAMY COLE SLAW (page 97)

TACO SALAD (page 107)

BLACKBERRY OR BLUEBERRY COBBLER (page 253)

Watermelon

SELECTED SOURCES

Following is a list of the most helpful books from among the scores I went through. There was considerable overlapping in recipe books; many of my adaptations are composites of several versions of classic recipes. Books that provided additional lore and literature to accompany the recipes, beyond those cited on the pages themselves, are also listed here.

Barringer, Maria M. *Dixie Cookery*. New York: R. Worthington, 1882.

Begue de Packman, Ana. *Early California Hospitality*. Glendale, Calif.: Arthur H. Clark Co., 1938.

Bergen, Fanny D., ed. *Animal and Plant Lore*. Boston: HoughtonMifflin/American Folklore Society, 1899.

Beverly, Robert. *The History and Present State of Virginia*. Reprint of 1705 edition. Chapel Hill, N.C.: University of North Carolina Press, 1947.

Botkin, Benjamin. *A Treasury of New England Folklore*. New York: Crown Publishers, Inc., 1964.

Bowles, Ella S., and Towle, Dorothy. *Secrets of New England Cooking*. New York: M. Barrows & Co., 1947.

Brown, Nellie I. *Recipes from Old Hundred: 200 Years of New England Cooking*. New York: M. Barrows & Co., 1939.

Buckeye Cookbook, The. Originally titled *Practical Housekeeping: A Careful Compilation of Tried and Approved Recipes*. Minneapolis: Buckeye Publishing Co., 1883.

Burdette, Kay. *Cookery of the Old South*. Self-published, no date.

Byrd, William. *Natural History of Virginia*. Richmond, Va. Dietz Press, 1940 (translation of 1737 edition by Richard C. Beatty and William J. Malloy).

Christian Women's Exchange. *The Creole Cookery Book*. New Orleans: T.H. Thompson, 1885.

Colquitt, Harriet R. *The Savannah Cookbook*. Olmstead, N.Y.: 1933.

Dictionary of Americanisms. Chicago: The University of Chicago Press, 1966.

Eustic, Celestine. *Cooking in Old Creole Days*. New York: R.K. Russell, 1903.

Flexner, Marion W. *Dixie Dishes*. Boston: Hale, Cushman and Flint, 1941.

Flexner, Stuart Berg. *I Hear America Talking*. New York: Simon and Schuster, 1976.

Frederick, J. George. *The Pennsylvania Dutch and Their Cookery*. Philadelphia: The Business Bourse, 1935.

Frost, Annie, ed. *The Godey's Lady's Book Receipts*. Philadelphia: Evans, Stoddart & Co., 1870.

Gilbert, Fabiola Cabeza de Baca. *The Good Life: New Mexican Food*. Santa Fe, N.M.: San Vincente Foundation, 1949.

Good, Frank, ed. *Rare Recipes and Budget Savers*. Wichita, Kans.: Wichita Eagle and Beacon, 1961.

Hearn, Lafcadio. *"Gombo Zhebes": Little Dictionary of Creole Proverbs Selected from 6 Creole Dialects*. New York: W.H. Coleman, 1885.

Hibben, Sheila. *The National Cookbook: A Kitchen Americana*. New York: Harper & Bros., 1932.

Hiller, Elizabeth O. *The Corn Cookbook*. Chicago: P.F. Volland Co., 1918.

Hughes, Phyllis. *Pueblo Indian Cookbook*. Santa Fe, N.M.: Museum of New Mexico Press, 1977.

Kaufman, William I., and Cooper, Sister Mary Ursula. *The Art of Creole Cookery*. New York: Doubleday & Co., 1962.

Kitchen Guild of the Tullie Smith House Restoration. *Tullie's Receipts*. Atlanta, Ga.: Atlanta Historical Society, 1976.

Ladies of the Second Presbyterian Church. *Recipes of Georgia Housekeepers*. New York: Trow's Printing and Bookbinding Co., 1883.

Land, Mary. *Louisiana Cookery*. New York: Bonanza Books (Crown Publishers, Inc.), 1954.

Leslie, Eliza. *Directions for Cookery in Its Various Branches*. 49th edition. Philadelphia: Henry C. Baird, 1853.

Mariani, John F. *The Dictionary of American Food and Drink*. New York: Ticknor & Fields, 1983.

Maylie, Eugenie Lavedan. *Maylie's Table d' Hote Recipes*. New Orleans: Self-published, 195-?

Morrow, Kay. *The New England Cookbook of Fine Old Recipes*. Reading, Pa.: Culinary Arts Press, 1936.

New Mexico College of Agriculture. *Historic Cookery*. Santa Fe, N.M.: Agricultural Extension Service, May 1939.

Parloa, Maria. *Miss Parloa's Kitchen Companion*. Boston: Estes and Lauriat, 1887.

Penner, Lucille Recht. *The Colonial Cookbook*. New York: Hastings House, 1976.

Piercy, Caroline. *The Shaker Cook-Book*. New York: Crown Publishers, Inc., 1953.

Porter, Mrs. M.E. *Mrs. Porter's New Southern Cookery Book*. Philadelphia: John E. Porter & Co., 1871.

Randolph, Mary. *The Virginia Housewife*. Edited by Karen Hess. Facsimile of 1824 edition. Columbia, S.C.: University of South Carolina Press, 1984.

Rice Industry. *Rice: 200 Delightful Ways to Serve It*. New Orleans, La.: Southern Rice Industry, 1937.

Rutledge, Sarah (attributed to). *The Carolina Housewife*. Charleston, S.C.: W.R. Babcock, 1951.

Scott, Natalie V. *200 Years of New Orleans Cooking*. New York: Jonathan Cape, 1931.

Simmons, Amelia. *American Cookery*. Edited by Gail Weesner. Facsimile of 1796 edition. Boston, Mass.: Rowan Tree Press, 1982.

Stern, Jane and Michael. *Goodfood*. New York: Alfred A Knopf, 1983.

Taylor, Archer, and Whiting, Bartlett J. *A Dictionary of American Proverbs and Proverbial Expressions, 1820-1880*. Cambridge, Mass.: Harvard University Press, 1967.

Taylor, Joe Gray. Eating, Drinking, and Visiting in the Old South. Baton Rouge, Louisiana: Louisiana State University Press, 1982.

Times-Picayune Publishing Co., Inc. *The Original Picayune Creole Cookbook*. New Orleans, La.: The Times-Picayune Publishing Co., 1901.

Trinity Mission. *Out of Vermont Kitchens*. Burlington, Vt.: Trinity Mission, 1939.

Tyree, Marion Cabell. *Housekeeping In Old Virginia*. Louisville, Ky.: John P. Morton & Co., 1870.

Works Progress Administration. *Louisiana: A Guide to the State*. Boston, Mass.: Houghton Mifflin Co., 1938.

Works Progress Administration. *Gumbo Ya-Ya: A Collection of Louisiana Folk-Tales*. New York: Bonanza Books (Crown Publishers, Inc.), 1945.

ACKNOWLEDGMENTS

Grateful acknowledgment is given to the following publishers for permission to reprint or adapt copyrighted materials from original sources.

American Heritage Publishing Co., New York:

From *The American Heritage Cookbook,* by the editors of *American Heritage,* ©1980: Black Bean Soup and Shoo-fly Pie, adapted by permission.

Lescher & Lescher, agents:

From *American Food: The Gastronomic Story* by Evan Jones, © 1981: Obijway Butternut Squash and Corn Chowder, adapted by permission.

Little, Brown & Co., Boston, Mass.:

From *How Many Miles to Galena?* by Richard Bissell, © 1968: A passage entitled "There's a Salad on the Floor," reprinted by permission.

MacIntosh & Otis, agents:

From *The Art of American Indian Cooking* by Jean Anderson and Yeffe Kimball, © 1965: Jerusalem Artichoke Salad, adapted by permission.

From *Recipes from America's Restored Villages* by Jean Anderson, © 1975: Brethren Cheddar Bread, adapted by permission.

New Directions Publishing Corp., New York:

From *A Member of the Wedding* by Carson McCullers, © 1946: A passage on "Hopping-John," reprinted by permission.

Random House, Inc., New York:

From *The New England Cookbook* by Eleanor Early, ©1954: Harwich Hermits and "Farmer's Cabbage," adapted by permission.

Simon & Schuster, New York:

From *The Best of Shaker Cookery* by Amy Bess Miller and Persis W. Fuller, ©1970: Herb Bread and Hancock Dill Bread, adapted by permission.

INDEX

Griddlecakes
   blueberry, 44
   cornmeal, lace-edged, 42
   rice and cornmeal, 43
   squash or pumpkin, 45
Grits, 25
   baked cheese, 164
   with fresh corn and tomatoes, 166
Guacamole, 110
   enchiladas, 211

Haliburton, Thomas C., 255
Harvard beets, 172
Harwich hermits, 241
Hazard, Thomas Robinson, 246
Herb bread, Shaker, 59
Hess, Karen, 48
High Life in New York (Stephens), 105
Hill's Manual of Social and Business Forms, 80
Hints on Etiquette (Day), 62, 79, 83, 156
History and Present State of Virginia, The (Beverly), 16, 128, 233, 250
Holmes, Oliver Wedell, 187
Holton, Edith, 155
Hominy
   with cheese and green chile, 168
   grits, 25
   muffins, 35
   with pink beans (Posole Y Frijoles), 167
   whole, 26
Honey, 27
Hoppin'-John (Black-eyed peas and rice), 141
How Many Miles to Galena? (Bissell), 109
Hubbard, Kin, 29, 56, 122, 242
Huevos Rancheros, 117

In the Tennessee Mountains (Craddock), 200
Indian pudding, baked, 246
Ingredients, 23-28

Jambalaya, 137
Jefferson, Thomas, 16, 170
Jerusalem artichoke salad, 112
Jicama salad with oranges, cilantro, and

   pumpkin seeds, 113
Jonny-Cake Papers of "Shepherd Tom" (Hazard), 246
Josh Billings Farmers' Almanac, 125
Journal of Travels in the U.S. (Palmer), 32

Kansas City Times, 40
Keywest black beans and rice, 144
Knickerbocker Magazine, 96
Knox, John A., 239

Lemony pound cake, light, 249
Leslie, Eliza, 17, 93
Lima bean(s), 25
   Amish potatoes with, 183
   Southern, 142
Louisiana cooking, 20-21

Maine rye pancakes, 40
Maine Woods, The (Thoreau), 124
Maple syrup, 28
Margarine, 26
Maryland Historical Magazine, 34
Mayonnaise, tofu, 96
McCullers, Carson, 141
McCutcheon, G. B., 237
Member of the Wedding, A (McCullers), 141
Menus
   brunches, 263-264
   soup and salad suppers, 262-263
   for special occasions, 265-266
   suppers with regional themes, 257-261
Mexican
   omelet, 118
   rice, 147
Migas (Scrambled eggs with tortillas), 120
Mince pie, mock, 237
Mirliton, stuffed, 199
Miss Parloa's Kitchen Companion, 17, 48, 94, 107
Molasses, 28
   corn bread, 50
Muffins
   apple, 36
   hominy, 35
   orange-cranberry, 38

ABOUT THE AUTHOR

Nava Atlas is the author and illustrator of several vegetarian cookbooks, including *Vegetariana*, *Vegetarian Soups for All Seasons*, and *The Vegetarian 5-Ingredient Gourmet*, among others. She has also written dozens of articles for food and health magazines, including *Vegetarian Times*, *Veggie Life*, and others. Nava lives with her husband and two sons in the Hudson Valley region of New York. She invites you to visit her popular web site, "In a Vegetarian Kitchen" at www.vegkitchen.com.